THE COMMON INTEREST IN INTERNATIONAL LAW

THE COMMON INTEREST IN INTERNATIONAL LAW

edited by

Wolfgang Benedek
Koen De Feyter
Matthias C. Kettemann
Christina Voigt

intersentia

Cambridge – Antwerp – Portland

Intersentia Ltd
Sheraton House | Castle Park
Cambridge | CB3 0AX | United Kingdom
Tel.: +44 1223 370 170 | Email: mail@intersentia.co.uk

Distribution for the UK:
NBN International
Airport Business Centre, 10 Thornbury Road
Plymouth, PL6 7PP
United Kingdom
Tel: +44 1752 202 301 | Fax: +44 1752 202 331
Email: orders@nbninternational.com

Distribution for the USA and Canada:
International Specialized Book Services
920 NE 58th Ave Suite 300
Portland, OR 97213
USA
Tel.: +1 800 944 6190 (toll free)
Email: info@isbs.com

Distribution for Austria:
Neuer Wissenschaftlicher Verlag
Argentinierstraße 42/6
1040 Wien
Austria
Tel.: +43 1 535 61 03 24
Email: office@nwv.at

Distribution for other countries:
Intersentia Publishing nv
Groenstraat 31
2640 Mortsel
Belgium
Tel.: +32 3 680 15 50
Email: mail@intersentia.be

The Common Interest in International Law
Wolfgang Benedek, Koen De Feyter, Matthias C. Kettemann and Christina Voigt (eds.)

ISBN 978-1-78068-271-6
D/2014/7849/3
NUR 828

GPRC
Guaranteed
Peer Reviewed
Content

The work reported on in this publication has been financially supported by the European Science Foundation (ESF), in the framework of the Research Networking Programme GLOTHRO.

European Science Foundation

British Library Cataloguing in Publication Data. A catalogue record for this book is available from the British Library.

EDITORS' PREFACE

This publication is part of the Research Networking Programme (RNP) 'Beyond Territoriality: Globalization and Transnational Human Rights Obligations' (GLOTHRO) which ran from May 2010 to May 2014 and was financially supported by the European Science Foundation (ESF). Over the course of its four years GLOTHRO has developed into one of the most important academic projects broaching questions of extra-territorial human rights protection and the obligations of multiple state and non-state actors.

This book is dedicated to one key aspect that connects the protecting of human rights and human dignity and the extraterritorial obligations of states under international law: the protection of the common interest. The book addresses several key questions that the issue engages: What is the common interest – or what *are* common interests? How does international law protect common interests? What are the obligations of states *vis-à-vis* each other and the international community? What role do different state and non-state actors have? And what can the protection of the common interest in different regimes tell us about the future of international law more globally?

The process of inviting contributions to this volume was particularly thorough and responsive. The contributions were presented at two workshops hosted by the University of Graz, on 11–12 October 2012 and 30–31 October 2013, and then extended and refined by the authors in light of discussions and comments. The introduction and the conclusions, written by all editors, frame and position the eleven contributions by both emerging and renowned scholars.

At the University of Graz the editors would like to thank Manuela Rusz for editorial support and co-editor Matthias C. Kettemann, who had the main role in reviewing the contributions. At Intersentia, we would like to thank the two reviewers for their comments and Tom Scheirs for his valuable support.

In his introduction into international law, Malcolm N. Shaw writes that "[i]n the long march of mankind from the cave to the computer a central role has always been played by the idea of law". In this book, we show that – transcending international legal regimes – the idea of a 'common interest' is just as important. Not only law – that is in Shaw's words "[the idea] that order is necessary and chaos inimical to a just and stable existence" – is necessary for the international community to flourish, but the common pursuance of issues of common interest through international law.

The contributors to this book show that it is time to turn the page when it comes to protecting the common interest in international law. To find out how, you will need to do the same.

Graz, Antwerp, Frankfurt am Main, Oslo
August 2014

Wolfgang Benedek, Koen De Feyter, Matthias C. Kettemann, Christina Voigt

CONTENTS

ABBREVIATIONS

AOSIS	Alliance of Small Island States
ARIO	Articles on the Responsibility of International Organizations
BCG	Boston Consulting Group
CCH	Common Concern of Humankind
CDP	Committee for Development Policy
CESCR	Committee on Economic, Social and Cultural Rights
CFI	Court of First Instance
CIR	Critical Internet Resources
COP	Conference of the Parties
CSR	Corporate Social Responsibility
DAC	Development Assistance Committee
DCD-DAC	Development Co-operation Directorate
DDos	Distributed Denial-of-Service
DNS	Domain Name System
DPI	Deep Packet Inspection
EBA	"Everything But Arms" Arrangement
ECHR	European Convention of Human Rights
ECJ	European Court of Justice
ECOSOC	Economic and Social Council
ECtHR	European Court of Human Rights
ESCRs	Economic, Social and Cultural Rights
ETO	Extraterritorial Obligations
GDP	Gross Domestic Product
GNI	Gross National Income
HDI	UNDP Human Development Index
HRC	Human Rights Committee
HTTP	Hyper Text Transfer Protocol
IBRD	International Bank for Reconstruction and Development
ICANN	Internet Corporation for Assigned Names and Numbers
ICCPR	International Covenant on Civil and Political Rights
ICESCR	International Covenant on Economic, Social and Cultural Rights
ICISS	International Commission on Intervention and State Sovereignty
ICJ	International Court of Justice
ICTs	Information and Communication Technologies
ICTY	International Criminal Tribunal for the former Yugoslavia
IDA	International Development Association

IHL	International Humanitarian law
ILC	International Law Commission
IMF	International Monetary Fund
IP	Internet Protocol
IXP	Internet Exchange Point
LDCs	Least Developed Countries
MDGs	Millennium Development Goals
MSI-DUI	Council of Europe's Committee of Experts on Rights of Internet Users
NAM	Non-Aligned Movement
NGOs	Non-Governmental Organizations
ODA	Official Development Assistance
OECD	Organisation for Economic Co-operation
R2P	Responsibility to Protect
SDGs	Sustainable Development Goals
SIDS	Small Island Developing States
TCP	Transmission Control Protocol
TRIPS	Agreement on Trade-Related Aspects of Intellectual Property Rights
UDHR	Universal Declaration of Human Rights
UK	United Kingdom
UN	United Nations
UNCTAD	United Nations Conference on Trade and Development
UNDP	United Nations Development Program
UNESCO	United Nations Educational, Scientific and Cultural Organization
UNFCCC	United Nations Framework Convention on Climate Change
UNHRC	United Nations Human Rights Council
UNSC	United Nations Security Council
UPR	Universal Periodic Review
USA	United States of America
VDPA	Vienna Declaration and Programme of Action
VCLT	Vienna Convention on the Law of Treaties
VoIP	Voice over IP
WB	World Bank
WSIS	World Summit on the Information Society
WSO	World Summit Outcome
WTO	World Trade Organisation
WWW	World Wide Web

INTRODUCTION

Wolfgang Benedek, Koen De Feyter,
Matthias C. Kettemann and Christina Voigt

1. 'COMMON INTEREST' IN INTERNATIONAL LAW

The main purpose of this publication is to investigate to what extent a common interest can be identified in various fields of international law and what legal instruments have been developed to address and implement such common interests. In particular, the authors look for new methods to realize the protection of the common interest. Though not the book's only focus, the contributions show how international law, and human rights law in particular, is progressively moving away from a system based on territorial sovereignty to a system based on shared responsibilities among states and other actors.

The question of how international law defines and protects collective interests is subject to numerous current discourses in international law. The book attempts to tie them together to a new – or renewed – understanding of 'common interest' reflective of contemporary challenges in international law. The concept of 'common interest' suggests that more is at stake in international law than the individual self-interests of states. Such notion might hold the key to transforming international law away from the dominance of sovereignty into a system which truly serves the interest of the "community", including all relevant actors. It is 600 years since the Council of Constance, when votes were first taken nation by nation. It is a little less than 400 years since the Thirty Years' War broke out that ended in the Peace of Westphalia, often considered as the starting point of an international order founded on sovereign states. Time has come for a review of the status quo. The concept of an 'international community', on which that of 'common interest' is based, is a legal fiction, presently comprising not only states, but also of international organizations and arguably also private actors.

Such a wide basis for common interests also has bearings on the way that common interests are constructed and deconstructed and endowed with international legal protection. The protection of common interests can be identified as a key element motivating the emergence of new rules in international law across all sources.

Though there is no authoritative list of global common interests in international law, a number of international treaties refer explicitly to the protection of common interests, although the terminology varies. If we take 'common interest' as an umbrella term, references to notions such as 'common concern', 'common interest', 'common heritage of mankind', 'crimes against humanity', erga omnes obligations, ius cogens norms, are all relevant.[1] Such common legal opinion – which goes well beyond the subjective element of custom – might be captured by general principles that aim at the fulfilment of the public interest and the realization of the common good of the international community as a whole.

International jurisprudence also recognizes common interests. The ICJ has made reference to the concept on several occasions, yet the nature and scope of 'common interest' remain somewhat unclear. In its 1951 *Reservations to the Convention on Genocide* advisory opinion, the ICJ found that

> In such a convention [Genocide Convention] the contracting states do not have any interests of their own; they merely have, one and all, a common interest, namely, the accomplishment of those high purposes which are the *raison d'être* of the convention.[2]

[1] Examples of provisions in international treaties and other instruments include: "armed force shall not be used, save in the common interest" (Preamble to the UN Charter); "The Area and its resources are the common heritage of mankind" (Art. 136 of the UN Convention on the Law of the Sea); "The exploration and use of the moon shall be the province of all mankind and shall be carried out for the benefit and in the interest of all countries, irrespective of their degree of economic or scientific development" (Art. 4 (1) of the Moon Agreement); "Such heritage constitutes a world heritage for whose protection it is the duty of the international community as a whole to cooperate" (Art. 6 (1) of the UNESCO Convention concerning the Protection of World Cultural and Natural Heritage); "Any state other than the injured state is entitled to invoke the responsibility of another state if (...) the obligation breached is owed to the international community as a whole" (Art. 48 (1) of the Articles on state Responsibility); "A peremptory norm of general international law is a norm accepted and recognized by the international community of states as a whole" (Art. 53 of the Vienna Convention Law of Treaties); "In order to liberate mankind from such an odious scourge, international cooperation is required" (Preamble of the Genocide Convention); "We recognize that, in addition to our separate responsibilities to our individual societies, we have a collective responsibility to uphold the principles of human dignity, equality and equity at the global level" (para. 2 UN Millennium Declaration); "Acknowledging that change in the Earth's climate and its adverse effects are a common concern of humankind" (preamble UN Framework Convention on Climate Change); "Affirming that the conservation of biological diversity is a common concern of humankind" (preamble UN Biodiversity Convention); "Proclaims that the Universal Declaration of Human Rights is a common standard of achievement for all peoples and all nations, to the end that every individual and every organ of society (...) shall strive" (preamble UDHR); "Determined to these ends and for the sake of present and future generations, to establish an independent permanent International Criminal Court (...) with jurisdiction over the most serious crimes of concern to the international community as a whole" (preamble ICC Statute).

[2] ICJ, *Reservations to the Convention on the Prevention and Punishment of the Crime of Genocide* (Advisory Opinion), ICJ Reports 1951, p. 15.

In the much-celebrated dictum of the *Barcelona Traction* case, the ICJ introduced a distinction between international obligations of a bilateral and of a community interest nature by stating that

> [an] essential distinction should be drawn between the obligations of a state towards the international community as a whole, and those arising vis-à-vis another state in the field of diplomatic protection. By their very nature the former are the concern of all states. In view of the importance of the rights involved, all states can be held to have a legal interest in their protection; they are obligations erga omnes.[3]

The Court developed this line of argument further in *Belgium v. Senegal*:

> As stated in its Preamble, the object and purpose of the Convention is "to make more effective the struggle against torture ... throughout the world". The states parties to the Convention have a common interest to ensure, in view of their shared values, that acts of torture are prevented and that, if they occur, their authors do not enjoy impunity. The obligations of a state party to conduct a preliminary inquiry into the facts and to submit the case to its competent authorities for prosecution are triggered by the presence of the alleged offender in its territory, regardless of the nationality of the offender or the victims, or of the place where the alleged offences occurred. All the other states parties have a common interest in compliance with these obligations by the state in whose territory the alleged offender is present. That common interest implies that the obligations in question are owed by any state party to all the other states parties to the Convention. All the states parties "have a legal interest" in the protection of the rights involved (*Barcelona Traction, Light and Power Company, Limited, Judgment, ICJ Reports 1970*, p. 32, para. 33).[4]

These obligations may be defined as "obligations erga omnes partes" in the sense that each state party has an interest in compliance with them in any given case. As the Court explains:

> The common interest in compliance with the relevant obligations under the Convention against Torture implies the entitlement of each state party to the Convention to make a claim concerning the cessation of an alleged breach by another state party. If a special interest were required for that purpose, in many cases no state would be in the position to make such a claim. It follows that any state party to the Convention may invoke the responsibility of another state party with a view to ascertaining the alleged failure to comply with its obligations erga

---

3 ICJ, *Barcelona Traction, Light and Power Company, Limited (Belgium v. Spain)* (New Application: 1962) (2nd phase) (Judgment), ICJ Reports 1970, p. 3, para. 32 (emphasis added).

4 ICJ, *Questions Relating to the Obligation to Prosecute or Extradite (Belgium v. Senegal)* (Merits), ICJ Reports 2012, p. 422, paras. 68–69.

> omnes partes, such as those under Article 6, para. 2 and Article 7, para. 1 of the Convention, and to bring that failure to an end.[5]

In *Gabčíkovo-Nagymaros*, the Court recognized the common interests in healthy ecological systems (river and estuary systems in this case) as well as the collective need to reconcile economic development and the protection of the environment when it stated:

> Throughout the ages, mankind has, for economic and other reasons, constantly interfered with nature. In the past, this was often done without consideration of the effects upon the environment. Owing to new scientific insights and to a growing awareness of the risks for mankind – for present and future generations – of pursuit of such interventions at an unconsidered and unabated pace, new norms and standards have been developed, set forth in a great number of instruments during the last two decades. Such new norms have to be taken into consideration, and such new standards given proper weight, not only when states contemplate new activities but also when continuing with activities begun in the past. This need to reconcile economic development with protection of the environment is aptly expressed in the concept of sustainable development.[6]

The Court further developed this idea by accepting a general requirement under international law to carry out an environmental impact assessment when there are risks of significant transboundary impacts. In *Pulp Mills*, the Court noted that

> [in] this sense, the obligation to protect and preserve, under Article 41 *(a)* of the Statute, has to be interpreted in accordance with a practice, which in recent years has gained so much acceptance among states that it may now be considered a requirement under general international law to undertake an environmental impact assessment where there is a risk that the proposed industrial activity may have a significant adverse impact in a transboundary context, in particular, on a shared resource. Moreover, due diligence, and the duty of vigilance and prevention which it implies, would not be considered to have been exercised, if a party planning works liable to affect the régime of the river or the quality of its waters did not undertake an environmental impact assessment on the potential effects of such works.[7]

The Court has identified some principles of international law, which are part of the obligations owed by individual states to the international community as a whole,

---

5 Ibid.

6 ICJ, *Case Concerning the Gabĉíkovo-Nagymaros Project (Hungary v. Slovakia)* (Judgment), ICJ Reports 1997, p. 7, para. 140.

7 ICJ, *Pulp Mills on the River Uruguay (Argentina v. Uruguay)* (Judgment), ICJ Reports 2010, p. 14, para. 204.

consequently implying that there is a 'common interest' for such obligations to be properly discharged by each state. In the words of the Court

> [such] obligations derive, for example, in contemporary international law, from the outlawing of acts of aggression, and of genocide, as also from the principles and rules concerning the basic rights of the human person, including protection from slavery and racial discrimination. Some of the corresponding rights of protection have entered into the body of general international law (*Reservations to the Convention on the Prevention and Punishment of the Crime of Genocide, Advisory Opinion, ICJ Reports 1951*, p. 23); others are conferred by international instruments of a universal or quasi-universal character.[8]

Two other legal terms used by the Court that are inherently linked to the concept of 'common interest', if not explicitly meant to give expression to it, are those of 'sacred trust of civilization' and 'elementary considerations of humanity'. The term 'sacred trust of civilization' has been used in cases concerned with the process of decolonization and self-determination of peoples, as expressing the 'common interest' of the international community that this process be finalized in accordance with the genuine will of the people concerned.[9] Another legal term used by the Court which expresses values protected under the 'common interest' is that of 'elementary considerations of humanity', originally meant to express a basic standard of state behaviour vis-à-vis all members of the international community.[10]

This brief review of the ICJ's case law shows that the protection of the 'common interest' has taken hold to a certain extent in the cases brought before the principal judicial organ of the UN, although the Court's findings are not always encouraging.

It is therefore important to gain a better understanding of the nature and scope of the 'international community' and 'common interests' in order to be able to properly assess whether and to what extent such interests are being safeguarded by international law.

---

8 ICJ, *Barcelona Traction* (note 3), p. 32, para. 34.

9 See among others ICJ, *Legal Consequences for States of the Continued Presence of South Africa in Namibia (South-West Africa) notwithstanding Security Council Resolution 276 (1970)* (Advisory Opinion), ICJ Reports 1971, p. 16.

10 ICJ, *The Corfu Channel Chase (United Kingdom of Great Britain and Northern Ireland v. Albania)* (Merits), ICJ Reports 1949, p. 4.

2. THE OBJECT, PURPOSE AND STRUCTURE OF THE BOOK

The book raises several related general *research questions*: What do we understand by common interest and what is its relationship to similar concepts? Which are the main areas of international law where a common interest has been or could be identified? In which ways has the common interest found recognition in various fields of international law? How do different aspects of the common interest relate to each other? Who defines common interests and what is the legitimacy of actors involved in this process? Which remedies exist, if the common interest is violated or ignored by states or international organizations? What are the responsibilities of the different actors involved?

In pursuing this research, certain *methodological principles* were followed:

1. The contributions focus on global common interests mainly from a legal and political science perspective. The areas covered range from the international environment and security to international economic law and international litigation.
2. The book deals with global common interests in public international law. It is therefore not concerned with specific joint interests of states as defined in bilateral treaties, nor with constitutional values as defined in the constitutive documents of international organizations, nor with national interests – unless such interests overlap with global common interests.
3. The objective of the book is to investigate whether and how a system of law (i.e. international law) that historically is state-centric and consensual can – today and *de lege ferenda* – protect common interests of humanity, when such common interests can only be safeguarded with the commitment and cooperation of all state and non-state actors.
4. Apart from explicit references to the common interest in various sources of international law, the book also identifies mechanisms that fit within a common interest approach in other sources that do not explicitly use a common interest terminology.

Despite the complexity of the task, the book sets out from a number of *working hypotheses*. These include:

1. Global common interests appear to be recognized mainly in three fields of international law: the law of international peace and security (encompassing for our purposes international humanitarian law, international criminal law, and universal jurisdiction issues), the law of sustainable development (with economic growth, environmental protection and social justice as its pillars), and international human rights law. The global common interest

in international law cannot be reduced to one single field (i.e. the common interest in international law does not equal 'peace' nor 'human rights' nor 'sustainable development').
2. The identification of global common interests is an actor-driven process: it is therefore necessary to assess whether the relevant actors can legitimately define an interest as a global common interest (as there is a risk that what is presented as a global common interest in fact serves a particular interest).
3. A global common interest approach requires a clarification of the role of various actors. First and foremost, of the role of the state exercising jurisdiction (if there is any such state): to what extent is that state in its exercise of sovereignty required to take the global common interest into account? But also: how should the role of other states and of other actors be defined? Are they entitled or required to act (i.e. to provide assistance or to intervene) when the global common interest is endangered through acts, omissions or lack of capacity of the state exercising jurisdiction?

The book is divided into four main parts. It sets out with a theoretical part which investigates the definition and identification of common interest (Voigt, Schaumburg-Müller, De Feyter, Buggenhoudt). This general part is followed by thematic pieces that are loosely clustered around the following themes: peace and security (Todeschini, Vidmar), (sustainable) development (Scholtz, Barros, Kettemann) and human rights (Benedek, Sørensen).

The authors come from different legal fields, though most of them are prominent scholars and practitioners in public international and human rights law. Importantly, however, they bring together a wide spectrum of views, allowing a fruitful exchange on strengthening the safeguarding of common interests through the rule of law.

We hope that the book will provide international law scholars, students, researchers, lawyers, judges and civil servants with compelling new perspectives upon the pressing issue of improving the protection of common interests. However, while focusing on international law, the book also provides important insights as to the law's potential for scholars working in other fields of law as well as for political scientists and scholars and practitioners in international relations who are not lawyers. As such, the book is a contribution to the discourse on common interests, which aims at stimulating debate and further research on how to advance the protection of common interests by the international community across geographical as much as disciplinary boundaries. Protecting common interests, as this book shows, transcends borders both real and imagined.

CHAPTER 1

DELINEATING *THE* COMMON INTEREST IN INTERNATIONAL LAW

Christina Voigt

1. INTRODUCTION

Can international law be described as a legal regime that pursues states' common interests? Is it a purposive system that aims at bringing about a common good or addressing a common concern? Or is it – as it may seem – an eclectic, self-centered, ad hoc "hotch potch" of norms with overlapping and even conflicting objectives?

Some may say that international law is about peace. But perhaps it is becoming more accurate to say that international law is eventually about humanity's survival?

Certainly, in the Grotian tradition international law is reflective of an "idea of peace". Hersch Lauterpacht – a prominent scholar in international law – noted that "international law should be functionally oriented towards both the establishment of peace between nations and the protection of human rights".[1] The modern concept of international peace treaties is often dated back to the 1648 Peace of Westphalia, which marked the end of the Thirty Years' Wars. The war involved all the major countries of Europe, and terminated with the signing of two peace treaties, consisting of detailed provisions that attempted to ensure a peaceful development.[2] The treaties established a system based on the coexistence of a plurality of states exercising unlimited authority within their own territory,[3] emphasizing inter alia the equality of states, the freedom to choose religion without intervention from other states, and the right to enter into agreements

1 H. Lauterpacht, 'The Grotian Tradition in International Law' (1946) 23 *British Yearbook of International Law* 1, 51.

2 A. Cassese, *International Law*, 2nd ed, Oxford University Press, Oxford 2005, p. 24.

3 F.X. Perrez, *Cooperative Sovereignty: From Independence to Interdependence in Structure of International Environmental Law*, Kluwer, The Hague 2000, p. 22.

with other states.[4] Since then, the international law on and for peace has grown and been diversified.[5]

While at the time of its Westphalian conception it can be said that international law first and foremost pertained to securing the interests of the sovereign in a way that aimed at ensuring orderly (if not always peaceful) coexistence, much has since changed. Industrialization, amongst other things, has created the means for human societies to prosper and expand. However, industrialization and economic as well as trade liberalization are resource and energy intensive. This is even more so, as many (if not all) environmental costs of this development remain economically unaccounted for ("externalities").

The collective pressure that states currently put on natural resources and ecological systems is starting to exceed – and is partly already exceeding – ecological thresholds.[6] This development points to inconvenient questions as to the sustainability of the current economic and political model pursued by most states. It has become clear, that significant political and legal interventions are necessary to realign development with the limits set by those thresholds.

The international legal system can thus no longer be seen as promoting mere co-existence according to the Westphalian model, but as a law of cooperation between nations in order to serve certain functions or to solve global problems.[7] In such context, the conventional view that international law is not a purposive system based on the principle of 'everything is allowed unless explicitly prohibited' is not only an outdated 'fossil' but an invalid and potentially destructive premise.[8]

Modern international law has to deal with a far wider variety of challenges than those deriving exclusively from forcible intervention in the affairs of other states.

---

4 M. Ruud and G. Ulfstein, *Innføring i folkerett*, 4th ed, Universitetsforlaget, Oslo 2011, p. 32.

5 See, for example, the Briand-Kellogg Pact of 1928, The Hague Conventions of 1899 and 1907, the UN Charter, the OAS Charter, the African Charter on Human and People's Rights, the Protocol to the African Charter on the Rights of Women in Africa, the UN Declaration on Principles of International Law Concerning Friendly Relations and Cooperation Among States, the Declaration on the Strengthening of International Security, the Definition of Aggression, the UN General Assembly Resolutions on Peace, UNESCO declarations, and the current UN Human Rights Council Advisory Committee on the Right to Peace Draft Declaration on the Right to Peace etc.

6 See, for example, OECD, *Environmental Outlook to 2050: The Consequences of Inaction*, OECD, Paris 2012; OECD, *Millennium Ecosystem Assessment, Living Beyond Our Means*, OECD, Paris 2005 and J. Rockström et al., 'Planetary Boundaries: Exploring the Safe Operating Space for Humanity' (2009) 14 *Ecology and Society 2*, 32.

7 P. Sands, 'Turtles and Torturers: The Transformation of International Law' (2001) 33 *New York University Journal of International Law and Policy 2*, 527–559; Perrez (note 3); W. Friedmann, *The Changing Structure of International Law*, Columbia University Press, New York 1964.

8 See J. Pauwelyn, *Conflict of Norms in Public International Law*, Cambridge University Press, Cambridge 2003, p. 154.

Various pressures of a modern, globalized world are forcing the international community of states (as the 'legislators' of international law) to think anew and recognize a more collectively oriented international legal system; socially oriented in the sense of recognizing international actors in their capacity to act in concert for the 'common good of all'. The concepts of 'global commons', 'common concern' or the 'common interests of mankind' are strong indicators of such a shift. In particular, the recognition of fundamental human rights and of environmental needs has been a crucial catalyst for a change. Global environmental threats, such as ozone depletion, global climate change, loss of biodiversity and advancing desertification damage not only individual states, but the world at large. Pollution knows no national boundaries, nor does the problem of a changing global climate. There is a high risk of climate change impacting on the stability of the global community, and the challenges facing international law to construct equitable and cooperative global responses to shared problems are already in sight.[9]

The cooperation needed to tackle the climate change challenge is, in Judge *Weeramantry's* words, 'not merely passive cooperation, but rather active cooperation. If we are to save our global inheritance, we must do so actively. We need, for this purpose, to be willing to surrender some part of sovereignty to the rest of the world, accepting common guidance by the global community'.[10] In this globalized and interdependent world, the recognition has therefore grown that states need to cooperate – to actively engage with each other – in standing a chance of addressing global challenges of an unprecedented nature.

In this chapter, we will investigate the notion of 'commonness' in international law. Particular attention will be given to the term "common conscience" as prescribed to general principles of international law. We then will continue to reflect over types of common interests as we see included in contemporary international legal treaties – with a special focus on international environmental law.

In the end, however, we arrive at the conclusion that there really is only *one* overarching common interest in international law: the interest of ensuring the long-term survival of humankind as expressed in the principle of sustainable development, based on equity, dignity and the rule of law.

---

9 See Wang, 'Sustainable International Climate Change Law: A Future Legal Research Agenda' in M.C. Cordonier-Segger and A. Khalfan (eds), *Sustainable Development Law: Principles, Practices and Prospects*, Oxford University Press, Oxford 2004, p. 353 et seq. See also, as a practical example, IEA report, *Energy Technology Perspectives: Scenarios and Strategies to 2050*, June 2006, providing a ground-breaking analysis of the prospects of global energy security and supply, which calls for the urgent and decisive cooperation on the promotion and implementation of energy efficiency and renewable energy technologies.

10 Ibid., p. xi.

2. EVOLUTION OF THE COMMON INTEREST IN INTERNATIONAL LAW

Studies of honeybees and ants suggest a common interest among the workers of complex insect societies and indicate how it might evolve.[11] Honeybee workers express a common interest in raising their queen's, rather than their half-sisters', eggs. Workers of large, complex ant colonies also serve their common interest.[12] Army ant *(Eciton burchelli)* workers choose their queen and her mate by their productivity, which benefits all in terms of collective survival, mutual defense against predators and reuse of resources (nests).[13]

What does ecology tell us? Apart from the fact that collective well-being is confined by ecological limits, these studies show that the reconciliation of individual advantage with the group's good is a result of evolution; it is not naturally inherent in individuals. But what is the striking difference between insect colonies and human society? Arguably it is automatism. Once started, the mechanisms of a beehive or of an ant hill do not require conscience or intelligence. Habits and customs are automatically learned and handed down. This ensured their being preserved unchanged.

Human societies, undergoing changes, interruptions and diversification, will have to consciously make decisions and align their activities for the common good, if so desired. Already Adam Smith proposed that individuals can share sufficient interest in their society's welfare to profit by cooperating for its benefit and by jointly suppressing behavior hurtful to it. In other words, if individuals had sufficient common interest in their group's good, they would combine to suppress the activities of members acting contrary to the group's welfare.[14] In human societies, arguably, the common interest is not an automatic reflex, but presupposes a (more or less) conscious decision, which again, presupposes conscience.

If this applies to human societies, it does even more so to human-made collectives, one of them being collectives of states. For states, the conscience that determines their actions and behavior is to a certain extent expressed in the law that governs their relations – international law. As mentioned, this law has since its inception increasingly been complemented by international legal rules and principles

---

11 E.G. Leigh, 'Genes, Bees and Ecosystems: The Evolution of a Common Interest Among Individuals' (1991) 6 *Trends in Ecology and Evolution* 8, 257–262.

12 K.R. Foster and F.L.W. Ratnieks, 'Convergent Evolution of Worker Policing by Egg Eating in the Honey Bee and Common Wasp' in (2001) *Proceedings of the Royal Society*, 169–174.

13 N.R. Franks and A. Ants, 'A Collective Intelligence' (1989) 77 *American Scientist*, 139.

14 A. Smith, *The Theory of Moral Sentiments*, A. Millar, London 1759. See also R. Axelrod, *The Evolution of Cooperation*, Basic Books, New York 1984, on reconciliation of individual advantage with the group's good.

facilitating the cooperation of states and other actors at the international level. Wolfgang Friedman and, later, Franz Xaver Perrez,[15] famously pointed to this development. Friedman also observed that the law of cooperation demanded a certain community of interests or values of the legal subjects.

2.1. COMMON INTEREST IN INTERNATIONAL LAW AS EXPRESSED IN "GENERAL PRINCIPLES"

Common interests have been a part of international law for a long time. For example, the discussion on the inclusion of general principles in Article 38 of the Statute of the International Court of Justice gives evidence of the long standing tradition to give account to certain issues that are of general interest.

General principles are recognized as distinct sources of international law.[16] Article 38 (1) (c) of the Statute of the International Court of Justice refers to general principles of law recognized by civilized nations.

The inclusion in and the wording of Article 38(1)(c) of the ICJ Statute reveal however a fundamental controversy in public international law. The Committee that prepared the Statute could not find a definite consensus on the role and significance of general principles. This situation is indicative of the division in international law between a concept of natural law and positive law. Baron *Descamps*, the President of the Committee, had supposedly a natural law concept in mind[17] when suggesting 'rules of international law as recognized by the legal

15 Friedmann (note 7), and Perrez (note 3).

16 See H. Thirlway, 'The Sources of International Law' in M.D. Evans (ed), *International Law*, Oxford University Press, Oxford 2003, p. 132; I. Brownlie, *Principles of Public International Law*, 6th ed, Oxford University Press, Oxford 2003, p. 15; M. Bogdan, 'General Principles of Law and the Problem of Lacunae in the Law of Nations' (1977) 46 *Nordic Journal of International Law* 42; B. Cheng, *General Principles of Law as Applied by International Courts and Tribunals*, Cambridge University Press, Cambridge 1953; P. Hulsroj, 'Three Sources – No River: A Hard Look At the Sources of Public International Law with Particular Emphasis on Custom and "General Principles of Law"' (1999) 54 *Zeitschrift für öffentliches Recht* 244; B. Simma and P. Alston, 'The Sources of Human Rights Law: Custom, Jus Cogens and General Principles' (1991) 12 *Australian Yearbook of International Law*, 102; M. Bos, 'The Recognized Manifestation of International Law' (1977) 20 *German Yearbook of International Law*, 33.

17 Whether or not Baron Descamps was an advocate for natural law is somewhat contentious. Descamps believed in the importance of 'civilization' in international law. His notion of civilized nations or 'legal conscience' refers to a concept of objective justice. Whether such objective justice is pre-imposed onto the conscience of civilized nations or a product or consequence of civilization is not clear. See Bos (1977), p. 37. This vagueness has given rise to critique. For a critique of the notion "civilized nations" as having a racist undertone by effectively excluding the interests of decolonized states see: A. Anghie, *Imperialism, Sovereignty and the Making of International Law*, Cambridge University Press, Cambridge 2004, pp. 226f.

conscience of civilized nations' as one of the (four) rules[18] to be applied by the judge in the solution of international disputes.[19] These rules, he stated, constitute 'objective justice' by being 'the rules necessary for the system of international relations'.[20]

On the other hand, *Root*, another member of the Commission, took a rather positivistic stance in expressing the concern of whether 'a Government would agree to allow itself to be arraigned before a Court who bases its sentences on its subjective conception of the principles of justice'.[21] *Descamps* countered the argument by clarifying that 'the fundamental law of justice and injustice is deeply engraved on the heart of every human being and is given its highest and most authoritative expression in the legal conscience of civilized nations'.[22]

Despite the various views, the Committee was able to prepare a text intended to give the Court a certain power to develop and refine the principles of international jurisprudence.[23] This text, suggesting 'the general principles of law recognized by civilized nations' as one of the sources of international law, was finally transposed into Article 38 of the Statute of the ICJ.

When discussing how such principles are identified, an element of *recognition by states* is required.[24] In can thus be said that general principles are norms adopted by the international community, whether the norm is derived from municipal law or not.[25] They are norms 'of general validity which is manifested not in a single statutory provision, but by a group of mutually interdependent legal rules or their system'.[26]

General principles are principles that are recognized by a *common sense* of nations. There is a shared understanding in the international community of their existence and their implications.

---

18 The other three rules were 1) conventional international law, whether general or special, being rules expressly adopted by the states; 2) international custom, being practice between nations accepted by them as law; and 3) international jurisprudence as a means for the application and development of law, Permanent Court of International Justice, Advisory Committee of Jurists, *Procès-Verbaux* of the Proceedings of the Committee, 16 June – 24 July 1920, with Annexes, 306.

19 Ibid., p. 306.

20 Ibid., p. 323.

21 Ibid., p. 309.

22 Ibid., pp. 310–311.

23 Brownlie (note 16), p. 16.

24 See for further discussion on the provenance of general principles: Ch. Voigt, *Sustainable Development as a Principle of International Law*, Martinus Nijhoff, Leiden 2009, p. 153ff.

25 Hulsroj (note 16), p. 245. Simma and Alston (note 16), p. 102, note 85.

26 G. Herczegh, *General Principles of International Law and the International Legal Order*, Akadémiai Kiadó, Budapest 1969, p. 11ff.

Such a view is based on a 'common legal conscience'; an *opinio juris communis.*[27] The initial phrases suggested by *Descamps* 'manifestation la conscience juridique des peuples civilizées' may be translated into English as 'the sense common to all civilized peoples of what is juridically right or wrong' or simply as 'the *opinio juris communis* of civilized mankind'. Others[28] refer to it as 'Rechtsbewußtsein der Menschheit'.

Whose legal conscience is relevant in this regard? There is evident difficulty attributing conscience to an entity like a state. With regard to custom, it is acknowledged that the legal 'state of mind' has to be deduced from state conduct, that is, pronouncements, statements, actions by foreign ministers, civil servants, judges etc. However, the establishment of general principles includes an *opinio juris communis* which not only embraces a 'state of mind' of state actors but a 'legal animus' supported by a wider spectrum of actors. *Hulsroj* contends in this context [t]hat every actor on the international law scene is relevant – and that the need for broad consensus means that it will be the attitude of a mix of categories of actors that will be formative of a 'general principle'.[29]

Given *Descamps* proposal that 'the sense common to all civilized peoples' can be exchanged with the 'opinio juris communis of mankind', a suggestion can be made that includes actors at sub-national levels, e.g. indigenous peoples, communities, national NGO's or cross-national levels, e.g. international NGOs, other international organizations, such as WTO, IMF, WB etc. The expression 'nations' that is now to be found in the text of Article 38(1)(c) of the Statute of the International Court of Justice originates from an amendment made by *Root*. The original text of the proposal referred to 'peuples', i.e. 'peoples' or 'mankind'. In the sound of the tone of the original proposal, the word "nation" in Article 38(1)(c) ICJ Statute should be understood not in its politico-legal sense, as it is used in "League of *Nations*", "United *Nations*" or "Inter*nation*al Law" but in its more general sense of a people, as for instance, the Scottish *nation*, the French *nation*, the Maori *nation* etc.

What can be concluded here is that general principles depend on recognition by states. In addition, however, their recognition is based on an opinio juris communis, a general global consensus, about what is just and what is unjust. This common legal conscience is inferred from the *'opinion universelle'* about justice. The universality applies not only horizontally – *all* states – but exhibits a vertical dimension as well – general opinion shared by a larger variety of actors. Finding

27 Ibid.

28 See J.C. Bluntschli, *Das moderne Völkerrecht der civilisirten Staaten: als Rechtsbuch dargestellt*, C.H. Beck, Nördlingen 1868, p. 65. He sees this *Rechtsbewußtsein* as the all-embracing concept for all non-written international law.

29 Hulsroj (note 16), p. 246.

how and where to look for general principles is partly overlapping with finding opinio juris of states. But the search will also have to cover a wider variety of texts, ideas and facts than those accepted by states. Statements of NGOs, indigenous peoples, local governments, for example, may be indicative of a general legal conscience, given it is widely enough expressed.

2.2. COMMON INTERESTS PROTECTED THROUGH INTERNATIONAL LAW

A prominent example of a common interest protected through international law is world peace and security. In relation to the maintenance of international peace and security, the term 'common interest' has entered the Charter of the United Nations. Its preamble states that the peoples of the UN are determined 'to ensure ... that armed forces shall not be used, save in the common interest ...' (at recital seven). Obligations aiming at the preservation of this common good are the obligation to refrain from the use of force (Article 2(4) UN Charter) or the obligations arising from disarmament treaties.

What is new, however, is that the structure of international law is undergoing changes – from a network of reciprocal and bilateral obligations to a system that increasingly accommodates the notion of obligations owed to an international community of states – and ultimately of all humankind. These structural changes occur at the same time as we see international norms expanding into more and more areas of state policy and deeper and deeper into the regulatory texture of states. Simultaneously, we can observe a transformation of the moral stance of international law: from an order that was largely indifferent to the concerns of individuals, or of human life and activities in general to a legal order which promotes individual human rights. This is all the more important, given that international law evolved from an order that permitted governments to cause or tolerate human sufferings that would not be accepted within their own societies to one centrally concerned with human wellbeing.[30]

We see this in the fields of maintenance of peace and security, protection of the environment, human rights, the most atrocious crimes, and minimal degree of economic solidarity. Judge Bruno Simma, in his celebrated Hague lectures "From Bilateralism to Community Interest in International Law" (2008) put it this way:

---

30 B. Kingsbury and M. Donaldson, 'From Bilateralism to Publicness in International Law' in U. Fastenrath, R. Geiger, D.-E. Khan, A. Paulus, S. von Schorlemer and Ch. Vedder (eds), *From Bilateralism to Community Interests, Essays in Honour of Judge Bruno Simma*, Oxford University Press, Oxford 2011, p. 81.

> International law has undoubtedly entered a stage at which it does not exhaust itself in correlative rights and obligations running between states, but also incorporates common interests of the international community as a whole, including not only states but all human beings. In doing so, it begins to display more and more features which do not fit into the ... 'bilateralist' structure of the traditional law. In other words, it is on its way to being a true public law.

The essential characteristic of common interests is that they transcend the interests of single states and instead correspond to the needs, hopes and fears of all human beings. It has been suggested that the importance of the interests makes it a common one. Common interests are those that transcend the boundaries of a single state.

Others define common interests as encompassing "fundamental values as well as interests shared by groups of states collectively".[31] The subset of rules of international law that protects and pursues such shared interests and values are referred to as "community interest norms".[32] Others, again, differentiate between community interest norms that seek to protect common goods (international peace, the environment) or common values (human rights) – although the dividing line is rather blurred.[33]

At the same time it needs to be noted, however, that common interests are not disconnected from states' egocentric interests. Rather, common interests are the result or the sum of "coinciding individual interests".[34]

While international law has or is about to incorporate common interests of the international community it has not clearly defined the relationship of these interests to each other. Neither has it – different from the natural laws of an ant hill or beehive – shown any sign of delineating and/or incorporating *the primary* common interest of collective survival. We will come back to this towards the end of this chapter.

While collective survival naturally should be an interest, it has rather become a concern – a concern because the survival of human kind may be something,

31 I. Feichtner, 'Community Interest' in R. Wolfrum (ed), *Max Planck Encyclopedia of Public International Law*, Oxford University Press, Oxford (online ed), paras. 1–12.

32 Ch. Tams, 'Individual States as Guardians of Community Interests' in U. Fastenrath, R. Geiger, D.-E. Khan, A. Paulus, S. von Schorlemer and Ch. Vedder (eds), *From Bilateralism to Community Interests, Essays in Honour of Judge Bruno Simma*, Oxford University Press, Oxford 2011, p. 380.

33 Ibid., p. 380.

34 J. Brunnee, '"Common Interests" – Echoes from an Empty Shell? Some Thoughts on Common Interest and International Environmental Law' (1989) *Zeitschrift für ausländisches öffentliches Recht und Völkerrecht*, 793.

which not only is, and should be, in the interests of all – but because it is something that increasingly requires collective action and responses in order to be addressed properly.

3. FROM COMMON INTEREST TO COMMON CONCERN

This brings us to the difference between common interest and common concern.

One writer notes that "common interests" are reflected in global environmental law by the concept of "common concern".[35] Another sees "common concern of humankind" as being "only one facet of common interest".[36] But what makes a common interest a common concern? And are the two notions the same or do they differ?

The semantic difference "interest"/"concern" suggests a difference in normative meaning and force. This view finds support by those writers that claim that the distinction lies in the "importance of the values at stake".[37]

It has been suggested that "common concern" may "indicate a *higher normative status inasmuch* as it addresses issues of fundamental value. The notion "common concern" emphasizes the potential dangers underlying the global problems of climatic change, the destruction of the ozone layer or decimation of biological diversity. This could imply that international governance regarding these "concerns" is not only necessary or "nice to have" but rather essential for the survival of humankind.[38]

At this place it is important to note that also the opposite argument could be made: That "concerns" indicate more general issues related to the environment, as opposed to "interest" which may pertain to a specific issue. It might be easier for states to agree on a common concern than on a common interest, thereby reserving "common concerns" for those issues where despite global attention no specific legal interest can be identified or no concrete commitment is made. In jurisprudence "common concern" is accordingly hardly used. In the field of human rights the notion of human rights concerns is often used, which does not

---

[35] E. Hey, 'Global Environmental Law: Common Interests and the (Re)constitution of Public Space' (2009) 1 *Iustum Aequum Salutare*, 41–57, 42.

[36] Brunnee (note 34), p. 792.

[37] D. Shelton, 'Common Concern of Humanity' (2009) 1 *Iustum Aequum Salutare*, 33, 34, referring to A. Kiss.

[38] F. Biermann, '"Common Concerns of Humankind": The Emergence of a new Concept of International Environmental Law' (1996) 34 *Archiv des Völkerrechts* 426, 431.

mean that there is an pre-existing interest, but that the mobilization around the common concern – for example human rights of disabled persons – develops a common interest which then is translated into legal instruments.

While this might be the case in human rights law, in the field of international environmental law "concern" entails a stronger imperative than "interest". "Concern" indicates that we are dealing with an issue of urgency, potentially devastating, possibly irreversible environmental impacts and wide-ranging and long-time socio-economic effects. The importance of an issue may make it a concern, but it does not necessarily make it a "common" one. Instead, issues of common concern are those that inevitably transcend the boundaries of a single state and require collective action in response. And here is the main difference: Common concerns require collaborative, concerted *action!* They require cooperation. Furthermore, they necessarily imply a constraint on states' sovereignty. Concerns cannot be addressed by all states agreeing that there is a concern – like an interest – but by *doing* something about it. Yet, common concerns presuppose common interests. "No state can resolve the problems they pose or receive all the benefits they provide. Harm to a matter of common concern is often widespread and diffuse in origin, making it difficult if not impossible to rely on traditional bilateral notions of state responsibility to enforce international norms. When the harm is mitigated, all or at least large parts of the community benefit."[39]

It is thus no surprise that common concern norms evolved at a time in international law, where it is "at a turning point from a system balancing conflicting sovereign interests to one of constructive interaction for the common good".[40] Neither is it surprising that the notion (or concept) of "common concern" evolved in international environmental law. It is *this* area of law, which "will need to go beyond weighing the rights and obligations of parties within a closed compartment of individual state self-interest, unrelated to the global concerns of humanity as a whole".[41]

Environmental issues are common ones because they often cannot be managed effectively by national or regional efforts. Moreover, environmental benefits and burdens are shared by all persons. The climate, the ozone layer, the oceans, biodiversity, indeed the entire physical world form an interdependent ecological system, much of which can only be protected at the global level, making it a common concern of all humanity.[42] Illustrative examples of international norms protecting common goods are found in international environmental law. The

39 Shelton (note 37), p. 34.
40 Brunnee (note 34), p. 793.
41 Shelton (note 37), p. 33, 34.
42 Ibid., p. 35.

United Nations Framework Convention on Climate Change affirms in its first paragraph of its preamble that "change in the Earth's climate and its adverse effects are a common concern of humankind". Slightly differently, the 1992 Convention on Biological Diversity proclaims "the importance of biological diversity for evolution and for maintaining life sustaining systems in the biosphere" and affirms "that the conservation of biological diversity is a common concern of humankind". What we see here can be described as a negative and a positive (if there is such a thing) concern. The point is, however, that both conservation (of biodiversity) and change (of the Earth's climate) are processes which either need to be maintained (conservation) or stopped (climate change). Both are directed at specific processes. Both mean that something *has to happen* in order to address these concerns. And both suggest that international cooperation is necessary to address conservation of biodiversity (or the loss thereof) and climate change. Because, if not, the consequences will be dire – for all, the international community, including states, human and (arguably in these two examples) also non-human communities.

4. LEGAL IMPLICATIONS OF COMMON CONCERNS

What are the legal implications of these common notions? The question is contentious, of course. Because we find explicit notions of common interest and common concern mainly in treaty provisions, the theme of sovereignty and sovereign rights remains largely intact.[43] Moreover, the concepts of common interest and common concern also leaves existing jurisdictional regimes intact. It rather requires that states *cooperate* with each other on the basis of equity in addressing the identified issues.[44]

Common concerns do not connote specific rules and obligations (neither of result nor of conduct), but establish the general basis (or entitlement or even mandate) for the concerned community to act cooperatively to address the concern. Yet, "the right and duty of the international community to act in matters of common concern must be balanced with respect to sovereignty. States retain sovereignty *subject* to the requirements of international law developed to ensure the common interest".[45] In other words, the concept of common concern signals that a state's freedom of action may be subject to limits even where other states' sovereign

43 Ibid., p. 37.
44 Hey (note 35), p. 43.
45 Shelton (note 37), p. 38.

rights are not affected. Where the common concern is recognized, the matter is no longer solely an internal affair of a State.[46]

In this context it has been suggested by several writers that the concept of common concern could widen the range of environmental protection obligations owed erga omnes.[47] This issue is not resolved. Here, we want to point out that the invocation of an obligation owed to the international community as a whole, requires just that: an obligation. As mentioned above, so far it is difficult to derive concrete obligations from common concerns. Which does not mean that some obligations exist that are of the common concern of all states and that "with a view of the importance of the rights involved, all states can be held to have a legal interest in their protection".[48] But common interests must first lead to an obligation and when that obligation is breached, liability might follow.[49]

Another, related question is whether common concern could be used as a justification for unilateral actions that have implications for other states' sovereignty. While treaty law is existent, common concerns could also find expression in customary law or as a general principle. "The unilateral enforcement of law in the common interest is the facet, where the common interest (or concern) gains particular importance as a legal concept, since states wishing to enforce universally applicable (customary) standards would no longer have to prove any specific legal interest other that the protection of the interests of the community as a whole."[50]

Yet, treaty negotiations may be more conducive to forging the content or form of cooperation.[51] For example, if something were of common concern, for example the "protection of the natural environment" (ILA Declaration 2002), absent a treaty, the legal implications would be subject to debate.[52] But treaties can also help crystallize the legal consequences that generally attach to common concerns and, thereby, contribute to the development of a customary norm.

After all this has been said, there is one important observation to make: The striking absence of an expressed common concern regarding the fundamental conditions that have to be in place for ensuring collective welfare – and eventually

---

46 N. Matz, 'Comment: The Common Interest in International Law: Some Reflections on its Normative Content' (2002) *Zeitschrift für ausländisches öffentliches Recht und Völkerrecht*, 17, 19.

47 Shelton (note 37), p. 37.

48 ICJ, *Barcelona Traction, Light and Power Company, Limited (Belgium v. Spain) (New Application: 1962)* (2nd phase) (Judgment), ICJ Reports 1970, p. 3, para. 33.

49 Matz (note 46), p. 18.

50 Ibid.

51 For a similar view, see Brunnee (note 34), p. 565.

52 Ibid., p. 566.

survival – of humanity. Changes in the atmosphere and the effects thereof as well as the conservation of biological diversity are all critically important. Yet, they need to be woven together. How do they relate to each other and to other collective interests, for example the liberalization of trade and raising the standards of living?

5. THE MISSING LINK: SUSTAINABLE DEVELOPMENT

All common interests and concerns we identified so far do not in themselves constitute the ultimate goal of the international society – but are means to improve the moral and economic well-being of humanity as a whole.[53] The missing link is their relationship to that overall goal; a relationship that also defines priorities.

The ultimate goal of human society is, arguably, the meeting of the needs of a growing, diverse global population – now and in the future – within the fragile confines of healthy ecological systems and a safe global climate. This goal is aptly captured in the principle of sustainable development. Sustainable development is commonly defined as "development that meets the needs of the present without compromising future generations to meet their own needs".[54]

But "unsustainable practices are woven deeply into the fabric of modern life", as Kofi Annan aptly expressed.[55] Unsustainable development has increased the stress on Earth's limited natural resources and on the carrying capacity of ecosystems. No legal document exists – yet – which affirms the common global concern of unsustainable development (or on a more positive note: the common interest of/in sustainable development); only fragmented concerns, which can only be "pieces of the puzzle".

The closest we get to the recognition of such concern is the ILA New Delhi Declaration of Principles of International Law Relating to Sustainable Development of 2 April 2002.[56] This document emphasizes that sustainable development is a matter of common concern both to developing and industrialized countries and that, as such, it should be integrated into all relevant fields of policy in order to realize the goals of environmental protection, development and respect for human rights.

---

53 Shelton (note 37), p. 38.

54 Report by the World Commission on Environment and Development, "Our Common Future", 1987.

55 Statement by Secretary General Kofi A. Annan, Johannesburg South Africa (3 September 2001). UN Press Release SG/SM8358, AFR/468, ENV/DEV/693.

56 UN Doc. A/CONF.199/8 (9 August 2002).

The document further noted that sustainable development is now widely accepted as a global objective and that the concept has been amply recognized in various international and national legal instruments, including treaty law and jurisprudence at international and national levels.

The promotion of sustainable development through international law recognizes that our collective, long-term survival matters and that collective development and well-being is confined by ecological limits. The Brundtland report already warned 25 year ago: "But ultimate limits there are." and "There are objective limits to what nature can bear". The report succinctly warned that "Human laws must be reformulated to keep human activities in harmony with the unchanging and universal laws of nature". This was and is a tough call – and states still have to figure out how to practically and effectively implement this insight.

Sustainable development has been amply recognized in various international and national legal instruments, including treaty law and jurisprudence at international and national levels.[57] What is the legal status of sustainable development then? Is it an objective, a concept, a process, a principle, or all of those things?[58] My argument is that it already is a general principle of law – reflective of a common conscience of the international community. Its normative force, broad scope and support in the international community are indicative of its principled character. It is reflected in a large number of binding international agreements as well as being used as a legal instrument by international courts and tribunals in the interpretation of treaties and settlement of disputes.[59]

Sustainable development has a normative content which is defined by the reconciliation of present and future economic, social and environmental interests within the limits set by certain essential ecological functions. In this way, sustainable development has been recognized widely both by international and national legislatures and jurisprudential practice. The general recognition of its normative content can be understood as forming an opinio juris communis. The classification of sustainable development as a general principle of law is legitimized by its widespread use in many national legal systems and in international law – signifying a common conscience, and the jurisprudence of international courts and tribunals, as well as by its moral necessity.

The reflection of sustainable development in the legal conscience of the international community is an important indicator for its evolution into a

---

57 See for an overview Cordonnier Segger and Khalfan (note 9).

58 P. Sands, *Principles of International Environmental Law*, Oxford University Press, New York 1994, p. 305.

59 For a comprehensive overview of international laws and other legal development on sustainable development see Voigt (note 24).

general principle of law. It must suffice here to refer to my writing elsewhere where I observed that the objective of sustainable development is part and parcel, sometimes even purpose, of a large number of binding and non-binding international texts and documents.[60] In uncountable ways, states, IGOs, NGOs, business associations, even multinational corporations have made reference to sustainable development. Global education programmes, e.g. the UN Decade, and the Earth Charter, national legislation, political declarations and administrative guidelines incorporate the objective of sustainable development. Global Summits have elaborated on sustainable development. Sustainable development as an integrationist principle has been endorsed by nearly all areas of society: politics, law, ethics, economics, corporate responsibility, communication, education, agriculture, architecture etc.

Based on this rich evidence, it can be concluded that the principle of sustainable development has become part of the 'universal public opinion', opinio juris communis. As a general principle, sustainable development – in particular its key aspect of integration – plays an important role in the application and enforcement of international and national law, especially in the solution of legal disputes. General principles play a normative role not only with regard to determining State conduct or the design of a policy measure, guiding legislative or regulatory action. Principles also have a normative function if they are perceived as influencing directly or indirectly the outcome of judicial decisions.[61]

6. SUSTAINABLE DEVELOPMENT AS *THE* COMMON INTEREST IN INTERNATIONAL LAW

The *rule of law* is pre-eminent to the achievement of global sustainable development. Sustainable development needs to be promoted through a variety of media, i.e. education, political decision making, research etc. – but also through law. In this context *Weeramantry* states that 'judges being such an important part of the legal establishment must necessarily be involved in this – and sensitively involved'.[62]

---

60 Voigt (note 24).

61 Koskenniemi recognizes a normative role of principles even in their indirect effect on the substance of the decisions through a Court's background theory, i.e. "when they provide knowledge of the values and goals of the legal order. Hereby they set limiting conditions for the construction of the background theory. They characterize the legal order in a very general fashion allowing the Court to perceive it in a meaningful way". M. Koskenniemi, *From Apology to Utopia: the Structure of International Legal Argument*, Cambridge University Press, Cambridge 2006, p. 381.

62 C.G. Weeramantry and M.C. Cordonier Segger (eds), *Sustainable Justice: Reconciling Economic, Social and Environmental Law*, Martinus Nijhoff, Leiden 2005, p. 444.

The judiciary assumes a particular responsibility to ensure the balanced hearing of powerful and not so powerful or even voiceless interests, i.e. where the interests of generations unborn, ecological systems or the poor are involved. The principle of sustainable development will in these cases be a working tool for the judiciary. In this sense, sustainable development as a legal principle awaits the craftsmanship of concerned and serious judges to shape it into a practical means of ensuring development based on sustainability. The practical implications of the principle will depend on the case in question and develop on a case-by-case basis. But judges can elevate the standing of the principle 'by moving it up the hierarchy of legal norms and principles, thus preventing it from being lightly brushed aside by political, commercial or other interests that seek to advance "development" whatever the cost'.[63] *Weeramantry* notes in this context:

> Sustainable development is yet an infant concept, at least so far as modern law is concerned. As an infant concept it needs to be fostered and developed. Treaties and legislation cannot anticipate the nuances of the myriad practical problems that could arise. When cases involving sustainable development arise the judiciary will find itself called upon to apply a broad general principle, the detailed implications of which have not yet been considered. ... In short the judges are at the cutting edge of the development of this concept and both domestically and internationally will need to show imagination, initiative and vision in handling a matter so deeply fraught with implications for the global future.[64]

There is still much work to be done on questions of doctrinal construction. Sustainable development is the conceptual framework that can be applied by courts and tribunals in situations where various interests intersect. In applying the principle, the different interests (and respective norms) need to be seen as equal and integral parts. The reconciliation of interests then needs to be set against the absolute limit of non-interference with certain fundamental ecological functions (that need to be protected 'at all costs').[65] In this sense, sustainable development as a legal principle of integration has been and will be applied by courts and tribunals. Good jurisprudence will be essential to its more frequent use. The judiciary is a key player in securing the construction of a mechanism that ensures the reconciliation of various interests under the framework of sustainability. Judges and arbitrators can – under certain circumstances – better defend long-term, common and global interests against the short-sighted sovereign interests often pursued by states in treaty negotiations. By developing the law the judiciary

63 Ibid., p. 445.
64 Ibid.
65 See Ch. Voigt, 'The principle of sustainable development: Integration and ecological integrity' in Ch. Voigt, *Rule of Law for Nature*, Cambridge University Press, Cambridge 2013, pp. 146ff.

could carry out punctual legislative functions and replace 'non-sustainable' law.[66] Judges thereby might become guarantors of sustainable development.[67]

Reconciliation might take a number of forms, from filling 'white spots' in the applicable law, enabling treaty interpretations that take account of this development in international, national and transnational law and to, as *Lowe* suggested, 'rewrit[ing], rather than strik[ing] down, a bargain struck by the parties that is shown to lead to unsustainable development'.[68]

An overview over the potential use of the concept by judges is found by *Frerichs*:

> Dennoch sprechen einige Argumente für die rechtliche Verwendung des Konzepts nachhaltiger Entwicklung, nämlich als Metanorm für den gerichtlichen Gebrauch. Gemeint sind damit Normen zweiter Ordnung, die den Richtern Argumentations- und Entscheidungshilfen in solchen Fällen bieten, in denen (gewohnheitsrechtliche und/oder vertragliche) Normen erster Ordnung konfligieren, also Abwägungsentscheidungen zu treffen sind. Auch wo das Leitbild nachhaltiger Entwicklung noch nicht kodifiziert ist, kann es über die Urteilsbegründungen in die Rechtsprechung einfließen und normative Kraft und institutionelle Wirkung entfalten.[69]

It is this function of the principle of sustainable development that makes it currently one of the most vibrant elements of international law. A coherent, normative theory of sustainable development which combines arguments of sociological, governance, democratic, economic and moral theories could elicit its key role in the transformation process of international societies. In whichever 'legal fold' it will fall in the end – a recognition as a common interest might pave the way for a stronger legal footing. As a consequence, it may then require international action to address unsustainable practices and necessitate new forms of law-making, compliance techniques and enforcement. Here, all

---

66 S. Frerichs, *Die rechtliche Dimension einer nachhaltigen Entwicklung in der Europäischen Union*, Otto-Friedrich-Universität Bamberg, Bamberg 2003, pp. 13–14. With regard to the responsibilities of the European Court of Justice she suggests that '[w]enn dem Gemeinschaftsgesetzgeber … keine generelle Untätigkeit vorgeworfen werden kann, jedoch eine manglende (sekundärrechtliche) Operationalisierung des Nachhaltigkeitsziels, könnte der EuGH somit zum regulativen Einschreiten legitimiert sein' (ibid., 14).

67 See also M. Decleris, *The Law of Sustainable Development: General Principles: Report produced for the European Commission*, Office for Official Publications of the European Communities, Luxembourg 2000, pp. 9–10, 38–48, 69–79. He notes: 'But for public law to become sustainable, as it must, legal methods must become sustainable first. The process will begin with court decisions, which are a sensitive index of the changes taking place' (ibid., 9).

68 V. Lowe, 'Sustainable Development and Unsustainable Arguments' in A. Boyle and D. Freestone (eds), *International Law and Sustainable Development: Past Achievements and Future Challenges,* Oxford University Press, Oxford 1999, pp. 39–60.

69 S. Frerichs, *Nachhaltige Entwicklung als Forschungsziel – Fragen an die Soziologie der Wissenschaft*, Center for European Studies, University of Trier, Trier 2002.

who are forming the law: legal scholars, law makers, judges, civil servants, civil society – all have a responsibility. That is defining and delineating *the* common interest in the 21st century and beyond.

CHAPTER 2
TO WHAT EXTENT DOES INTERNATIONAL LAW OBSTRUCT THE PROTECTION OF COMMON INTERESTS?

Sten SCHAUMBURG-MÜLLER

1. INTRODUCTION

The question posed in the title may make one think of the problems of how to promote common interests in a world consisting of sovereign states, each pursuing their own goals and interests (or the goals and interests of their rulers). However, states are not and have never been the only units in international society, nor are they the only relevant actors in international law. Consequently the only relevant questions to pose are not how to protect common goals in a world of states or how to make more than 180 states act in pursuance of common interests. The legal world has never only consisted in sovereign states, playing the game of international relations ruled by international law. All along there were empires, companies and individuals, empires which may have played the sovereignty game at home, but disregarded sovereignty elsewhere whenever interference suited their interests, companies executing power overseas and individuals in need of having their property rights defended, no matter the state borders. In addition to states, also empires, companies and individuals have played important parts at the world stage and in international law, parts which tend to be ignored if one conceives international relations as relations among states and international law as law between states. I am not arguing that states are not important, and I recognize the fact that the world is divided into states, legally and de facto, and I recognize that that division has its problems in relation to pursuing common interests. However, I argue that the world is more than states, that international relations are more than relations among states, that international law is more than law between states, and that this 'more' generates its own problems in relation to the pursuit of common goals. I am not arguing that it is totally mistaken to perceive the world as consisting of sovereign states, I am only claiming that it is partly wrong – which is bad enough as it prevents us from seeing some of the pertinent problems.

For the purposes of this contribution I shall refer to the idea that the world basically consists of sovereign states as the conventionalist view,[1] and to the system of sovereign states as *Westphalia*.[2] The aim of the present contribution is therefore to focus on obstacles to protect common interests stemming from non-*Westphalian* traits and traditions of international law, traits that have been largely ignored by conventionalist views. One may of course argue that after the UN Charter and the decolonization process, the *Westphalian* model of equal sovereign states constitutes the basic principle of international law, and that even if the European powers upheld an imperialist regime for centuries, this is simply no longer the case. And similarly one may argue that even though the UN Charter contains a chapter on an International Trusteeship System, such systems have become obsolete as all territories are now members of the United Nations and as such sovereign and equal according to the UN Charter Article 78. A strong counterargument against this view claims that international law was shaped in times of imperialism and that imperialism is still an inherent component of international law, even as we know it today.[3] If this claim is true, certainly international law is in itself an obstacle to protect common interests. I shall deal with this question in section 3. A less radical counterargument claims that in addition to *Westphalia* with its system of sovereign states, we have had a non-*Westphalian* system all along, consisting of ideas and practices of shared sovereignty and extraterritorial application of law, especially property rights. Previously, the two systems were applied in different parts of the world, *Westphalian* in most of Europe and non-*Westphalian* in the remainder, but now both systems have expanded and cover the entire globe, even though the two categories of ideas and practices are mutually irreconcilable.[4] I shall deal with this position in section 4. Based on the analyses of sections 3 and 4 I shall come up with some conclusions and perspectives in section 5. Before doing this, I shall briefly outline some theoretical considerations, immediately below section 2.

2. THEORETICAL INSPIRATIONS

The present contribution is inspired by what is sometimes referred to as path dependence. This term indicates "that where we go next depends not only on

1 Within international relations theory, Hedley Bull is a conventionalist, see infra note 10. Within international law Antonio Cassese draws a conventional picture of international law, bringing in "emerging trends", which in fact may have been there for as long as we have had international law, *International Law*, 2nd ed, Oxford University Press, Oxford 2005.

2 I am not thereby making any precise historical claims as to the Treaties of Westphalia. I merely assume that there is such a connection between the treaties and the system of sovereign states that it makes sense to apply the term.

3 A. Anghie, *Imperialism, Sovereignty and the Making of International Law*, Cambridge University Press, Cambridge 2004.

4 E. Keene, *Beyond the Anarchical Society*, Cambridge University Press, Cambridge 2002.

where we are now, but also upon where we have been",[5] implying that we are likely to make choices according to past experience and that societal institutions and institutional memory are bound to influence our choices, no matter whether we are aware of the various paths that we previously have taken. For the present purpose I am not interested in isolating determinants, and in fact I am only making a rather banal claim, namely that history tends to be sticky. Patterns of behavior may repeat themselves, even when they are no longer relevant, and also when we are not aware of them; and patterns of conceptions are part of a collective process.[6]

In addition, I am inspired by constructivism in international relations, the relevant idea being that ideas and beliefs matter. If state leaders tend to conceive the world as anarchical, they tend to behave accordingly, thereby reinforcing anarchical traits in world politics.[7] Combining the two, the main idea is that where we are able to go, i.e. how we are able to solve problems such as dealing with the protection of common interests also depends on where we believe we have been. If we believe that the world has only recently been globalized, thus failing to include past globalization in our conception, we are more likely to go astray in the future. And similarly, if we believe that the world has for the past centuries mainly consisted of sovereign states, thereby making it difficult to pursue common goals because of competition and anarchy among states, we are not able to understand that all along empires sought (or at least claimed) to take care of larger goals than the interests of the mother country, thereby ignoring that taking care of common interests may be dysfunctional and unsuccessful. It is therefore necessary to include path dependence and constructivism when dealing with obstacles to protect common interests.

Last but not least, I am inspired by the international relations school of International Society as set out by Hedley Bull and others, the core idea being that there is, in fact, an international society, imperfect and with obvious shortcomings, but an international society nevertheless, including norms, rules, laws and institutions.[8] This perspective has its advantages: Firstly, it perceives law to be an integrated part of international society, implying that law plays a part and is not a mere epiphenomenon. Secondly, by claiming the factuality of an international society, the protection of common interests is not only

5 S.J. Liebowitz and M. Stephen, *Encyclopedia of Law and Economics*, Edward Elgar Publishing, Cheltenham 2000, p. 981.

6 L. Wittgenstein points to the social aspect of judgment: "Zur Verständigung durch die Sprache gehört nicht nur eine Übereinstimmung in den Definitionen, sondern (so seltsam dies klingen mag) eine Übereinstimmung in den Urteilen", *Philosophische Untersuchungen*, Suhrkamp, Frankfurt am Main 1977 (orig. 1953), p. 139, para. 242.

7 A. Wendt, 'Anarchy is What States Make of It: the Social Construction of Power Politics' (1992) 46 *International Organization* 2, 391–425.

8 H. Bull, *The Anarchical Society*, MacMillan, London 1977.

perceived as an ideal but seen also as part of contemporary international law and international relations, no matter its shortcomings. The school of International Society is divided into two sub-branches, often referred to as solidarism and pluralism, respectively;[9] solidarists emphasize shared values, including the obligation to protect common interests, whereas pluralists emphasize the plurality of values, being skeptical towards the possibility of a larger amount of shared values. Obviously, the protection of common interests is a solidarist project towards which I am sympathetic. It is a part of my present argumentation that pluralists misread history by only accepting *Westphalia* as the international society, plainly disregarding other contrary characteristics.[10] However, solidarists and other proponents of universalism may make the much more fatal mistake of claiming some values as shared, global values, when they, upon closer scrutiny, are nothing but local, particular and even biased interests. In other words, the project of protecting common interests seems to be in constant danger as universal values and self-interest are easily mixed up, and the danger is exacerbated by actors who appear very apt at dressing up their particular interests in the guise of universalism and common interests. In order to illustrate my point, it is necessary to take a closer look at history and its conception by international lawyers.

3. IMPERIALISM LINGERS ON IN INTERNATIONAL LAW

According to Antony Anghie imperialism and colonialism is still a prominent feature of international law, and he conceives the main problem of international law not as a question of how to create order among sovereign equal states or how to make them cooperate in concert action in order to protect common interests. For Anghie the most prominent problem of international law is the issue of dominance under the guise of noble goals, pursuing particular interests in the name of lofty ideals, pleading universal application of neutral rules which upon closer scrutiny prove to be mere promotion of self-interests. He conceives international law as inherently biased towards the weaker players, especially the former colonies, and he conceives a large bulk of international lawyers as more or less successful tricksters and conmen, expressly advocating neutral and shared

9 H. Bull, 'The Grotian Conception of International Society' in H. Butterfield and M. Wight (eds), *Diplomatic Investigations. Essays in the Theory of International Politics*, George Allen & Unwin Ltd., London 1966, pp. 51–73.

10 In his seminal *The Anarchical Society* (note 8), Bull is arguing *contra* the realists that there is in fact an international society. However, he sees this in terms of a society of states, thereby ignoring non-state entities which have played a part in international society as well. The same goes for H. Bull and A. Watson (eds), *The Expansion of International Society*, Oxford University Press, New York 1985, which makes an attempt at accounting for the history of international relations as a history of an expanding *Westphalia*, thereby ignoring that history of international society is more than a history of states.

rules while in fact implicitly advocating the particular interests of their home country.

3.1. VITORIA'S TRICK

Anghie claims that international law has been imperialist from the outset. His first take is Francisco de Vitoria's conception of the encounter, the Spanish encounter with and conquest of the Americas. Vitoria (1483–1546) rejected the idea that the Spaniards had any pre-existing right to conquer the Americas, in contradistinction to i.e. Columbus who merely took possession of the newly discovered lands by unfurling the royal standard. According to Vitoria, the Indians were not subjects of a Spanish king and they were not under papal jurisdiction. They had their own king, their own law, and their own institutions, they had reason and were to be treated on equal footing. They even had their own religion which certainly was not the right one; however, this deplorable fact had repercussions mainly for their irredeemable souls but not for their earthly laws and lives. Even though the laws of the Indians did not have a divine origin, they had laws nevertheless. So far, Vitoria is a *pluralist*, recognizing and acknowledging different laws and different versions of the good life,[11] rejecting a hierarchical order and thereby rejecting any right of interference, let alone conquest. By acknowledging the differing Indian law exactly as law, there is also a common ground. Indians are human beings on equal footing, they have souls and they have reason. And because they have reason, they are also bound by ius gentium,[12] the natural law pertaining to all human beings as rational creatures. And being bound by natural law, they of course have to abide by the obligations ensuing from ius gentium, such as allowing for foreigners to travel and sojourn and allowing the foreigners to trade,[13] just as the Spaniards would have to allow the Indians to travel and trade in case the Indians came to Spain. Thus, for Vitoria there is a common ground, a common law including Indians as well as Spaniards, a law pertaining equally to all; and this common law is neither Spanish, nor papal but a law for all peoples, a ius gentium. In this respect Vitoria is a *solidarist*, claiming common interests and mutual obligations worldwide. He rejects any rights for Spain or any other power to merely conquer other people, disregarding the sovereignty of the king and disregarding the natural equality

---

[11] BULL (note 9).

[12] At this time, the term *ius gentium* does not refer to later ideas of international law. The term probably vacillates between the Roman concept of the law pertaining to non-Roman citizens and the idea of a law pertaining to the relation between peoples (A. NUSSBAUM, *A Concise History of the Law of Nations*, Macmillan, New York 1947, pp. 19–20.). Importantly, Vitoria applies the term to a common law, pertaining to all creatures endowed with reason, including Indians and Spaniards alike.

[13] Ibid., p. 21.

of peoples.[14] Everybody is under the rights and obligations of the common law. Vitoria's position makes sense and is even laudable: All peoples have their own laws and king, and they ought to be respected. In addition, there is also common ground as we are all human beings; we are similar, we all have reason and soul, and consequently we share *some* common norms.

However, this common law comes in a particular version. Upon closer scrutiny, the alleged ius gentium is not genuinely everybody's; rather it is somebody's, it is Vitoria's conception or construction of a particular European legal tradition. Here Vitoria did not look for any commonalities, nor did he ground his findings in agreements or negotiations between various peoples of the earth or amongst the involved parties. In fact the proclaimed common law was a mere reflection of the ideas and practices of the Spaniards, a sort of localized version in universal disguise. And once Vitoria has established the basic ideas of ius gentium, he has no difficulty in pointing out the Indians' violations of the law and the ensuing rights for the Spaniards to sanction such violations. When the Indians do not honour their obligations under international law, it is for the Spaniards to take action, to secure, by all necessary means, e.g. that sojourners, travelers and traders are protected in their enterprise, and that property is protected. Waging war, conquering territories and even the taking of slaves, all of which were not allowed according to the pluralistic respect for other systems of law, are now allowed according to Vitoria's solidarist position, claiming one law for all, a law which, alas, is framed on the traditions and in the interests of one party, providing this party with practically unlimited rights. It is thus possible to see Vitoria as a humanitarian defender of Indian rights, and at the same time as a mere totalitarian suppressor. Not only do the Spaniards have the means to conquer and exploit, they also have the right, and not only the right of the stronger, but a right based on a law which is common to all peoples and natural to all men.

Thus, Vitoria is not vacillating between a pluralistic position on the one hand, recognizing the norms and laws of the Indians, and a solidarist on the other, claiming *some* norms to be common. And he is not mediating the two positions, making a case for common interests and paving the way for the protection thereof. Rather he proves to be a pluralist in disguise, pretending to apply common norms when in fact he is merely applying local norms, backing up the traditions and the interests of his mother country, thus not only forfeiting the option of protecting common interests but actively engaging in furthering local interests in the name of mankind.

---

14 Vitoria may not be clear as to who is the actual sovereign, and I do not have a clear picture of his understanding of a people and its king. For the present purpose, this problem is immaterial. What matters is the equal footing of the different entities.

Anghie claims that the colonial encounter and the ensuing construction of legal concepts basically inform international law. According to Anghie the unequal encounter and Vitoria's insidious interpretation are integral parts of international law, which cannot be (or at least have not been) done away with by granting all territories equal sovereignty. In Anghie's view, international law was shaped by this unequal encounter, sovereignty was created not only as a part of *Westphalia*, producing equal entities, but as a part of colonialism and imperialism, producing unequal "sovereignty" which persists no matter the UN treaty's formal dealing with the matter. Inequality and hierarchy are inherent traits of in international law, and so is the readiness to dress it up.

3.2. THE CONSTANT TRICK

Not only was international law shaped by the unequal colonial encounter between the Europeans and the Amerindians; conmen continued to abound and tricks continued to be played.

In the latter half of the 19th century, the European great powers were engaged in a struggle for empires especially in Africa, and according to Anghie legal positivist international lawyers were engaged in legitimizing the conquests, the dominance and the use of force in relation to the non-European world.[15] They mainly argued along two lines: In the first place they claimed to be scientists basing their observations on empirical data, in this case the practices, customs and treaties of *states*, thereby distinguishing themselves from previous less scientific international lawyers who were dependent on the dubious concept of natural law. However, via this focus on states large tracts of the globe were excluded from international law and it was not possible to identify proper states in most of the non-European world. In this way, law by definition only pertained in and between (mainly European) states, whereas the relation to the remainder of the world was outside the scope of law and according to one international lawyer should be dealt with on the basis of discretion.[16] The relation between mother country and colony was seen as an entirely domestic affair and closed to external legal regulation. In this way an alleged scientific approach allowed for existing empires as they were

[15] One may question whether the international lawyers were in fact pure positivists even if they claimed to be so, and one may point to the fact that not all international lawyers were favorable to colonialism, M. Koskenniemi, *The Gentle Civilizer of Nations. The Rise and Fall of International Law 1870–1960*, Cambridge University Press, Cambridge 2001, Chapter 2 and pp. 130–131. For the present purpose, however, it suffices to point to the fact that many international lawyers were engaged in defining international law in such a way that dominance was ignored.

[16] Ibid., p. 81, referring to L. Oppenheim, *International Law. A Treatise*, 2nd ed, Longman, London 1912, pp. 34–35.

conceived as states and international law was only dealing with relations between states.

As for the expansion of empires, the international lawyers had more trouble. Basing the right of the empire to acquire new colonies on actual conquest or occupation implied a mere equation of might with right. This is an awkward position for lawyers, especially when they boast to be scientific. Therefore cessation worked better as a legal basis for the expansion of the European empires, and there are many examples of treaties signed by local chiefs and alleged representatives of the empire such as Cecil Rhodes.[17] However, treaties presuppose legal standing, and the positivist international lawyers had difficulties in explaining how European states could acquire rights by entering agreements with actors outside the scope of international law.[18] Anghie points out that the positivists' legitimization of empire and the rights of the European states was less convincing than Vitoria's more coherent argument based on natural law. This problem of explaining how non-states could enter into binding treaties led to yet another argument, namely the distinction between the civilized and the uncivilized. By introducing the concept of civilization, large part of the non-European world was not only excluded from the protection of international law because of lacking statehood. Being uncivilized, they also fell under the protection of the civilized nations, which for their part had not only a right but also a duty to bring civilization to the uncivilized. Anghie is not very impressed by this device, either. It proved difficult, not to say impossible, to produce any workable definition of civilization, and attempts to introduce stages of civilization, and consequently of legal capacity, did not bring any clarity.[19]

For the present purpose, the introduction of the 'civilization mission' – 'white man's burden', as Rudyard Kipling framed it – exposes a problematic aspect of the protection of common interests, namely the question whether in fact the alleged common interests are truly common or whether they are somebody's interests, the interests of the powerful or the strong. In hindsight, it is easy to criticize late 19th century European imperialism and its concomitant racist ideology, but the problem of presenting own interests as common interests is, I claim, ever present[20]

---

17 Cecil Rhodes acquired extensive rights for his British South African Company through a treaty with the local chief in what is now Western Zambia. R. Hall, *Zambia*, Praeger, London 1966.

18 Similarly, ibid., p. 169: 19th century international lawyers did not succeed in producing an operational concept of sovereignty.

19 It is tempting to compare Nazi-Germany's problems of defining 'Jews'. Excluding Jews or uncivilized certainly may serve unsympathetic political purposes, but it does not work in a scientific or legal context.

20 For an updated version, see Condoleezza Rice in *Foreign Affairs*, January/February 2000: "Since American values are really universal, one can advance good things in the world by promoting American values."

and not easily solved. Anghie is of the opinion that what he calls the dynamics of difference is still a salient feature of international law. Even if this is not the case,[21] the idea of the civilizing mission of the (mainly) European powers points to the problem of how to identify common interests and not merely assume certain local or even biased values to be universal.

According to Anghie, international law continued to support dominance and hierarchy, and international lawyers continued to produce convenient arguments. After the First World War, the European powers had lost some military strength, and the distinction between the civilized and the uncivilized appeared less convincing after four years of unprecedented killings, the use of chemical weapons, etc. Hence, the administration of the former colonies and territories of the losers of the war was handed over to an international organization, whose task it was to develop the territories and make them ready for sovereignty.[22] Anghie points to the irony that an international organization was created in order to develop the territories into sovereign states. The existence and the necessity of an international organization appear to be undermining state supremacy rather than creating and reinforcing it, and even though the handling of the mandate territories was in fact carried out by (mainly European) states, this fact only added to the confusion: An international organization handing over the practical task of administering territories with the purpose of developing the latter into future states, a situation not easily recognizable as a world consisting of sovereign states as unquestionable basic units.

Therefore positivism fell out of vogue and legal pragmatism entered the stage, conceiving law as a means to achieve desirable societal goals, in this case developing the territories into modern sovereign states. Social sciences were engaged for the purposes of collecting information, gathering knowledge, and making government more efficient and, in fact, more totalitarian.[23] The tasks of the mandatory powers were therefore to protect the welfare of the backward peoples, who were so unfortunate as not yet to have developed their own sovereign states, to assist in making the peoples ready for sovereignty, a task that the mandatory powers did not always take too seriously,[24] and to integrate the

21 See further discussion below, section 3.3.

22 Wilson's ideas of self-determination were not intended to include the former colonies of the losing powers, let alone the colonies of the winners, cf. E. Manela, *The Wilsonian Moment. Self-Determination and the International Origins of Anticolonial Nationalism*, Oxford University Press, New York 2007.

23 Anghie seems to vacillate between a more radical position, claiming that the mere gathering information for governmental purposes is suppressive, and a less radical position pointing to the fact that the mandate territories were governed undemocratically with little inclusion of the governed, thereby rendering the bulk of information into a means of governing and suppressing.

24 Anghie notes the difference between the approach taken by the USA on the one hand and by the European powers and South Africa on the other. The British approach is indicated

territories into the world economy. Anghie notes that this resembles Vitoria's trick: Acknowledging the rights of the non-Europeans, yet claiming an underlying more profound law, the existence of which Europeans have a privileged knowledge and to whose execution European powers are best suited. In *Vitoria's* case the underlying law was the natural law of ius gentium, in the mandate period (and later) it is the law of development, especially economic development. Thus, Anghie claims, international law and international lawyers continue the dynamics of difference reserving unfettered sovereignty for themselves while providing others with an unclear mix of shared sovereignty, making sure to reserve the upper hand for themselves. And they continue playing tricks by claiming a universal law of development, merely assisting the backward peoples to reach the modern stage, while in fact international law favors mainly European interests in having access to the raw materials and the markets of the territories.

Even after the Second World War and the establishing of the United Nations with its basic principle of sovereign equality of member states, Article 2 (1) of the Charter and the acquisition of statehood by almost all former colonies and mandates, international law is still biased. According to Anghie there is still dominance and hierarchy, and there are different types of sovereignty – not in spite of the demands of international law but because of it.[25] He bases his view on a number of observations: The former colonies are held to be bound by all sorts of previous treaties even though these were not entered into by a sovereign but by a colonial master or by a chief who for all other purpose has been denied legal standing. In addition, existing treaties, and especially the ones not favorable to the former colonies, are valid no matter if they were entered into under threat of use of force or other similar circumstances which normally would render a treaty void. And when former colonies enter into agreements with transnational companies of Western origin, they are held to relinquish their sovereign rights even though it is easily arguable that a state cannot rightfully give up its sovereignty in an agreement with a non-state party. When such agreement is decided upon by international arbitration, the international lawyers resort to 'general principles of international law', which in fact is no more than an application of English natural law.[26] And there is no reference to United Nations General Assembly resolutions, which of course is only soft law but on the other hand has been agreed upon by the involved party. Here, Vitoria's trick is easily recognizable: Two equal parties each with their laws and values, yet bound by an underlying law which appears neutral and general but which in fact serves the interest of only one party and

in F. Lugard, *The Dual Mandate in British Tropical Africa*, William Blackwood and Sons, Edinburgh and London 1922, the dual mandate being the protection of the natives and expanding trade into the territories, p. 157, whereas the American approach emphasized development to self-government, pp. 140 and 280 f.

25 Ibid., pp. 117–118.

26 Ibid., p. 238.

upon closer scrutiny appears to be a mere reflection of the customs of the stronger party. And Anghie certainly emphasizes the continuation of imperialism: Though former colonies have acquired sovereignty, it is a sovereignty of a different and far less valuable kind than the one for the former empires and greater powers. Furthermore, the requirements to the political and economic performance of poorer countries as held by the International Monetary Fund and the World Bank Group are yet another application of a newer kind of natural law, namely the law of economic development, dressed up as neutral and scientific, but in fact serving the interests of the former empires, now including the United States, to have access to raw materials and markets for their products.

By ignoring the past, Anghie claims, international law and international lawyers are reproducing the past instead of overcoming it. And the past is (also) one of imperialism, colonialism, hierarchy and dominance, at best a kind of paternalistic liberalism, in turns ostracizing less fortunate people or including them by force or other means of coercion.[27]

3.3. DOES INTERNATIONAL LAW CONSTITUTE AN OBSTACLE TO THE PROTECTION OF COMMON INTERESTS?

According to Anghie, international law at least in its present condition is inherently biased and as a consequence not able to take care of common interests. This does not follow from the fact that the world is divided in numerous autonomous states not being able to cooperate – an aspect which is not in Anghie's focus – but from the fact that international law has been biased from the outset and continues to be so, promoting some interests to the detriment of others. If Anghie is correct, international law is indeed an obstacle, and the prospect of protecting common interests seems very bleak as it requires profound changes in international law, changes that are not likely to be carried out in any near future

However, I am of the opinion that Anghie exaggerates his points.[28] No doubt we can find examples of outright injustice and gross disregard of the interests of the ones affected by the law, but even gross examples of injustice do not allow for the conclusion that international law *per se* is unjust, and striking examples of pursuit of particular interests do not preclude the possibility of international law protecting common interests. I believe that Anghie is right in pointing out concrete examples of injustice and of misrepresentations of common interests,

27 Anghie notes that even Kant, who strongly opposed colonialism, in his *Perpetual Peace* held that people not living in a legal civil state but in a state of nature, injures its civil neighbours by their mere existence. Ibid., p. 295.

28 I am not the only one. A reservation is even indicated in the foreword to his book, p. xii-xiii.

and I believe that he has a particularly valid point in showing *patterns* of injustice and misrepresentations reappearing in different historical epochs. Still, even patterns do not cover all international law at all times. To make such a conclusion is to make the inductive fallacy.

Secondly, Anghie simply assumes that there is no way international law can avoid being imperialistic and suppressive only because of the fact that international law was caught up in imperialism from the outset. However, genesis does not equal function. Even if modern international law – modern in the broad sense of the word from the age of the discoveries – was framed exactly as a reaction to the discoveries and the encounters and as a justification for the emerging imperialism and an apt construction aiming at accommodating i.e. the right to colonies, it does not automatically follow that international law will always play the part of being an instrument for suppression in disguise. Concepts and institutions may change over time, and in fact they all do. As for international law, it has changed tremendously, most conspicuously in relation to the use of force. At least from the 19th century the use of force was seen as a natural quality of sovereignty, and kings and princes could fight in order to solve their disagreements. With the Kellogg-Briand Pact of 1928 and Article 2 (4) of the United Nations Charter the legal situation is completely reversed and the use of force is no longer a legitimate means of acquiring aspired goals even though this started out to be the case. Obviously, this example does not show that all dislikeable features of international law will turn into more appreciable ones, but it does show that international law is changeable and in fact has changed tremendously.

Thirdly, no matter its historical development, contemporary international law is not only hierarchy and dominance even when Anghie is correct in pointing out often ignored suppressive traits. International law also features equality of states, respect for treaties and even respect for individual human rights. There is in fact a difference between a normative requirement of the sovereign equality of states, as stated in the UN Charter Article 2 (1), and a normative claim of civilization, categorizing some states as being civilized and others as uncivilized and stating the former's right to dominate the latter. Similarly, there is a difference between on the one hand criticizing actors or structures for preventing the implementation of the law, such as pointing to examples of different types of sovereignty among formally equal states, and on the other hand criticizing the law itself, such as pointing to the absurdity of the distinction between civilized and uncivilized. Anghie mixes up the two situations, and he does not make it clear when he is criticizing the law and when he is criticizing violations of the law or lack of implementation.

Fourthly, in relation to Anghie's critique of engaging the disciplines of social science and law with the purpose of gathering precise and useful information in order to be able to govern more efficiently, it is important to keep in mind that efficient governance is not in itself suppressive. Obviously, information may be used for suppressive purposes, and obviously, an efficient suppressive regime is worse than a less efficient one. However, the gathering of information is necessary in order to be better able to protect common interests. Without proper knowledge we shall not be able to take care of common interests, even if knowledge is by no means sufficient for that purpose.[29]

No matter the exaggerations, Anghie definitely has some valid and relevant points: International lawyers have been engaged in legitimizing oppression and inequality, and they seem to have a perpetual propensity for dressing up exploitation and injustice as neutral application of the most excellent rules and principles. And even if international law is not inherently imperialist, neither is it a perfectly neutral institution, always working towards the benefit of the common interests. For the present purpose, I think I can safely conclude, firstly, that international law is not *per se* an obstacle to the protection of common interests. Secondly, and importantly, international law features traits of biased interests, and they are often dressed up as noble common goals and values. The question of whether imperialism is still a salient feature of international law thus turns into a challenge of being aware and being able to handle the permanent risk of mistaking particular and biased interests for shared interests and universal values. This is less of a problem for the pluralists of the International Society school of thought as they tend to minimalize universal and shared values and consequently have little interest in the protection of common interests except for the importance of an established world order – which of course is a highly relevant, albeit insufficient concern.[30] The solidarists in contradistinction emphasize common values and shared interests, and they are more prone to the risk of making the mistake of conceiving particular interests as universal interests. This hinges on the conception of an international society: As long as international society is conceived merely in terms of a state system, *Westphalia*, the obstacle to the protection of common interests is exactly the partition of the world into sovereign states. But *Westphalia* is only a part of the picture, and solidarists as well as pluralists of the International Society school of thought appear to be little aware of the danger of imperialism, here taken to indicate the danger of presenting and even advocating the execution of common interests, which upon closer scrutiny prove to be little more than the execution of particular interests.

29 I tend to think that Anghie is misled by Foucault or at least by his reading of Foucault's works: Truly enough, information is linked with power, but power is also required in order to promote common goods.

30 Cf. the curiously ignored Art. 28 of the Universal Declaration of Human Rights: "Everyone is entitled to a social and international order in which the rights and freedoms set forth in this Declaration can be fully realized."

I therefore agree with Anghie in his pointing out that by ignoring the imperial traits in international law, we forfeit the chance to get rid of them.[31]

4. NON-WESTPHALIA STILL LINGERS ON

In his *Beyond the Anarchical Society*,[32] Keene also focuses on the non-*Westphalian* part of the world: He agrees that we can identify an anarchical society, consisting of self-contained entities, i.e. sovereign states each with its own jurisdiction within its territory, states that constitute a society,[33] but an anarchical one since there is no central government. However, in addition to this anarchical society of *Westphalia* we also have a world beyond, a world which features shared sovereignty (in contradistinction to *Westphalia*'s unpartitioned sovereignty) and extraterritorial protection of certain rights, especially property rights (in contradistinction to exclusively domestic jurisdiction) and whose basic value is not toleration of equal states and their equally valid norms, but a value of civilization, indicating certain basic substantive norms plus the idea of progress.

Thus, Keene agrees with Anghie that it is insufficient and misleading to grasp the world in terms of a European *Staatensystem*[34] which by now has expanded to cover the whole world. All along there have been other systems with different characteristics which conventionalist international lawyers and international relation theories have failed to include. But Keene does not conceive non-*Westphalia* merely in terms of imperialism – which, one may add, tends to portray the state of affairs in a rather one-dimensional way. For Keene it is not mainly a question of dominance and suppression – even though, of course, these traits are easily recognizable – but in a sense a more profound question of understanding sovereignty not only in the misleading *Westphalian* terms of mere self-determination, of understanding extraterritorial protection of basic rights and, consequently, of understanding the competing and conflicting ideals of toleration and civilization, which previously were allocated special compartments of the world, but now are not territorially divided but all over, making an incoherent

---

31 Interestingly, ANGHIE (note 3), p. 133, mentions Sigmund Freud. And in fact the point of acknowledging disquieting facts such as the biases of some part of international law and the machinations of some international lawyers as a means of getting rid of them is a truly Freudian approach. Repressions hit hard if not openly confronted.

32 KEENE (note 4).

33 For BULL (note 8), p. 4, a society is "a pattern that leads to a particular result, an arrangement of social life such that it promotes certain goals and values".

34 Keene conceives the system of sovereign states, for which I here apply the term *Westphalia*, as an apt political invention of the beginning of the 19th century, well-suited for the interests of the 'concert of Europe', keeping the Napoleonic empire at bay while ignoring the British by constructing British colonies as a part of British internal affairs.

mess out of international law and international relations – a mess that is not comprehensible from a conventionalist view.

Keene points out that the ideas of shared sovereignty and of protection and even defence of private property in foreign jurisdictions were central already to Grotius' thinking. Even though Grotius refers to Bodin and the notion of undivided sovereignty, he continues to elaborate on various forms of shared sovereignty: The people can transfer some rights to a king, sovereignty can be divided e.g. between a king and other institutions, and Grotius' defence of the Dutch right to wage war against the Spanish king did not rely on any right to revolt, a right which Grotius rejected downright, but on the right to levy taxes, which was held by the Dutch even though they were under the sovereignty of the Spanish king. When the king overstepped his authority and wanted to levy taxes, this constituted an infringement of that particular sovereign right which belonged to the Dutch. As for the protection of property, Grotius developed the notion of '*occupatio duplex*': occupation either by a public authority or by a private party. Both could rightly acquire land e.g. in the Americas where land was neither under *occupatio* nor *dominium*, i.e. land was neither occupied or under recognized ownership, and therefore private persons could acquire land under a foreign sovereign, an acquisition valid under domestic as well as international law. Thus, private parties were agents under international law and extraterritorial defense of property a lawful remedy. According to Keene, these particular points in Grotius' writing have been forgotten at least since the mid-20th century – Keene notes that the bulk of Grotius' writing is enormous and that he was not always consistent – or they have been dismissed as medieval relicts.[35] Contrary to this view, Keene maintains that these traits are not mere pre-modern leftovers but in fact active features of modern international law, and easily recognizable if one does not reduce one's focus to the anarchical *Westphalia*.

For the sake of his argument Keene points to two different examples: In colonial North America there was "considerable confusion about the ultimate location of sovereignty":[36] the king, proprietors with some seigneurial rights, companies such as the Massachusetts Bay Company, and local settlers with some public rights regarding taxes, defence, courts etc. And upon independence the Northwest Ordinance of 1787[37] laid out guidelines for a demarcated territory paving the way for the territories' future status as states within the 'Confederacy of the United States of America'. The Ordinance provides for protection of property before and after statehood and even some specific regulations as to succession of property; it lays out rules for temporary government to be divided between the Congress of the

35 Bull (note 8).
36 Ibid., note 67.
37 "An Ordinance for the Government of the Territory of the United States Northwest of the River Ohio."

United States and local legislature when the number of inhabitants reaches 5,000 male freeholders. Conditions for statehood are stipulated, conditions to "forever remain unalterable unless by common consent", including a bill of rights – in a way sovereign rights for the settlers, such as freedom of religion, protection of property, habeas corpus, prohibition of inhumane treatment etc. – and a right to form a state when their number exceeds 60,000. The Ordinance also provides for protection of the Indians,[38] perhaps the least effective part. Keene emphasizes the conspicuous features of diluted sovereignty in contradistinction to the *Westphalian* model of a prince or a people holding absolute sovereignty; he notes the difference of recognition: the Ordinance does not require capacity of full control of the territory or self-defence, as these matters are not solely under the authority of the coming states; and he notes that this way of acquiring new territory is different from the European imperial model and is, in fact, part of international law as it is not solely domestic legislation. In addition, individuals are legal agents even before statehood, and private property and other basic rights are protected no matter the status of the territory. One could add that the idea of developing statehood resembles the Mandate system of the interwar period (see section 3.2 above) and the system related to development organization such as the World Bank and the IMF: statehood can be developed – thus no pre-existing state units as basic elements – territories are to be civilized, and certain basic rights for the individual are in force regardless of the status of the territory. This does not look *Westphalian*.

Keene points to another example, colonial East India, which differed from the North American situation i.e. in terms of settlement, but with conspicuous similarities as regards shared sovereignty and extraterritorial protection of individual rights, especially property rights. In the early phases of European presence, the European powers treated the local princes as sovereigns with whom they traded and concluded treaties. Later, as the European powers became stronger towards the end of the 17th century, chunks of sovereignty were taken over by the Europeans; but even at the peak of British colonial rule in India about two fifths of the territory consisting of about 600 native states enjoyed a certain degree of sovereignty under the rule of local princes. The relations varied, but most often the local prince had a degree of internal sovereignty limited by British geopolitical interests (mainly relating to foreign policy) *and* by British economic interests including of course protecting the property of British traders and

[38] Art. 3: 'The utmost good faith shall always be observed towards the Indians; their lands and property shall never be taken from them without their consent; and, in their property, rights, and liberty, they shall never be invaded or disturbed, unless in just and lawful wars authorized by Congress; but laws founded in justice and humanity shall from time to time be made for preventing wrongs being done to them, and for preserving peace and friendship with them.'

companies within the local territory.[39] In the 19th century the idea of civilizing mission emerged, and the colonial powers reserved their rights to intervene in case of corrupt local princes who mismanaged their realm and maltreated their subjects. Interestingly, the liberals – the ones resembling the solidarists of the International Society school – were the ones favouring intervention, whereas the conservatives – resembling the pluralists – saw the local princes as important agents for the maintenance of local law and order. In the course of the 19th century the colonization was held to serve two purposes: to extract profit through trade and/or taxation at the lowest cost possible *and* to civilize, encourage good government, entrepreneurship and technological progress. Or put in more general terms: the colonial empires must serve the particular interest of the colonizing mother country and at the same time the perceived interests of the colonized peoples to become more civilized and more developed, a kind of common interest framed paternalistically by one party. Keene notes that the same general picture of shared sovereignty pertained to Dutch East India: A patchwork of different solutions in different parts of the colonial empire, with various degrees of sovereignty and the mother country vacillating between securing economic profit at the expense of even starving the local population on the one hand or protecting the interests of the local population at the expense of profit for the mother country on the other.

To recapitulate on Keene's points, he agrees that a *Westphalian* society has emerged, a decentralized system of delimited sovereignties, an anarchical society with institutions like the balance of power, diplomacy, and law. However, in addition a more centralized and hence less anarchical system has also emerged with conspicuous features of shared sovereignty, shared values such as civilization and progress, and the option of extraterritorial protection of individuals and especially property at the expense of the local sovereign. Here international order was less strict and limited to protection of trade and securing economic interests, and the distinction between national and international law was less clear.[40] Conventionalist views have failed to include these important aspects of international relations and international law. By focusing on Europe with its *Westphalian* system, conventionalists simply fail to get the whole picture. Besides, not only have the conventionalists excluded large parts of the world from their conception of world affairs and of international law, they also failed to see how the European system of states emerged in constant engagement with their colonies, with the development of shared sovereignty and the extraterritorial protection of

39 Interestingly, in his *Ancient Law*, Henry Summer Maine, who worked in the colonial administration in India for several years, pointed to the facts of divided sovereignty, arguing against John Austin who, as a former officer in the British army, claimed sovereignty to be perceived in terms of orders backed by threat.

40 Keene does not explicitly make this point, but it follows from his ideas of shared sovereignty, shared values and extraterritorial protection of property.

property and economic interests. In other words, the two identifiable systems did not emerge in isolation but in mutual interdependence.

Thus, Keene criticizes conventionalists for a rather gross misreading of history. However, it is not only a question of getting the history right, the conventionalists also misunderstand the present: By only seeing the expansion of *Westphalia*, which was the only system visible to them in the first place, they ignore that the non-*Westphalian* system has equally expanded. Keene agrees that we now have a worldwide *Westphalian* system with sovereign states constituting a type of anarchical society. But we also have non-*Westphalian* institutions worldwide: Shared sovereignty is a feature in federal states such as the USA and even in Europe – of all places. (Keene notes the peculiarity of the European Union having large powers regarding internal affairs whereas the member states are still sovereign in foreign affairs, the reverse situation of the one in North America and colonial East India). Protection of individual rights in preference of sovereignty is also prevalent, either in form of humanitarian intervention or less dramatically via commercial contracts;[41] and last but not least the overarching idea of civilization and progress, whether dramatically excluding rogue states from civilized society or more mainstream by providing development aid and assistance to less civilized and less progressed countries (even though phrases such as 'backward people' are no longer used, at least not in public). Thus, we have a world in which two opposing systems abound, one of toleration, the anarchical *Westphalian* model tolerating a plurality of different entities and diverging norms, and one of civilization, a more centralized, less anarchical system with solid values. Keene notes that many scholars are involved in solving this difficult problem, e.g. in terms of sovereignty versus human rights, only that they most often fail to grasp the historical roots of the problem by conceiving the present situation as post-*Westphalian*, whereas in fact there is nothing 'post' in this regard. Neither is the system of states collapsing, firstly, because it never covered the world but only a smaller part, and secondly because it also expands.

Keene points to two problems: One, that the existence of non-*Westphalia* is ignored, which is bad enough but mendable, and two, that we now have two conflicting systems and sets of ideas at work, toleration and civilization respectively, not only at the same time but also at the same places, and in fact all over the place. Keene readily admits that he does not know how to solve this second, pressing and overwhelming problem. All he can do is to correct the first problem of misunderstandings thereby hoping to pave the way for solving also the second. In the perspective of International Society and its division into pluralists and solidarists, Keene is indicating that the pluralists are mistaken in their historical

41 See also above, section 3.2, on Anghie's critical position towards agreements between weaker states and transnational companies.

view as well as in their conception of the contemporary situation: International society is and has been more than a society of sovereign states, and all along there have been features of shared values. Thus, implicitly, Keene supports a solidarist view by demonstrating the existence of shared or at least uniform values in the past as well as today, values which are, at least under certain circumstances, executed extraterritorially. Still, he falls short of supporting a solidarist approach as he does not present any solution to the deadlock of tolerance and shared values.

5. CONCLUSIONS AND PERSPECTIVES

I agree with Keene's pointing to the existence of more than one type of international society and that we are misreading the present as well as the past if we only see an anarchical society. The world has never been purely *Westphalian* and it is a mistake to conceive international society purely as a society of relatively isolated, sovereign states, by and large tolerating different sovereigns' different ways – and it is equally mistaken to perceive international law merely in terms of agreements between and customs created by states. It is important to realize that we had and still have a non-*Westphalian* world featuring shared sovereignty, extraterritorial protection of certain rights, especially property rights, and the 'active' value of civilization and progress rather than the 'passive' value of toleration. The existence of these features is important for our dealing with problems of protecting common interests.

I take it that the problems pertaining to *Westphalia* are rather well-known: The construction of a state system based on self-contained ever competing units implies problems with coordination, toleration is a weak ordering principle – the outbreak of the First World War, which was mainly a war fought on *Westphalian* territory, is a sobering example[42] – and furthermore, the protection of common interests is almost absent in a mere tolerating international society. Even the creation of common (solidarist) institutions may not help much, as the various actors within the institutions still behave in a pluralistic, anarchical way, mending the interests of their home state.[43] But as Keene points out, we also have a non-*Westphalian* world with its features of shared values and a certain level of extraterritorial protection of rights, especially property rights. Keene deserves credit for pointing to this important fact. However, his idea that we now have a problem because the *Westphalian* toleration and the non-*Westphalian* civilization are now mixed geographically is less convincing. I simply do not see why only one value is possible, rather on the contrary, one value is hardly ever possible as it is

[42] I tend to perceive the later ban on the use of force in international relations as a non-*Westphalian*, civilizational feature.

[43] See e.g. the contribution by A. Barros, in the present volume, at 143.

most often both counterbalanced and contested. As an example, Western Europe between 1945 and 1990 may be conceived as a rather successful coexisting of on the one hand a *Westphalian* toleration and pluralism in form of single states existing side by side *and* on the other hand a non-*Westphalian* sphere of civilization, shared values and solidarism in form of the overall protection by the US American army and the creation of solidarist institutions such as the Council of Europe including the European Convention of Human Rights and later the European Coal and Steel Community eventually turning into the European Union. Of course, the two sets of values, toleration and civilization, pluralism and solidarism, do not automatically exist in harmony, but neither are they incompatible.

Keene's valuable contribution lies in his demonstrating that in addition to the anarchical society with the pluralist value of toleration we also have a civilizational society (or perhaps societies) with shared values of protection of property etc. Perhaps the problems of this non-*Westphalian* civilization are less known: Civilization points more in the direction of common interests than does toleration, and indeed civilization proved to be an efficient way of creating order in e.g. North America. However, this is only a part of the picture: Among the Indians the taking possession of land in order to create civilization and progress created disorder, chaos and disaster, and in other colonies, such as Keene's example of India, the imperial project of civilization was equally disorderly. Besides, the idea of civilization has largely been a particular perception of civilization, not necessarily furthering common interests. This takes us back to Vitoria's problem: How to identify or create common law and common interests which are genuinely common and not merely particular interests and local norms in disguise? This is exactly where Anghie leaps in: The allegedly shared values may in fact not be properly shared, civilization may serve as a euphemism for control and power, and the so-called common interests may upon closer scrutiny prove to be particular values dressed up in a solidarist disguise. Anghie deserves credit for this out presentation. However, his idea that common interests and international law are inherently incompatible is less convincing. He sees international law as imperialist, suppressive, and biased with a core value of dominance rather than equality. Sovereignty does not apply equally but is unequally distributed with a full-fledged sovereignty for the strong states, the mother countries of the former empires, and an ineffective sovereignty for the poor states, the former colonies whose sovereignty is continuously infringed by all sorts of machinations by powerful states and international lawyers alike. As indicated in section 3.3, I find this position exaggerated: Even though we may find imperialistic traits and suppressive features in contemporary international law, this does not imply that international law is inherently and unescapably imperialistic and suppressive. What I do find useful is, firstly, Anghie's demonstration of patterns of injustice, suppression and the setting aside of common interests. The existence of a pattern indicates that we are not only dealing with isolated instances of unfortunate dominance and injustice but with more deeply rooted problems. Secondly, I find his pointing to 'Vitoria's trick' very important. Lawyers have for ages been engaged in legitimizing all sorts of suppression and dominance by references to common norms, which upon closer scrutiny turn out to be little more than home-grown norms and self-interest in disguise.

One may of course question whether we need a historical account in order to understand that actors, including states, have a propensity to promote their self-interest. Is the problem of balancing self-interest and common interest – or the problem of taking care of common interests at all – not a structural problem rather than a historical one? The answer to this is twofold: First, Anghie does not only point to the problem of promoting self-interest at the expense of common interests or the interests of others; he is also pointing to the propensity and the danger of presenting particular interests as common interests, of presenting homey norms and laws as common norms and laws. It is often legitimate to promote self-interests, but it is not legitimate to present them as common interests, and it is not legitimate to play a trick, pretending to follow common laws and pursue common interests when in fact this is not the case. By pointing to 'Vitoria's trick' and to innumerous tricks later on in history, Anghie enables us to better understand the problem. He provides us with sensitivity towards common interest tricks, enabling us to identify them. It should be emphasized that the trick is not necessarily intentional. Vitoria probably believed that he was applying plain old straight forward common law when he was providing legitimate reasons for waging war against the Indians, suppressing their norms etc., even though he in fact was applying his native laws as if they were common. This is no doubt a common feature: to assume the existence and the naturalness of home-grown norms and thereby confusing them with common norms: Anghie has little interest in distinguishing between intentional and unintentional tricks. But for the present purpose his identification and exposition of the existence and the danger of mistaking local norms and self-interest as common norms and common interest are highly useful and important.

Secondly, in a more general sense history matters, and dealing with self-interest and common interest is not only a structural problem. The ones in the receiving end of paternalistic imperialism and 'for your own good' suppression are likely to be skeptical towards renewed attempts of formulating common interests, especially of course when followed by action. If law is experience much more than mere structures and logic,[44] the ones who have experienced suppressive law presented as common law pursuing common interests are more likely to maintain and defend local rules, norms and interests to the detriment of common interests.

[44] As stated in O.W. Holmes' famous introductory passage, in *The Common Law*, Little, Brown & Company, Boston 1881, Lecture One, first and second paras.

Common interests are, so to speak, in bad standing. This is an apprehensible reaction, but unfortunately not very conducive to the protection of common interests. And at least part of this problem is connected to the continual protection of particular interests with unashamed references to common interests. Improved performance requires sensitivity of Vitoria's trick.

When dealing with issues of common interests and international law, I find it important to realize that not only do we have *Westphalia* with its problems of coordinating the plural interests of the single units but we also have non-*Westphalian* features of shared values, civilization and solidarism (Keene). And it is no less important to realize that non-*Westphalia* carries its own problems of tricks and presenting particular interests as if they were common (Anghie). The latter point does not imply that common interests are always fake. After all, wolves dressed up in sheep's clothing only works because sheep exist and we sort of know how they look. Being aware that wolves may dress up as sheep and that particular interests may dress up as common interests is important. The awareness does not necessarily solve the problem but is a prerequisite for being able to cope with it.

CHAPTER 3

DIFFERENTIATION BETWEEN DEVELOPING AND DEVELOPED COUNTRIES IN INTERNATIONAL LAW

Koen De Feyter

1. PRELIMINARY OBSERVATIONS

The protection of global common interests, as defined in international instruments dealing with sustainable development and peace and security, requires the commitment and cooperation of all states and other public and private entities.

Treaties on global common interests depend on wide state ratification to reach their objective. As states decide freely whether or not to consent to a treaty, achieving (near) universal ratification is not self-evident. Differentiation of state obligations may help. States with lesser capacities may be willing to participate in the protection of a common interest if they have fewer obligations, and/or receive implementation aid from states with stronger capacities. States with stronger capacities may accept more onerous obligations if they are convinced that a global commitment is necessary to protect an interest which they deem sufficiently important.

Nevertheless, differentiation remains exceptional in international law,[1] given the centrality of the concept of sovereign equality. During the decolonization era, formal equality of states was of crucial importance to states emerging from colonial rule.[2] Sovereign equality ensured that the newly independent states were

---

1 A historical example is Art. 19 (3) of the Constitution of the International Labour Organization, 28 June 1919: 'In framing any Convention or Recommendation of general application the Conference shall have due regard to those countries in which climatic conditions, the imperfect development of industrial organization, or other special circumstances make the industrial conditions substantially different and shall suggest the modifications, if any, which it considers may be required to meet the case of such countries.'

2 Pahuja notes that new states were only included in the international community 'on the understanding that they would change to become the same' as Western states. See S. Pahuja, *Decolonising International Law*, Cambridge University Press, Cambridge 2011, p. 31 and

equal to the former colonial powers, and free to engage in domestic decision-making. Even if control of important sectors of the economy remained in foreign hands, at least in law, decision-making power shifted to domestic governments. Economic sovereignty and state equality shielded against third state interference, and served as preconditions for ensuring that natural resource exploitation could one day benefit domestic societies.

In international law sovereign equality implied not only that the new states could decide whether or not to consent to a treaty[3] (and thus ensure that the interests of their populations could be better served by future treaties), but also that, once concluded, the treaty applied uniformly to all states, regardless of their power. International treaties offered a constraint on the exercise of power by states with stronger capacities. Formal equality served as a response to substantive inequality. In addition, some treaties offered flexibility through the mechanism of reservations that allowed acceding states to unilaterally exclude or modify the legal effect of certain provisions provided the reservation was compatible with the object and purpose of the treaty. Submission to a compliance mechanism was not compulsory in all treaties either, but might be subject to an additional declaration by the state.[4]

Proponents of differentiation, however, argue that sovereign equality and the flexibility offered by international treaty law are not enough. Substantive inequality between states is such, so the argument goes that it can only be addressed through non-uniform obligations.

Differentiation between states and other entities is part and parcel of public international law. The International Court of Justice famously held that only the state possesses the totality of international rights and duties recognized by international law. The rights and duties of intergovernmental organizations depend on their purposes and functions as specified or implied in their constituent documents and developed in practice.[5] The international personality of private

pp. 110–111. Compare also Y. Onuma, *A Transcivilizational Perspective in International Law*, Brill/Nijhoff, Leiden 2010.

3 For a thorough discussion, see M. Craven, *The Decolonization of International Law*, Oxford University Press, New York 2007.

4 Further elements of flexibility are included in the chapter in the Vienna Convention on the Law of Treaties (23 May 1969) on the invalidity, termination and suspension of the operation of treaties, and in particular Art. 61 (supervening impossibility of performance) and Art. 62 (fundamental change of circumstances), although these provisions tend to be interpreted restrictively. Stone points out that weakly motivated countries may also be convinced to join treaties through 'side payments' taking the form of development aid, or a diplomatic credit. See C. Stone, 'Common but Differentiated Responsibilities in International Law' (2004) 98 *American Journal of International Law*, 283.

5 ICJ, *Reparation for Injuries Suffered in the Service of the United Nations* (Advisory Opinion), ICJ Reports 1949, p. 174.

actors – individuals, groups, companies, non-governmental organizations – is limited, and 'determined by political exigencies'.[6] Private actors become international persons to the extent that international law recognizes their rights and duties, and enables them to bring a claim and holds them accountable for wrongful acts. The attainment of international legal personality is a gradual process that depends on the willingness of the entities and of established international legal persons to make international law applicable to their relationships.[7]

From a common interest perspective, the problem thus is not too little, but too much differentiation between states and other entities. Lack of international legal personality acts as an obstacle, because it may prevent other entities from acting at the international level for the protection of the common interest, and may obstruct the establishment of responsibility when actions of these entities run counter to the common interest.[8]

The remainder of this text focuses on differentiated responsibility among states in current treaty law. It contains three main sections. The first section discusses various ways of differentiating. This is followed by an analysis of classifications of states used for the purposes of differentiation. Subsequently, justifications offered for differentiation are reviewed. Findings from the different sections contribute to a forward-looking conclusion.

---

6 J. Klabbers, *International Law*, Cambridge University Press, Cambridge 2013, p. 88.

7 There is thus a circular dimension to Art. 3 of the Vienna Convention on the Law of Treaties, 23 May 1969 that provides that international agreements concluded between states and other subjects of international law can have legal force. Entities become 'other subjects of international law' to the extent that they conclude agreements to which international law applies. Nevertheless, Art. 3 of the VCLT is an important provision in that it clarifies that there is no obstacle to making international law applicable to a variety of transboundary relationships, as long as the parties consent. For an interesting analysis of international agreements and non-state actors, see A.-K. Lindblom, *Non-Governmental Organizations in International Law*, Cambridge University Press, New York 2005, pp. 487–509.

8 For example, the polluter-pays principle in international environmental law often operates as a principle for the establishment of state responsibility, even when pollution is caused by industry. Nevertheless, some international civil liability regimes for high risk activities which are likely to create environmental damage seek to hold private operators (such as shipowners and carriers) directly liable. See P. Schwartz, 'The Polluter-Pays Principle' in M. Fitzmaurice, D.M. Ong and P. Merkouris (eds), *Research Handbook on International Environmental Law*, Edward Elgar, Cheltenham 2010, p. 252. Art. 6 of Annex VI to the Protocol on Environmental Protection to the Antarctic Treaty: Liability Arising From Environmental Emergencies (17 June 2005, not yet entered into force) thus provides that a private operator that fails to take prompt and effective response action to environmental emergencies arising from its activities shall be liable to pay the costs of response action taken by the Parties to the treaty.

2. DIFFERENTIATION THROUGH VARIOUS WAYS

Treaties organize differentiated responsibility in various ways:

- by including uniform, but contextual obligations;
- by allowing some states a grace period in the fulfillment of uniform obligations;
- by combining uniform general obligations with obligations of some states to assist other states in implementation;
- by making obligations of recipient states conditional on the prior fulfillment of obligations of assistance by other states;
- by including non-uniform core obligations.

These approaches are not mutually exclusive; they may be combined in one and the same treaty.

2.1. CONTEXTUAL OBLIGATIONS

Contextual obligations are uniform obligations that apply equally to all parties to a treaty. Differences in implementation are, however, not deemed unlawful, as it is recognized that implementation will be impacted upon by domestic context. As domestic contexts vary, differentiation at the level of implementation is acceptable. The aspects of domestic context that are deemed legally relevant in order to assess implementation may be spelled out in greater or less detail in the relevant treaty.[9]

Article 2 (1) of the International Covenant on Economic, Social and Cultural Rights[10] provides a uniform obligation applicable to all state parties to progressively realize economic, social and cultural rights to the maximum of their available resources. In this example 'available resources' is the element in the domestic context that is taken into account to assess implementation of the uniform obligation. The availability of resources (even when supplemented by international assistance and cooperation) differs from country to country, and

9 On contextual obligations, see D.B. Magraw, 'Legal Treatment of Developing Countries: Differential, Contextual and Absolute Norms' (1990) 1 *Columbia Journal of International Environmental Law & Policy*, 69–99.

10 Art. 2 (1) of the International Covenant on Economic, Social and Cultural Rights, 16 December 1966, reads: 'Each State Party to the present Covenant undertakes to take steps, individually and through international assistance and co-operation, especially economic and technical, to the maximum of its available resources, with a view to achieving progressively the full realization of the rights recognized in the present Covenant by all appropriate means, including particularly the adoption of legislative measures.' The Covenant lacks a mechanism that ensures international assistance and co-operation for the realization of the treaty's objectives.

therefore the expectation of the actual level of realization of these rights at a given point in time also differs. According to the UN Committee on Economic, Social and Cultural Rights, the reference to progressive realization is 'a necessary flexibility device, reflecting the realities of the real word and the difficulties involved for any country in ensuring full realization of economic, social and cultural rights'.[11] The Committee hastens to add, however, that in order for a state party to be able to attribute its failure to meet at least its minimum core obligations to a lack of available resources it must demonstrate that every effort has been made to use all resources that are at its disposition in an effort to satisfy, as a matter of priority, those minimum obligations.[12]

The UNESCO Convention concerning the Protection of the World Cultural and Natural Heritage provides another example of an approach based on contextual obligations[13] that allows broader flexibility, but also provides a solidarity mechanism. According to the Convention, every state party is required to invest the utmost of its resources in measures for the protection of cultural and natural heritage that are appropriate for the country. Again, all states are bound by the obligation to commit resources and to adopt measures, but what is deemed sufficient may vary greatly from to country. States enjoy a considerable margin of discretion in implementing the Convention. As a corollary to domestic efforts, the Convention sets up a collective body, the World Heritage Committee, to which requests for assistance can be addressed. One of the factors taken into account by the committee in considering applications for funding is 'the resources available to the states on whose territory the threatened property is situated and in particular the extent to which they are able to safeguard such property by their own means'.[14] The Convention also creates a Fund to support the Committee's activities, to which all state parties are required to contribute – although a reservation to the relevant provision is permissible.

2.2. GRACE PERIOD

Another way of maintaining uniform obligations while taking into account state variety is to allow a category of states a grace period for implementation.

---

11 UN Committee on Economic, Social and Cultural Rights, General Comment No. 3: The Nature of States Parties Obligations, UN Doc. E/1991/23, para. 9.

12 Ibid., para. 10.

13 UNESCO Convention concerning the Protection of the World Cultural and Natural Heritage (1972). Art. 4 requires (in part) that each state party 'will do all it can' to protect cultural and natural heritage, 'to the utmost of its own resources and, where appropriate, with any international assistance and co-operation, in particular, financial, artistic, scientific and technical, which it may be able to obtain'. Art. 5 requires that each state party 'shall endeavor, in so far as possible, and as appropriate for each country' a range of measures.

14 Ibid., Art. 13, para. 4.

In this approach, non-compliance only results in a wrongful act after the grace period elapses. Article 5 (1) of the Montreal Protocol on Substances that deplete the Ozone Layer thus provides that a developing country with a low level of consumption of controlled substances was 'on the date of entry into force of the Protocol for it, or any time thereafter until 1 January 1999 (...) in order to meet its basic domestic needs, entitled to delay for ten years its compliance with the control measures (...)'.

A more sophisticated approach to phasing in obligations – but one that proves difficult to manage – is inherent in the special and differential treatment accorded to developing countries in the context of WTO law.[15] Article XXXVI (8) of GATT 1947 established the principle of non-reciprocity, stating that 'developed contracting parties do not expect reciprocity for commitments made by them in trade negotiations to reduce or remove tariffs and other barriers to trade of less-developed contracting parties'. In 1979, the GATT Decision on Differential and more favourable treatment,[16] also known as the Enabling Clause, took note of the expectation of the 'Less-developed contracting parties'[17] that their capacity to make contributions or negotiated concessions under GATT would improve with the progressive development of their economies and improvement in their trade situation. Developing countries were thus expected to graduate into full participation in WTO obligations. No clear criteria for graduation were laid down, however, and developing countries are unwilling to graduate out of special and differential treatment on their own initiative. It has been argued that graduation at the country level is too blunt an instrument, and that instead, countries should be graduated out of specific provisions on special and differential treatment, when economic need no longer justifies non-compliance with the relevant rule.[18]

---

15 It may be contested whether WTO law is geared towards the protection of a global common interest. The Preamble to the Agreement establishing the World Trade Organization (15 April 1994) recognizes that trade and economic relations should be organized in such a way as to contribute to the achievement of the objective of sustainable development. Nevertheless, Stone points out that in trade law bargaining on conditions of trade access rather than the protection of global public goods is typically at issue. See STONE (note 4), p. 276, note 1.

16 GATT Contracting Parties Decision on Differential and More Favourable Treatment, Reciprocity and Fuller Participation of Developing Countries (28 November 1979).

17 Ibid., para. 7. The Enabling clause decision applies to developing countries. Some of its provisions apply only to least-developed countries as defined by the United Nations. In para. 7, the unusual term 'less developed countries' is used in contradistinction to the term 'developed countries', and was most probably intended to apply to all developing countries. Compare S.E. ROLLAND, *Development at the WTO*, Oxford University Press, Oxford 2012, 82.

18 A. KECK and P. LOW, *Special and Differential Treatment in the WTO: Why, When and How?* WTO Staff Working Paper ERSD-2004-03 (2004), pp. 9–10.

2.3. IMPLEMENTATION AID

Uniform treaty obligations may be complemented with obligations of a certain category of states to assist another category of states in complying with the treaty. Such duties of assistance may be financial in nature, require transfer of technology or knowledge, or aim at capacity-building. They may apply directly between the state parties or they may be governed by a collective body.

The UN Convention to Combat Desertification (17 June 1994) establishes a direct link between the states bearing the duties of assistance and the beneficiary states. Next to general obligations in the Convention applying to all states, developed states are required to actively support the efforts of developing countries affected by desertification.[19] Developed states undertake to provide substantial financial resources and other forms of support to assist affected developing country Parties, particularly those in Africa, effectively to develop and implement their own long-term plans and strategies to combat desertification and mitigate the effects of drought. Duties of assistance are thus directed at building the capacity of affected developing states to engage in their own decision-making on the issues addressed in the Convention. Countries affected by desertification, including the developing countries that are entitled to implementation aid, have the duty to allocate adequate resources to combat desertification 'in accordance with their circumstances and capabilities' (Article 5).

Article 10 of the Montreal Protocol on Substances that Deplete the Ozone Layer (16 September 1987; Article 10 was included in the 1990 Amendments) creates a Financial Mechanism that provides financial and technical co-operation including the transfer of technologies to developing countries[20] with a low level of consumption of the substances controlled by the Protocol. The Financial Mechanism strives to meet all agreed incremental costs developing countries face in order to comply with the control measures of the Protocol. A multilateral fund supports the mechanism. The fund is financed by contributions from Non-Article 5 Parties. The level of contribution required from each such Party is calculated on the basis of the United Nations scale of assessments. The creation of the Financial Mechanism was crucial to attracting the participation of developing countries in the Protocol.[21] In 2009, the Montreal Protocol achieved universal ratification.

---

19 UN Convention to Combat Desertification (1994), Art. 6. See also Arts. 19 and 20 on financial resources and financial mechanisms.

20 See Art. 5 of the Montreal Protocol on Substances that Deplete the Ozone Layer (16 September 1987, as amended), entitled 'Special Situation of Developing Countries'.

21 Ph. Sands and J. Peel, *Principles of International Environmental Law*, Cambridge University Press, Cambridge 2012, p. 272.

Even when no duties of assistance provided for, states with stronger capacities may as a minimum be required to consider the interests of states with lesser capacities when they take unilateral measures that have an impact on those states. Article XXXVII: 3 of GATT 1947, for example, thus states that developed countries shall "give active consideration to the adoption of other measures designed to provide greater scope for the development of imports from less-developed contracting parties ...". The same Article also says that developed countries shall "have special regard to the trade interests of developing contracting parties when considering the application of other measures permitted under this Agreement to meet particular problems ...".

Article 15 of the WTO Anti-Dumping Agreement provides that developed countries give consideration to the special situation of developing countries before applying anti-dumping measures. Constructive remedies should be explored first when the essential interests of developing countries are at stake.[22] WTO dispute settlement system rulings, however, have interpreted the rule as not requiring that developed countries undertake a specific action or ensure a given outcome. What needs to be shown is only that other remedies than anti-dumping measures were explored.[23]

In the United States – Import Prohibition of Certain Shrimp and Shrimp Products (US Shrimp-Turtle case)[24] the WTO Appellate Body held that a US import prohibition of shrimp and shrimp products from non-certified countries constituted unjustified discrimination, because it did not take 'into consideration different conditions which may occur in the territories of those other Members'.[25]

22 Art. 15 of the Agreement on Implementation of Art. VI GATT (15 March 1994), reads: 'It is recognized that special regard must be given by developed country Members to the special situation of developing country Members when considering the application of anti-dumping measures under this Agreement. Possibilities of constructive remedies provided for by this Agreement shall be explored before applying anti-dumping duties where they would affect the essential interests of developing country Members'.

23 For a review, see A. Alavi, *Legalization of Development in the WTO*, Kluwer Law International, The Hague 2009, 163–166. Muchlinski notes that in the area of protection of foreign investment, arbitral tribunals rarely take into account the level of development of the host country in determining the investor's legitimate expectations as to treatment. See P. Muchlinski, 'Holistic Approaches to Development and International Investment Law: The Role of International Investment Agreements' in J. Faundez and C. Tan (eds), *International Economic Law, Globalization and Developing Countries*, Edward Elgar, Cheltenham 2010, p. 185. For a plea in favour of the inclusion of contextualized obligations in international investment law, see E. Alexander, 'Taking Account of Reality: Adopting Contextual Standards for Developing Countries in International Investment Law' (2008) 48 *Virginia Journal of International Law*, 815–839.

24 Appellate Body Report, United States – Import Prohibition of Certain Shrimp and Shrimp Products, WT/DS58/AB/R (6 November 1998), DSR 1998, VII, 2755.

25 Ibid., para. 164. See also Panel Report, United States – Import Prohibition of Certain Shrimp and Shrimp Products. Recourse to Art. 21.5 by Malaysia, WT/DS58/RW (15 June 2001), para. 5, 46: 'We believe that another reason for the Appellate Body finding is that the United

In addition, the United States should have engaged in 'serious, across-the-board negotiations with the objective of concluding bilateral or multilateral agreements for the protection and conservation of sea turtles, before enforcing the import prohibition against the shrimp exports of those other Members'.[26]

It has been suggested that WTO requirements on developed members to take into consideration the needs of developing members should be construed as obligations of due diligence on their part.[27]

The International Court of Justice has held – in utterly different circumstances – that what is required under a 'due diligence' standard depends on an assessment in concreto. According to the Court,[28] various parameters operate when assessing whether a state has duly discharged its due diligence obligation. This includes the capacity to influence the actions of others, which 'varies greatly from one state to another', and depends on geographical proximity and the strength of political and other links between the authorities of the relevant states. The capacity to influence may, the Court warned, be affected by the limits permitted by international law.

The UN Convention on the Law of the Sea encourages cooperation between states with regard to the conservation and management of living resources on the high seas. In jointly determining the allowable catch and other conservation measures, measures should be agreed to produce a sustainable yield, while taking into account i.a. 'the special requirements of developing states'.[29]

2.4. CONDITIONAL OBLIGATIONS

The Montreal Protocol for Substances that Deplete the Ozone Layer and several other international environmental treaties make developing country obligations conditional on the fulfillment of the developed states' duties of assistance.[30]

States, by unilaterally defining and implementing criteria for applying Section 609, failed to take into account the different situations which may exist in the exporting countries.'

26 Ibid., para. 166.

27 See ROLLAND (note 17), p. 122; note also pp. 166–169.

28 ICJ, *Application of the Convention on the Prevention and Punishment of the Crime of Genocide (Bosnia-Herzegovina v. Serbia and Montenegro) ('Bosnia Genocide Case')* (Request for the Indication of Privisional Measures) (Judgment), ICJ Reports 2007, p. 43, para. 430.

29 UN Convention on the Law of the Sea (1982), Art. 119 (1a). See also for a similar approach: Arts. 61–62 of the Convention.

30 See Art. 5 (5) of the Montreal Protocol for Substances that Deplete the Ozone Layer (16 September 1987 as amended) that makes developing country implementation of core obligations under the treaty dependent upon the effective implementation of the financial co-operation and transfer of technology obligations by developed countries. Even the mere identification of both the financial needs of recipient countries and of the financial resources made available by developed countries has not been straightforward; see UNEP/CBD/COP/11/

Conditional obligations of developing countries exert pressure on developed states to honor their own commitments to provide assistance if they wish developing states to comply.

The Convention on Biological Diversity (5 June 1992) requires that developed states provide access both to (bio-)technology to developing countries under fair and most favorable terms, including on concessional and preferential terms (Article 16 (2)), and obliges them to provide new and additional financial resources to enable developing country Parties to meet the agreed full incremental costs to them of implementing measures which fulfill the obligations of the Convention (Article 20 (2)). A Financial Mechanism (Article 21) is set up that manages the flow of financial resources, on the basis of an agreed indicative list of the incremental costs and a burden-sharing agreement among the contributing parties. Pressure on developed states to honor their duties to provide assistance is exerted through the inclusion of Article 20 (4):

> The extent to which developing country Parties will effectively implement their commitments under this Convention will depend on the effective implementation by developed country Parties of their commitments under this Convention related to financial resources and transfer of technology and will take fully into account the fact that economic and social development and eradication of poverty are the first and overriding priorities of the developing country Parties.

Conditional obligations raise intricate problems.[31] It is not straightforward to determine when developed countries have satisfied their obligations of financial and technological assistance: the concept of "full incremental costs" is open to debate, as is the assessment of the sufficiency of technology transfer. Given this difficulty, there is a risk that developing countries postpone fulfilment of their domestic obligations under the Convention indefinitely. The use by developing countries of the financial and technological transfers provided through the Convention mechanism may also be contested if domestic management of environmental protection shows no improvement.

2.5. NON-UNIFORM OBLIGATIONS

The most 'radical' form of differentiation within a single treaty regime is the inclusion of core substantive obligations that are binding for some state parties,

---

INF/16 (3 October 2012), State of Financing for Biodiversity: Draft Global Monitoring Report 2012 on the Strategy for Resource Mobilization under the Convention.

31 Compare L. Gündling, 'Compliance Assistance in International Environmental Law: Capacity-Building through Financial and Technology Transfer' (1996) 56 *Zeitschrift für ausländisches öffentliches Recht und Völkerrecht*, 796–809.

and voluntary or non-existent for other state parties. This form of differentiation is used in the international regulation of climate change. The United Nations Framework Convention on Climate Change (9 May 1992) introduced a distinction between 'all Parties' and 'the developed country Parties and other Parties included in Annex I'. The Kyoto Protocol to the Convention (11 December 1997) set quantified emission limitations for controlled greenhouse gasses and a timetable only for the Parties included in Annex I. In addition, all Parties were required to formulate policies and programs to monitor and mitigate climate change.[32]

Within the group of Annex I parties, further differentiation was negotiated. According to Article 3 of the Kyoto Protocol, Annex I parties were required to ensure individually or jointly that their aggregate emissions dropped by at least 5% below 1990 levels in the commitment period 2008 to 2012. The assignment of the contribution of each specific Annex I country to the reaching of this aggregate target was the subject of a separate negotiation. The Kyoto Protocol excludes the making of reservations.

The Kyoto Protocol was amended in 2012:[33] a second commitment period (2013–2020) was provided for, with Annex I Parties committing to a reduction of overall emission of controlled gasses by at least 18% below 1990 levels. The 'Doha amendment' has, however, not yet entered into force at the time of writing. It will only do so after acceptance by at least three fourths of the Parties to the Kyoto Protocol. The rate of ratification has been very slow.

Simultaneously, a process was set in motion for the adoption of 'a protocol, another legal instrument or an agreed outcome with legal force under the Convention applicable to all parties' to be adopted at the Conference of the Parties in December 2015, for it to come into effect and be implemented from 2020.[34] The new instrument will be directed at ensuring the highest possible mitigation efforts by all Parties.

The negotiation process on the follow-up to the Kyoto Protocol has been very difficult, due to division of opinion on the parameters on which to differentiate in the future. Developed countries have argued that in the 2015 instrument categories of countries and commitments should be realigned. Although the

---

32 Art. 26 of the Kyoto Protocol to the United Nations Framework Convention on Climate Change (1997). Note that the Protocol also introduces an element of differentiation into the regulation of the entry into force of the treaty. Art. 25 (1) requires that the Protocol will only enter into force on the ninetieth day after the date on which no less than 55 Parties have consented to the treaty 'incorporating Parties included in Annex I which account in total for at least 55% of the total carbon dioxide emissions for 1990'.

33 Art. 3 (1 bis) of the Doha Amendment to the Kyoto Protocol. Decision 1/CMP.8 (8 December 2012).

34 See Decision 1/CP.19 (23 November 2013), paras. 1–2.

2015 instrument is to be "applicable to all parties", which may suggest that all parties should make some commitment to reduce emissions domestically from 2020 onwards, a form of differentiation is bound to survive as the new instrument will be adopted under the UN Framework Convention on Climate Change that enshrines the principle of common but differentiated responsibilities and respective capabilities in its Article 3 (1).

An example of a treaty that differentiates at the gate is the Food Assistance Convention (25 April 2012):[35] this treaty is open only to developed states. The objective of the Convention is 'to save lives, reduce hunger, improve food security, and improve the nutritional status of the most vulnerable populations' by providing coordinated food assistance to the most vulnerable populations in 'eligible countries' (primarily countries on the OECD Development Committee Assistance list).[36] Each Party commits to making a minimum annual commitment (that it is free to specify), that is overseen by a Food Assistance Committee consisting of all the Parties to the Convention and deciding by consensus. Although the beneficiaries of food assistance live in countries outside of the territories of the ratifying parties, these countries are excluded from participation in decision-making under the Convention.[37]

3. VARIETIES OF STATES

Differentiation requires an identification of the states that are subject to different rights and obligations. States may be classified in certain categories, such as 'developing' and 'developed' countries. Differentiation may also be organized on a country-by-country basis, without any use of categories.

Categorization may be based on an assessment of whether a state meets certain objective criteria that are laid down in a treaty or in the rules of an international organization. Alternatively, ad hoc lists of states for the purposes of attribution of different obligations may be drawn up. During the listing process, use may be made of criteria or of certain factors, but the lists result mainly from political bargaining. Finally, it may be left to each state to self-identify as a member of a category. Examples of these different methods are discussed below.

---

35 Art. 12 of the Food Assistance Convention (2012). The Convention entered into force on 1 January 2013.

36 Ibid., Art. 4.

37 Art. 7 (6) of the Food Assistance Committee merely provides that the Food Assistance Committee 'should facilitate information-sharing with and dissemination to other stakeholders, and should consult with and receive information from them to support its discussions'.

Differentiation in international law is based mainly on the developed/developing state dichotomy. There is no generally applicable definition of these two categories in international law. Different instruments and organizations define the terms in light of their specific objectives.[38]

The United Nations Development Program (UNDP) uses a classification system for the purposes of measurement of progress made in human development. No legal consequences attach to the classification. The UNDP Human Development Index (HDI) currently distinguishes between four categories: countries with very high, high, medium and low human development. UNDP uses a single statistic that serves as a frame of reference for both social and economic development; it combines measurement of education, life expectancy at birth (health) and decent standard of living (income). The annual Human Development Reports also provide disaggregated HDIs illustrating gaps among regions, between the sexes, between urban and rural areas and among ethnic groups.

The 2013 Human Development Report is entitled 'The Rise of the South', which it describes as 'unprecedented in its speed and scale'.[39] The Report establishes that today the combined output of the developing world's three leading economies (Brazil, China and India) is about equal to the combined gross domestic product of Canada, France, Germany, Italy, the UK and the US. This 'represents a dramatic rebalancing of global economic power'. The projection is that by 2050 the global output of Brazil, India and China will far surpass the combined production of the traditional industrial North.[40] The Report also finds, however, that the pace of change remains slow in most least-developed countries.[41]

UNDP created the Human Development Index as an alternative to measuring development purely on the basis of income.[42] The World Bank's main criterion for classifying economies is gross national income (GNI) per capita.

Based on its GNI per capita, every economy is classified within an income group as a low income, middle (subdivided into lower middle and upper middle), or high income country. The World Bank refers to low-income and middle-income

---

38 Classifications used by authors writing in the field of international law and development also reflect the author's perspective on the field. Rumu Sarkar thus uses a three-tier classification among developing countries in her book based on degree of access to world capital markets: 'emerging economies', 'nations that are unable to attract sustained foreign direct investment and remain dependent on international aid' and 'nations that have collapsed or who suffer from an impaired international legal status'. See R. Sarkar, *International Development Law*, Oxford University Press, Oxford 2009, pp. 5–6.

39 UNDP, *Human Development Report 2013*, UNDP 2013, p. 1.

40 Ibid.

41 Ibid., 3.

42 Q. Qerimi, *Development in International Law*, Martinus Nijhoff Publishers, Leiden 2012, p. 5.

economies together as 'developing economies'. Countries with developing economies are eligible as IBRD/IDA clients. Lending categories do not fully coincide with income groups, although they too are partly based on GNI per capita. Lending categories are used to determine whether a country has access to IDA loans (that are concessional), to IBRD loans (that are non-concessional) or to both ('blend countries').[43] Classification for these categories is revised yearly.

The Development Assistance Committee of the Organization for Economic Cooperation and Development refers to the low and middle income groups as defined by the World Bank in order to determine which countries and territories it considers eligible for the receipt of official development assistance (ODA).[44] Only assistance to DAC recipient countries counts as development assistance, and thus contributes to reaching the 0,7% of gross national product as ODA target set by numerous UN soft law instruments.[45] The DAC revises its own list of eligible countries every three years. As already noted, the Food Assistance Convention uses the OECD DAC list in order to define eligible countries under the Convention.[46]

Candidate countries to the Development Assistance Committee itself are assessed on the basis of qualitative criteria: the existence of appropriate strategies, policies and institutional frameworks that ensure capacity to deliver a development co-operation program; an accepted measure of effort; and the existence of a system of performance monitoring and evaluation.

As is already apparent from the instruments discussed up to now, the group of 'developing countries' is far from homogeneous. In writings on international law and development, several authors nevertheless insist that the countries should be approached as a grouping, e.g. under the term the 'Third World'. It is argued that the identity of the Third World is rooted in its common history of subjugation, first to colonialism, and later to economic policies by hegemonic powers.[47] Pahuja explains that for her the term 'Third World' refers to a 'political grouping rather than a putatively 'objective' demographic or economic coalition'.[48] Celine Tan

[43] According to the World Bank website, in 2013, IDA countries were those that had a per capita income in 2012 of less than $ 1,205 and lacked the financial ability to borrow from IBRD. Blend countries are eligible for IDA loans because of their low per capita incomes but are also eligible for IBRD loans because they are financially creditworthy.

[44] G8 members, EU members, and countries with a firm date for entry into the EU are not eligible for ODA under OECD DAC rules.

[45] Originally in UN General Assembly Res. 2626 (XXV) (24 October 1970), para. 43.

[46] Art. 4 of the Food Assistance Convention (2012).

[47] As reflected in dependency theories that explain disparities in development as ensuing from a conscious effort by the West to create wealth by keeping the Third Wealth in a state of dependency, e.g. see QERIMI (note 42), p. 33.

[48] S. PAHUJA, *Decolonising International Law*, Cambridge University Press, Cambridge 2011, p. 261.

argues that the term should be retained as 'a continuing form of resistance to hegemonic attempts to disperse the collective voice and organizing unity of third world states and third world peoples'.[49] Both authors build on Antony Anghie's reading of the history of international law as continuously disempowering the non-European world'[50] through the maintenance of 'juridical mechanisms in the form, for example, of sources doctrine, personality doctrine, consent doctrine and so forth, which resist any challenge being made to the colonial past and sovereignty's role within it'.[51] Differentiation vis-à-vis developing countries serves to insulate developing countries from the adverse effects of a legal system (international law) that does not prioritize their interests.

The growing heterogeneity within the Third World has nevertheless led to the establishment of legal sub-categories allowing further differentiation within the group. The most frequently used sub-category is 'least developed countries'. Least developed countries are typically accorded more generous differential treatment, including preferences and exemptions from treaty obligations not granted to other developing countries.[52]

Within the United Nations, the Committee for Development Policy (CDP),[53] an ECOSOC subsidiary body, is responsible for reviewing the status of least developed countries. The CDP defines least developed countries (LDCs) as low-income countries suffering from the most severe structural impediments to sustainable development. Three criteria are currently taken into account: per capita gross national income (GNI), human assets and economic vulnerability to external shocks; the latter two criteria are measured through indices. To be added to the category, a country must score below a given threshold level for all three selected criteria and have a population no larger than 75 million inhabitants.[54] CDP reviews the list (currently consisting of 49 countries – South Sudan is the most recent addition) every three years. The review process results in a proposal to ECOSOC on revision.

---

49 C. Tan, *Governance through Development*, Routledge, London 2011, p. xv.

50 A. Anghie, *Imperialism, Sovereignty and the Making of International Law*, Cambridge University Press, Cambridge 2004, p. 312.

51 Ibid., p. 313.

52 Examples include: Art. 66 of the WTO TRIPS (Agreement on Trade-Related Aspects of Intellectual Property Rights (15 April 1994) provides a grace period for implementation of numerous TRIPS provisions to least developing countries; Art. 32 (1) of the International Tropical Timber Agreement (27 January 2006) that enables least developed countries to apply for special measures to the convention's governing body; the EU's "Everything But Arms" arrangement (EBA) gives all LDCs full duty free and quota-free access to the EU for all their exports with the exception of arms and armaments. The arrangement was created in 2001, see Council Regulation (EC) No. 416/2001 (28 February 2001).

53 ECOSOC Res. 1998/46 (31 July 1998), Annex IB.

54 See UN Doc. E/2011/33, Committee for Development Policy. Report on the thirteenth session (21–25 March 2011), para. 32.

The UN definition of least developed countries is used within the entire UN system [including by UNCTAD[55] – which produces an annual Least Developed Countries Report – and by the UN High Representative for the Least Developed Countries, Landlocked Developing Countries and the Small Island Developing States (UN-OHRLLS)], as well as by other international organizations, such as the World Trade Organization, the OECD or the EU, and in numerous international treaties. The definition of 'least developed country' thus invites little controversy.

Within the UN system other well-established sub-categories of developing countries include landlocked countries[56] and small island states.[57] Both categories are defined on the basis of geographical features.

In international treaties and instruments additional sub-categories of developing countries appear when they are deemed relevant to the subject at hand.[58] The Rio +20 Outcome Document that deals with all aspects of sustainable development contains an omnibus provision on all countries entitled to special attention that is so inclusive that it becomes self-defeating:

> We recognize that each country faces specific challenges to achieve sustainable development, and we underscore the special challenges facing the most vulnerable countries and, in particular, African countries, least developed countries, landlocked developing countries and small island developing states, as well as the specific challenges facing the middle-income countries. Countries in situations of conflict also need special attention.[59]

55 The first resolution on the subject of the least developed countries was adopted at UNCTAD II in 1968 (Res. 24 (II)). At the start of the second UN Development Decade, the General Assembly adopted special measures in favour of the least developed countries (LDCs) in UN General Assembly Res. 2626 (XXV) (24 October 1970), paras. 56–58.

56 The specific problems of landlocked countries – dependency on transit – were equally first identified in UN GA Res. 2626 (XXV) (24 October 1970), para. 59. In 2003, a 10-year action plan on landlocked countries was adopted, that is currently under review. See UN GA Res. 67/222 (3 April 2013). According to the UN-OHRLLS website, of 31 landlocked developing countries 16 are classified as least developed.

57 Small Island Developing States (SIDS) were recognized as a distinct group of developing countries facing specific social, economic and environmental vulnerabilities at the 1992 Rio Conference on Environment and Development (UNCED). Agenda 21 contains a Chapter 17G on sustainable development and Small Island States. The United Nations recognizes the 38 UN Member States belonging to the Alliance of Small Island States (AOSIS) as an ad hoc negotiating body that also includes other island entities that are non-UN Member States or are not self-governing or non-independent territories that are members of UN regional commissions. Small Island States are among the developing countries particularly affected by climate change as recognized in Art. 4 (8a) of the UN Framework Convention on Climate Change (1992).

58 E.g. the UN Convention to Combat Desertification (17 June 1994) in its Art. 7 establishes a priority for Africa 'in the light of the particular situation prevailing in that region, while not neglecting affected developing country Parties in other regions'.

59 UN GA Res. 66/288 (27 July 2012), para. 32.

'Vulnerability' is an intriguing criterion that is open to various interpretations, sometimes within the same treaty. In the Framework Convention on Climate Change countries with special needs include countries with opposite interests: countries physically affected by climate change (with low-lying coastal, arid or forested areas ...) as well as countries whose economies depend on fossil fuels and associated energy-intensive products, i. e. countries that may suffer economically from the measures addressing climate change provided for in the Convention.[60] Christopher Stone has suggested that vulnerability as an argument for differentiation works best in situations where there is both risk exposure and limited access to resources to mitigate the risk.[61]

'Countries with economies in transition' hold a position in the twilight zone between developing and developed countries. The concept stems from political economy, and refers primarily[62] to countries in Eastern Europe and those emerging from the dismemberment of the Soviet Union that transit from a plan to a market economy.

In international environmental law countries with economies in transition tend to be grouped with developed countries, but they are awarded more flexibility. The Biodiversity Convention thus encourages countries undergoing the process of transition to a market economy to voluntarily assume the obligations of the developed countries in terms of financial assistance to the developing countries.[63] In the Framework Convention on Climate Change, transition countries are included in Annex I, but they are allowed 'a certain degree of flexibility' in order to enable the ability of these Parties to address climate change.[64]

On the other hand a number of transition countries appear on the OECD DAC list of ODA recipients, and are ranked as 'medium human development' by UNDP. During negotiations on access to the World Trade Organization, transition countries may well seek special and differential treatment as accorded to developing countries.

At the World Trade Organization, the (unwritten) practice emerged that countries may designate themselves as 'developing countries' during the accession process, and thus claim an entitlement to special and differential treatment.[65] Other

60 Art. 4 (8) of the UN Framework Convention on Climate Change (1992).

61 Stone (note 4), p. 291.

62 Some Asian 'developing countries', such as Cambodia, Vietnam, Laos are also introducing elements of market economy into a state controlled economic system.

63 Art. 20 (2) of the Convention on Biological Diversity (1992).

64 Art. 4 (6) of the UN Framework Convention on Climate Change (1992). No definition of transition countries is included in the Convention, but the countries that qualify as such are marked with an asterisk in the Annex.

65 See Rolland (note 17), pp. 78–85.

countries may then challenge such a claim. Even if the Protocol of accession acknowledges the development status of the relevant country, the effect of the acknowledgment remains limited. Commitments made by the country in specific areas of WTO law (in order to gain accession) override development status; the specific commitments determine the degree of special and differential treatment that the country is entitled to. As already indicated, the self-identification procedure does not apply to least developed countries. The WTO refers to the UN classification of least developed countries, and WTO agreements often explicitly regulate the treatment of the least developed countries.

Differentiation can also be achieved without the use of criteria by agreeing ad hoc lists. In the Convention on Biological Diversity, the competence to decide and periodically review the list of developed country parties and other parties voluntary assuming the same obligations is entrusted to the Conference of the Parties.[66]

In the UN Framework Convention on Climate Change 'the developed country Parties and other Parties' required to limit greenhouse gas emissions are listed in an Annex to the Convention. Annexes are subject to the same amendment procedure as the Convention itself.

A final option is to avoid categorization, and to differentiate simply on a country by country basis. In such an approach, each party to a treaty would be allowed to indicate its level of commitment in light of its capacity (ideally matching its level of commitment with the population's sustainable development needs). The adequate tailoring of commitments and needs could be assessed by a relevant treaty body. In the negotiation process on the 2015 climate change instrument, all Parties have been invited to prepare 'intended nationally determined contributions'[67] in the context of the future instrument. The submission of this information is to facilitate the adoption of the 2015 instrument. It has been suggested[68] that national contributions could consist of greenhouse gas mitigation goals,[69] policies and projects.

---

66 Art. 20 (2) of the Convention on Biological Diversity (1992).

67 See Decision 1/CP.19 (23 November 2013), para. 2 (b). The submission of such intended national contributions is, however 'without prejudice to the legal nature of the contributions', ibid.

68 See K. Levin et al., *Ex-Ante Clarification, Transparency, and Understanding of Intended Nationally Determined Mitigation Contributions*, Working Paper. World Resources Institute, Washington, DC 2014, www.wri.org/publication/ex-ante-clarification-transparency.

69 Domestic mitigation goals consist of a commitment to reduce, or limit the increase of, GHG emissions (or emissions intensity) by a defined amount and by a specified point in time or over a time period. Ibid., 4.

4. JUSTIFICATION

International treaties may give reasons for why differentiation was deemed appropriate – typically in the preamble, or in provisions dealing with the objectives and principles of the treaty. Such reasons may include:

- Historical responsibility: past injury should be redressed through additional current effort;
- Harm caused: countries currently contributing more to the injury should contribute more to reparation;
- Availability of resources: countries with the financial (and/or other) capacity should contribute more;
- Sustainable development needs: efforts required under treaty commitments should not disable countries from satisfying the sustainable development needs of their population.

Reliance on historical responsibility for the purposes of differentiation makes sense particularly when past acts have continuous effects. At the World Conference against Racism, Racial Discrimination, Xenophobia and Related Intolerance, the responsibility of the former colonial powers to provide reparation for the continuous effects of slavery and colonialism, was a highly contested issue. In the end, the Conference acknowledged the 'massive human suffering' caused by slavery, the slave trade, the transatlantic slave trade, apartheid, colonialism and genocide. It took note of the initiative of some states to apologize and pay reparation, and expressed awareness of 'the moral obligation on the part of all concerned states [...] to take appropriate and effective measures to halt and reverse the lasting consequences of those practices'.[70] In climate change discussions, it makes a huge difference whether past or current harm is primarily taken into account. Past emissions by developed states, so the argument goes, have lasting effects because they: (a) caused irreversible damage, and (b) allowed the early industrializing countries to build wealth for their current generation.[71]

[70] Paras. 98–102, Declaration World Conference against Racism, Racial Discrimination, Xenophobia and Related Intolerance (8 September 2001). For a case-study, see L. Van Den Herik, 'Addressing Colonial Crimes through Reparations? Adjudicating Dutch Atrocities Committed in Indonesia' (2012) 10 *Journal of International Criminal Justice*, 693–705, J. Sarkin, *Colonial Genocide and Reparations Claims in the 21st Century: The Socio-Legal Context of Claims under International Law by the Herero against Germany for Genocide in Namibia 1904–1908*, Praeger Security International, London 2009.

[71] S. Carney, 'Justice and the Distribution of Greenhouse Gas Emissions' (2009) 5 *Journal of Global Ethics*, 133–135.

International instruments usually do not rely on a single factor such as historical responsibility as a justification for differentiation.[72] Principles 6 and 7 of the Rio Declaration on Environment and Development bring together various arguments for differentiation in order to construct higher expectations for developed countries:

(6) The special situation and needs of developing countries, particularly the least developed and those most environmentally vulnerable, shall be given special priority. International actions in the field of environment and development should also address the interests and needs of all countries.
(7) States shall cooperate in a spirit of global partnership to conserve, protect and restore the health and integrity of the Earth's ecosystem. In view of the different contributions to global environmental degradation, states have common but differentiated responsibilities. The developed countries acknowledge the responsibility that they bear in the international pursuit of sustainable development in view of the pressures their societies place on the global environment and of the technologies and financial resources they command.[73]

The combination of the degree of injury caused (the contribution to environmental degradation), the capacity to deal with the problem and the special needs of the developing countries results in the attribution of a heavier responsibility to developed countries. In these principles 'developed countries' are approached collectively as countries bearing a special responsibility – leaving open the possibility of further differentiation within the group when individual state responsibility for specific obligations needs to be attributed.

Political bargaining rather than a weighted application of criteria resulted in an exclusive focus on developed countries as major duty bearers.

The provision on Principles in the UN Framework Convention on Climate Change (9 May 1992) contains a similar mix of factors that are to be taken into account in future normative developments on the attribution of responsibility for climate change measures. Article 3 of the Framework Convention states that developed countries should take the lead in combating climate change, given their differentiated responsibility and capacity (para. 1); requires full consideration of the special needs and special circumstances of developing country parties, and of those parties that would have to bear a disproportionate or abnormal burden

---

[72] The Preamble of the Framework Convention on Climate Change thus refers to both *historical and current* global emissions of greenhouse gases in developed countries as a justification for differentiation. See third preambular paragraph, UN Framework Convention on Climate Change (1992).

[73] Principles 6 and 7, Rio Declaration on Environment and Development (14 June 1992).

under the Convention (para. 2); and notes that climate change measures should be appropriate for the specific conditions of each Party and should be integrated with national development programs, 'taking into account that economic development is essential for adopting measures to address climate change' (para. 4).[74]

Today, a combined use of criteria could easily support the conclusion that a number of UNDP high and even medium human development developing countries should accept responsibility as duty bearers: they contribute to environmental degradation, dispose of sufficient technological and financial resources, and are not particularly vulnerable in terms of satisfying the sustainable development needs of their population. Cristopher Stone criticizes the bundling of environmental policies with welfare goals. This, he argues, may lead to a suboptimal outcome to the achievement of both, and reduces transparency and accountability.[75] On the other hand, a sustainable development approach requires a balancing of the different dimensions of economic growth, environmental protection and social justice.[76]

One could also take the position that differentiation is justified whenever negotiators so agree: the process justifies the outcome. The assumption then is that participants in the negotiation process rationally agreed that differentiation was mutually beneficial. On the other hand, international negotiations have a notoriously asymmetrical structure, both among states, and between states and other actors, and therefore the quality of the process would need to be carefully scrutinized.[77] In addition, even a process that perfectly balances individual (state) interests may lead to an imperfect outcome from the perspective of the effective protection of global common interests.

5. FORWARD-LOOKING PERSPECTIVE

In international instruments aiming at the protection of global common interests differentiation serves the purpose of ensuring universal state participation.

74 Note that Art. 3 of the Framework Convention on Climate Change refers explicitly to economic development, but not to social justice.

75 Stone (note 4), p. 294.

76 Compare also Art. 3 of the International Law Association Declaration of Legal Principles relating to Climate Change (2014): 'In the context of addressing climate change and its adverse effects, sustainable development requires states to balance economic and social development and the protection of the climate system and supports the realisation of the right of all human beings to an adequate living standard and the equitable distribution of the benefits thereof. To that extent, policies and measures taken in response to climate change must integrate environmental, economic and social matters.'

77 Compare W. Benedek, 'Multi-Stakeholderism in the Development of International Law' in U. Fastenrath, R. Geiger, D.-E. Khan, A. Paulus, S. von Schorlemer and Ch. Vedder (eds), *From Bilateralism to Community Interest*, Oxford University Press, Oxford 2011, pp. 209–210.

Differentiation is deemed necessary because states have unequal capacities; addressing factual inequality arguably requires the creation of non-uniform obligations for different categories of states.

The terms 'developed' and 'developing' states are frequently used to describe these categories. The terms reflect the impact of colonialism and of post-colonial economic globalization on the development of international law. In treaties based on differentiation, developing countries are required to contribute less to the protection of the global common interest.

In today's world, the relevance of the dichotomy developing/developed countries is decreasing. Emerging economies are catching up with the early industrializing countries. Former colonies achieve faster progress in human development than the former colonial powers. Among developing countries, disparity grows. As a result, the category of 'least developed countries' will probably remain relevant, in practice, but also in law.[78] Legal differentiation on the basis of the dichotomy developing/developed countries will become increasingly contentious.

As an alternative, the use of contextual obligations holds promise. Contextualization allows taking into account variety at the country level, and avoids categorization of countries. The specific characteristics of variety that are deemed legally relevant can be defined in light of the issue at hand. Importantly, contextual obligations allow navigating between the global and the local. They imply a joint commitment to the protection of a common interest, while at the same time respecting policy space on how to take up responsibility at the domestic level. The use made of domestic policy space can be subject to review by a treaty body entrusted with both monitoring and assistance powers.

Treaty regimes for the protection of global common interests are ideally jointly owned by all states.[79] All states – regardless of their capacities – should be adequately involved both in the identification of global common interests as well as in the design of the protection system, in recognition of their mutual duty to cooperate for the protection of global common interests. As Rumu Sarkar puts it: '(…) both developed and developing nations should bargain with each other in good faith, and facilitate, where practicable, the development of other nations. More importantly, the act of cooperating with each other is more than joint or

---

78 Compare M. Irish, 'Least-Developed Countries, Climate Change and Trade' (2012) 5 *The Law and Development Review* 2, Art. 2 who concludes, with regard to LDCs, 22: 'The basis for differentiation remains strong and dictates special attention to their environmental, economic and social interests, viewed in an integrated manner in accordance with the objective of sustainable development.'

79 Inclusion of non-state actors in international law and institution-making is not discussed here, but it is clearly also of importance.

simultaneous action; it is the unity of action to a common end or a common result'.[80] If the (contextual) global norms and protection system are jointly owned, there is no reason why the regime should not apply equally to all (except the least developed countries). Such a global regime is preferable over a regime that is at its core geared towards the preferences of states with strong capacities, while carving out exceptions for states with weaker capacities – particularly if the expectation is that the latter group of states will gradually adhere to the obligations of the dominant states. In such a regime the asymmetries of postcolonial law are reproduced[81] by requiring from states with weaker capacity that they build up the capacity to fully comply with an international legal order that reflects the priorities of states with stronger capacities.

Inclusive decision-making and insistence on uniform but contextual obligations may imply that progress in the effective protection of global common interests is slow. There is thus a need to create mechanisms providing incentives to encourage all countries to strengthen their commitments to reaching global goals. As a minimum, the cumulative effect of efforts made towards achievement of global goals as originally agreed should be systemically measured, so that the gap between aspiration and success can, when necessary, be closed through additional agreements.

80 Ibid., p. 100. See also Principle 12, Rio Declaration on Environment and Development (14 June 1992).

81 Ibid., p. 27.

CHAPTER 4

THE COMMON INTEREST IN INTERNATIONAL LITIGATION

Claire BUGGENHOUDT

1. INTRODUCTION

In the last decades common interests such as peace and security and environmental protection have been explicitly recognized in public international law.[1] In spite of this formal recognition at the international level, the enforcement of such interests remains problematic. In this paper, the decisions of international judicial bodies will be examined to determine whether the current international case law encourages or impedes the enforcement of common interests. At first sight, the traditional adversarial and bilateral procedures adopted by most international courts and tribunals do not allow for considerations that are not explicitly recognized in the treaty that provides jurisdiction or that go beyond the direct interests of the parties. Furthermore, the functional differentiation of international law has led to a specialization of international judicial bodies that seems to encourage a judicial bias towards specific interests. The aim of the present paper is to investigate when and how international judicial bodies leave room for the consideration of common interests in their decisions. It analyses the case law of three inter-state mechanisms (the WTO Dispute Settlement Mechanism, the International Court of Justice and the International Tribunal for the Law of the Sea) to determine whether and how common interests are considered.[2] The findings demonstrate that, both in the procedural and the substantive decisions of the examined judicial bodies, methods have been developed to accommodate for an interpretation of international law that takes account of common interests. The paper is structured as follows: in the first section the emergence of common interests is sketched in the context of the international judiciary, the second

---

1 See notes 5 and 6.

2 These three bodies were chosen because they are all inter-state dispute settlement mechanisms. Although it is interesting to study the approach of other types of dispute settlement (for example international investment arbitration), a limitation to mechanisms that have similar procedural rules seemed preferable given the limited scope of this paper.

section analyses the case law of three inter-state judicial bodies and in conclusion the paper will briefly link these developments in international litigation to the enforcement of common interest in general.

2. THE EMERGENCE OF COMMON INTERESTS AND THE INTERNATIONAL JUDICIARY

The recognition of common interests was described by Wolfgang Friedmann as one of the features of the transition in international law from a law of 'coexistence' to a law of 'cooperation'.[3] It seems that in the process of a more intensified cooperation, states became aware of the importance of protecting certain common interests.[4] Besides solving disputes between sovereign interests, the aim of international law has now expanded to the preservation and protection of 'interests that transcend the boundaries of a single state and require collective action in response'; interests of which 'no single state can resolve the problems they pose or receive all the benefits they provide'.[5] An example of this evolution is the protection of peace and security, one of the first issues recognised as an interest of the international community as a whole, rather than that of an individual state.[6] Another example is environmental protection, which was first stated to be of 'common interest' in the 1972 Stockholm Declaration on the Human Environment.[7]

The main question addressed in this paper is how the international judiciary enforces respect for these common interests. Since the early ninety-nineties, there has been a significant expansion of international litigation and the number of specialized judicial bodies has multiplied. However, it is unclear how the consideration of common concerns fits into this proliferated judicial system that is governed by separate instances pursuing different goals, such as the promotion of free trade or the enforcement of the Law of the Sea. International law has always been a balancing act, in the sense that it continuously reconciles the public or national interests of different states with the shared interests that

---

3 See W. Friedmann, *The Changing Structure of International Law*, Columbia University Press, New York 1964, p. 367.

4 S. Villalpando, 'The Legal Dimension of the International Community: How Community Interests Are Protected in International Law' (2010) 21 *European Journal of International Law* 2, 393.

5 D. Shelton, 'Common Concern of Humanity' (2009) 1 *Iustum Aequum Salutare* 34.

6 The Preamble of the UN Charter states that its goal is 'to unite our strength to maintain international peace and security, and to ensure, by the acceptance of principles and the institution of methods, that armed force shall not be used, save in the common interest'.

7 The preamble of the Stockholm Declaration provides that '{a} growing class of environmental problems, because they are regional or global in extent or because they affect the common international realm, will require extensive cooperation among nations and action by international organizations in the common interest'. Declaration of the United Nations Conference on the Human Environment (16 June 1972), para. 7.

those states have identified by means of an international treaty. The question is how the new dimension of common interests, or interests of the international community as a whole, fits into this existing balance. This is especially true in the context of international litigation, which lacks the 'constitutional world court' that may seem necessary to enforce common interests at the international level. The institutionalisation of international law is, for the moment, incomplete. In particular in the field of common interests, states are generally reluctant to provide for strong global judicial dispute settlement.[8] As a result, the existing mechanisms are confronted with the issue of enforcing common interests.[9] Besides the fact that these bodies may be biased, the procedural as well as the substantive rules of the existing judicial mechanisms are generally not designed to deal with common interests other than those explicitly recognized in the treaty that gives them jurisdiction. In consequence, judicial bodies of different regimes are faced with the same, politically sensitive, demand of (re)interpreting their procedural and substantive rules in light of common interest issues.

3. COMMON INTERESTS IN RECENT CASE LAW

Against the background of the common interest in international law and the proliferation of the international judiciary, this section will analyse to what extent international judicial bodies can and have considered common interests in their decisions. The paper focuses on three inter-state dispute settlement bodies, the International Court of Justice, the International Tribunal for the Law of the Sea and the WTO Appellate Body. The results of the case law analyses show that there has been a gradual integration of the consideration of common interests in both the procedural and the substantive decisions of these judicial bodies. Although the consideration of common concerns can be found in most steps of the decision-making process, it will here be illustrated in the context of indicating provisional measures, granting standing to the claimant, permitting third party interventions and (substantively) considering environmental concerns.

8 C. Tams, 'Individual States as Guardians of Community Interests' in U. Fastenrath, R. Geiger, D.-E. Khan, A. Paulus, S. von Schorlemer and C. Vedder (eds), *From Bilateralism to Community Interest – Essays in Honour of Judge Bruno Simma*, Oxford University Press, Oxford 2011, p. 383. There exists, for example, no specialized international judicial body to enforce environmental protection or human rights law.

9 A. Paulus, 'Reciprocity Revisited' in U. Fastenrath, R. Geiger, D.-E. Khan, A. Paulus, S. von Schorlemer and C. Vedder (eds), *From Bilateralism to Community Interest – Essays in Honour of Judge Bruno Simma*, Oxford University Press, Oxford 2011, p. 128.

3.1. INDICATION OF PROVISIONAL MEASURES

Of the considered institutions only two bodies use provisional measures to protect the rights of the parties during the proceedings (the ICJ and the ITLOS); the WTO Appellate Body does not indicate provisional measures but works with a tight time schedule to prevent conflicts from deteriorating.[10] Nevertheless, it is of interest to look at this element here because recently the ICJ and the ITLOS have used the indication of provisional measures to go beyond the protection of the rights of the parties and into the realm of protecting common interests.

3.1.1. ICJ

The International Court of Justice has itself created an opening for the consideration of common interests in its procedure on provisional measures. According to Article 41 (1) of the ICJ Statute, the court has the power to grant binding provisional measures if it has *prima facie* jurisdiction over a dispute[11] and the court 'considers that circumstances so require to protect the rights which might form the subject matter of a judgment'.[12] Traditionally the court interpreted this to mean that measures are only justified if there is urgency, pending the final decision of the case, to protect the rights of the parties.[13] However, the ICJ widened its power to indicate provisional measures from protecting the rights of the parties to the prevention of (violent) intensification of a dispute.[14] In other words, it has broadened the purpose of its provisional measures to protecting the common interest of international peace and security. This evolution took place since the nineties when the court started motivating its indication of provisional measures in border conflicts by referring to the protection of the people living in the disputed areas.[15]

Two more recent cases show that the ICJ's focus on the prevention of violent conflict has far-reaching consequences on its case law on provisional measures.

10 Reports are circulated 90 days after the appeal, although it must be noted that recently the Appellate Body has not managed to consistently meet this deadline.

11 ICJ, *Armed Activities on the Territory of the Congo (New Application: 2002) (Democratic Republic of the Congo v. Rwanda)* (Provisional Measures) (Order), ICJ Reports 2002, p. 219; ICJ, *Pulp Mills on the River Uruguay (Argentina v. Uruguay)* (Provisional Measures) (Order), ICJ Report 2006, p. 113, para. 57.

12 Art. 41 (1) of the Statute of the International Court of Justice of 26 June 1945.

13 On urgency: ICJ, *Pulp Mills on the River Uruguay* (note 11), para. 62. On the protection of rights: ICJ, *Armed Activities on the Territory of the Congo* (note 11).

14 K. Oellers-Frahm, 'Article 41' in A. Zimmermann, C. Tomuschat and K. Oellers-Frahm (eds), *The Statute of the International Court of Justice: A Commentary*, Oxford University Press, Oxford 2006, pp. 931–932.

15 For example ICJ, *Case concerning the Frontier Dispute (Burkina Faso v. Mali)* (Provisional Measures), ICJ Reports 1986, p. 554, para. 21; ICJ, *Case concerning the Land and Maritime Boundary between Cameroon and Nigeria (Cameroon v. Nigeria)* (Provisional Measures) (Order), ICJ Reports 1996, p. 13, para. 39.

In the 2002 case concerning *Armed Activities on the Territory of the Congo (DRC v. Rwanda),* the court was asked by the Democratic Republic of the Congo to order provisional measures to end the armed aggression committed by Rwandan forces on its territory because, if not stopped immediately, this aggression 'would have humanitarian consequences which could never be made good again ... in the short term or in the long term'.[16] In this case, the court did not find that it had *prima facie* jurisdiction and therefore refrained from indicating provisional measures. Nevertheless, the ICJ went on to urge both parties to prevent grave violations of human rights and international humanitarian law.[17] In the 2011 *Request for Interpretation of the Judgment of 15 June 1962 in the Case concerning the Temple of Preah Vihear (Cambodia v. Thailand)* Cambodia asked the ICJ to order an immediate withdrawal of all Thai forces from the area of the Temple of Preah Vihear, a religious site situated near the border between the two countries.[18] The court, however, did not grant the requested measures. Instead, it indicated provisional measures addressed to both the parties and ordered the parties to respect a demilitarized zone around the Temple.[19] Although the power to indicate provisional measures that are not requested by the parties is supported by the ICJ's power to grant provisional measures *proprio motu*, it has been criticized for going beyond the court's mandate.[20] That the court, nevertheless, extended its provisional measures to include the prevention of (possibly violent) conflict can be seen as an incorporation of the common interest of peace and security, a fundamental interest of the international community, in its procedure.[21]

3.1.2. ITLOS

Like the ICJ Statute, Article 290 of UNCLOS provides that the ITLOS may prescribe binding provisional measures if the Tribunal has *prima facie* jurisdiction and if measures are necessary and urgent.[22] The necessity of provisional measures under UNCLOS is not limited to preserving the rights of the parties, but may

---

16 ICJ, *Armed Activities on the Territory of the Congo (New Application: 2002) (Democratic Republic of the Congo v. Rwanda)* (Provisional Measures) (Order), ICJ Reports 2002, p. 219, para. 11.

17 Ibid., paras. 54–56, 93.

18 ICJ, *Request for Interpretation of the Judgment of 15 June 1962 in the Case concerning the Temple of Preah Vihear (Cambodia v. Thailand)* (Provisional Measures) (Order), ICJ Reports 2011, p. 537.

19 Ibid.

20 Art. 75 of the ICJ Rules of the court of 14 April 1978, www.icj-cij.org. Criticized in Oellers-Frahm (note 14), p. 932.

21 M. Benzing, 'Community Interests in the Procedure of International Courts and Tribunals' (2006) 5 *The Law and Practice of International Courts and Tribunals*, 379–380. However, the decision may also be explained in light of protecting individual lives, without referring to a common interest.

22 Art. 290 of the United Nations Convention on the Law of the Sea (1982), *UN Treaty Series* 1833, 3. Measures appropriate pending ITLOS' final decision on the merits or pending the constitution of an arbitral tribunal.

also be aimed at preventing serious harm to the marine environment, a common interest. In the *Southern Bluefin Tuna (SBT)* Case, the Tribunal adopted a broad interpretation of the preservation of the marine environment.[23] The *SBT* dispute arose when Japan decided to carry out a scientific exploratory fishing program that violated the 1993 Conservation of Southern Bluefin Tuna Convention. In this case, the Tribunal stated that 'the conservation of the living resources of the sea is an element in the protection and preservation of the marine environment' which justifies provisional measures,[24] it thus established that the duty to preserve includes the conservation of endangered species and ecosystems.[25]

The common interest in preserving the marine environment also seems to affect the ITLOS' interpretation of *prima facie* jurisdiction and urgency. In the *SBT* case the applicants chose to bring the issue to the ITLOS rather than following the procedure explicitly established in the 1993 Convention. Nevertheless, the ITLOS established *prima facie* jurisdiction, which was later rejected by the Annex VII arbitral tribunal deciding on the merits.[26] A similar flexible interpretation is applied by the ITLOS in establishing urgency. In the *MOX Plant Case (Ireland v. United Kingdom)* Ireland asked the Tribunal to order the U.K. to suspend the authorisation of a MOX (Mixed Oxide Fuel) Plant in the North West of England and to stop the transport of radioactive materials over sea while the case was pending.[27] Although the ITLOS did not consider the circumstances to be urgent enough to answer Ireland's demand it did, remarkably, order provisional measures and instructed Ireland and the United Kingdom to 'cooperate in exchanging information concerning the risks or effects of the operation of the MOX plant and in devising ways to deal with them'.[28] It can be concluded that the Tribunal in both the *MOX* and the *SBT* orders offered the applicants 'the benefit of a great many doubts'.[29] The loose interpretation of the requirements of *prima facie* jurisdiction as well as urgency could be explained by considering the prevention of harm to the marine environment as the 'Tribunal's overriding objective' in these cases.[30]

---

23 ITLOS, *Southern Bluefin Tuna* Case *(New Zealand v. Japan; Australia v. Japan)* (Provisional Measures) (Order) (1999), Case Nos. 3 & 4, http://www.itlos.org/index.php?id=62.

24 Ibid., para. 70.

25 A. Boyle, 'The Environmental Jurisprudence of the International Tribunal for the Law of the Sea' (2007) 22 *The International Journal of Marine and Coastal Law* 3, 373.

26 Arbitral Tribunal constituted under part XV ("Settlement of Disputes") Annex VII ("Arbitration") of the UNCLOS, *Southern Bluefin Tuna* Case *(Australia and New Zealand v. Japan), Award on Jurisdiction and Admissibility* (2000).

27 ITLOS, *The MOX Plant* Case *(Ireland v. United Kingdom)* (Provisional Measures) (Order) (2001).

28 Ibid., 78–84.

29 B. Kwiatkowska, 'Southern Bluefin Tuna *(New Zealand v. Japan; Australia v. Japan)* (Provisional Measure) (Order), ITLOS Cases Nos. 3 and 4 (2000) 94 *American Journal of International Law*, 154.

30 Ibid., 155.

3.2. STANDING

A second element that may be influenced by common interest considerations is the requirement that the claimant has standing, the right to initiate a suit. Because all of the discussed judicial systems are inter-state mechanisms[31] the main question is whether a state needs a direct, individual, legal interest to bring a case; such a requirement would severely limit the possibility for a state to enforce obligations owed to the international community as a whole.

3.2.1. ICJ

The ICJ first discussed the issue of applications 'in the common interest' in the 1966 *South West Africa* Case *(Ethiopia and Liberia v. South Africa).*[32] In this case, the court had to decide whether Ethiopia and Liberia could file a claim against South Africa for not fulfilling its duties as a mandate holder over South West Africa (now Namibia).[33] The ICJ rejected the claim, holding that international law does not include a right for each state to take legal action in the common interest.[34] The court distanced itself from this decision with the recognition of erga omnes obligations in its *obiter dictum* of the 1970 *Barcelona Traction* Case *(Belgium v. Spain).*[35] In that case, the court established that obligations exist 'towards the international community as a whole' and that 'all states can be held to have a legal interest in their protection; they are obligations erga omnes'.[36] Until the 2012 case of *Questions concerning the Obligation to Prosecute or Extradite (Belgium v. Senegal)*, the question whether all states have standing in cases where erga omnes obligations are at risk remained completely unanswered.[37] In this case, Belgium asserted that Senegal was obliged, under the CAT, to prosecute or extradite Hissène Habré, the former president of Chad. Belgium argued that it had standing because of its specific interest as a home state of former victims of the regime and because of the erga omnes nature of the relevant obligations. The court focussed only on the latter argument and provided that 'the common interest in compliance with the relevant obligations under the Convention against Torture implies the entitlement of each state party to the convention to make a claim concerning the cessation of an alleged breach by another state party'.[38]

[31] An exception is included in Art. 187 of the UNCLOS, which grants standing to non-state entities before the Seabed Disputes Chamber.

[32] ICJ, *South West Africa, Second Phase (Ethiopia v. South Africa; Liberia v. South Africa)* (Judgment), ICJ Reports 1966, p. 6.

[33] Ibid.

[34] Ibid., para. 88.

[35] ICJ, *Barcelona Traction, Light and Power Company, Limited* (New Application: 1962) *(Belgium v. Spain)* (2nd phase) (Judgment), ICJ Reports 1970, p. 3.

[36] Ibid., para. 32.

[37] ICJ, *Questions Relating to the Obligation to Prosecute or Extradite (Belgium v. Senegal)* (Judgment), ICJ Reports 2012, p. 422.

[38] Ibid., para. 69.

Thus, at least for erga omnes partes obligations, the court does accept that each state party has the right to initiate legal proceedings in the common interest.

3.2.2. WTO

In the context of the WTO dispute settlement mechanism it is not clear whether the claimant must establish an (legal) interest to obtain the right of standing or whether the shared interest of the WTO member states in enforcing the obligations included in the WTO treaties suffices. Standing has only been an issue in a limited number of cases. In the Case of *European Communities – Regime for the Importation, Sale and Distribution of Bananas* the EC questioned the legal interest of the US because it is not an exporter of bananas.[39] The Appellate Body, however, held that neither the DSU nor the GATT require a legal interest to obtain standing.[40] The Appellate Body confirmed the panel's reasoning that 'with the increased interdependence of the global economy (...) any deviation from the negotiated balance of rights and obligations is more likely than ever to affect [other members], directly or indirectly'.[41] It may therefore be concluded that the WTO's judicial bodies interpret standing very broadly. A mere potential impact on the interest of the complainant was considered sufficient to establish standing in *EC-Bananas*.

3.2.3. ITLOS

Whether the UNCLOS requires a claimant state to have a direct legal interest in the dispute has not yet been raised before the ITLOS. In the context of the Tribunal's procedure for the prompt release of vessels, the UNCLOS does state that 'the application for release may be made only by or on behalf of the flag state of the vessel'.[42] Nevertheless, the ITLOS case law shows that the tribunal interprets this provision rather broadly to ensure that the common value of international peace and security is respected. In the *M/V "SAIGA" (No. 2)* Case *(Saint Vincent and the Grenadines* v. *Guinea)*, the tribunal had to pronounce itself on the legitimacy of the use of force in arresting a vessel.[43] During the disputed arrest, two members of the M/V Saiga's crew endured gunshot wounds. One of the first issues addressed by the tribunal was the capacity of Saint Vincent as the flag state of the M/V Saiga. Guinea argued that the ship did not have a nationality at the time of the arrest. Despite inconclusive evidence to the contrary,[44] the tribunal found that '[i]n the

39 WTO Appellate Body Report, *European Communities – Regime for the Importation, Sale and Distribution of Bananas*, WT/DS27/AB/R (9 September 1997).
40 Ibid., para. 132.
41 Ibid., para. 136.
42 Art. 292 (2) of the UNCLOS.
43 ITLOS, *The M/V "Saiga"* (No. 2) case (Judgment), 1999 (1 July 1999).
44 ITLOS, *The M/V "Saiga"* (No. 2) case, *Dissenting Opinion of Judge Warioba*, 1999 (1 July 1999), paras. 22–29.

particular circumstances of this case, it would not be consistent with justice if the tribunal were to decline to deal with the merits of the dispute'.[45] The tribunal took a similar approach when examining whether it could pronounce itself on issues that concerned crew members that did not have the nationality of Saint Vincent. In this context, the ITLOS found that the ship and everyone involved in its operations constitute one entity that is linked to the flag state.[46] The Tribunal justified this finding stating that 'undue hardship would ensue' if it would oblige each person to seek the protection of its own state.[47]

3.3. THIRD PARTY INTERVENTIONS

A procedure that could have a high potential for bringing common interest issues under the attention of judicial bodies, is the acceptance of third party interventions. In adversarial and interstate dispute settlement mechanism, third party interventions may introduce issues that have not been raised by the litigating parties. Especially in the context of public interest concerns, additional materials could provide relevant information and 'multilateralise' a bilateral dispute.[48]

3.3.1. ICJ

The ICJ's jurisdiction is strictly based on consent, which implies that access to the court is necessarily restrictive. In the court's contentious proceedings, third party interventions are reserved for states that have an individual legal interest under the mechanisms of Articles 62 and 63 of the ICJ Statute. The court does not consider an interest 'regarding the applicable general principles and rules of international law' as an interest allowing intervention.[49] Intervention is the only way in which states can participate in contentious proceedings; states may not act as *amicus curiae* before the ICJ.[50] While states have attempted to inform the court of their point of view by sending communications to the court, it is not clear whether the court uses this information.[51] Non-state actors can only submit information to the court in contentious cases if the court requests or accepts information of public international organizations under Article 34 para.

---

45 ITLOS, *The M/V "Saiga"* (No. 2) case (1999), para. 73.

46 Ibid., para. 106.

47 Ibid., para. 107.

48 Benzing (note 21), p. 298; D. Shelton, 'The Participation of Nongovernmental Organizations in International Judicial Proceedings' (1994) 88 *American Journal of International Law*, 625.

49 ICJ, *Continental Shelf (Libyan Arab Jamahiriya v. Malta), Application to Intervene* (Judgment), ICJ Reports 1984, p. 3.

50 The court does allow for *amicus curiae* briefs of third states and international organizations in its advisory proceedings in accordance with Art. 66 of the ICJ Statute.

51 P. Palchetti, 'Opening the International Court of Justice to Third states: Intervention and Beyond' (2002) 6 *Max Planck Yearbook of UN Law*, 166.

2 of its statute. However, this mechanism is not often used because the court has limited 'public international organizations' to intergovernmental organizations.[52] Moreover, IGO's do not take the initiative to make submissions and the court rarely requests information from them.[53]

Non-state actors other than intergovernmental organizations cannot intervene nor submit *amicus curiae* briefs to the court. Nevertheless, the ICJ did accept a limited amount of NGO involvement in the *Gabcikovo-Nagymaros* Case.[54] In this case, Hungary claimed that its suspension and abandonment of a major joint project with Slovakia was justified by environmental reasons. To strengthen its defence, Hungary attached several Hungarian, Slovakian and international NGO reports to its submission in the form of 'scientific reports'.[55] The court accepted Hungary's submission and (implicitly) the involvement of NGOs at the pre-trial stage. However, true *amicus curiae* briefs, i.e. submissions that are not directly endorsed by one of the parties, continue to cause disagreement within the Bench.[56] To date, *amicus curiae* submissions have not been accepted in the ICJ's contentious case law and it is unlikely that they will be accepted in the court's future case law without a change in the statute's provisions.[57] It could therefore be concluded that the court is reluctant to accept third party interventions that are purely based on common interest grounds in its contentious proceedings.

3.3.2. WTO

The intervention of third parties is arguably one of the most controversial procedural issues in the context of the WTO. This is especially true for third party interventions that could introduce (common) interests other than those of the parties. The Dispute Settlement Understanding explicitly allows member states to intervene in a dispute if they have a 'substantial interest in a matter before a panel'.[58] Because this substantial interest is not further qualified as a trade or legal interest, this provision could, hypothetically, be used to intervene in the common interest. In contrast, non-state entities do not enjoy the right to intervene and may

---

52 Art. 69 (4) of the ICJ Rules of the court of 14 April 1978, www.icj-cij.org.

53 P.-M. Dupuy, 'Article 34' in A. Zimmermann, C. Tomuschat and K. Oellers-Frahm (eds), *The Statute of the International Court of Justice: a Commentary*, Oxford University Press, Oxford 2006, p. 553.

54 ICJ, *Gabcikovo-Nagymaros Project (Hungary v. Slovakia)* (Judgment), ICJ Reports 1997, p. 7.

55 Memorial of the Republic of Hungary (Vol. 5, annexes, parts 1 and 2) (2 May 1994), www.cij-icj.org.

56 Gilbert Guillaume even argued that the ICJ should be protected against 'powerful pressure groups'. ICJ, *Legality of the Threat or Use of Nuclear Weapons* (Advisory Opinion) (Seperate Opinion Judge Guillaume), ICJ Reports 1996, p. 226.

57 Benzing (note 21), p. 403.

58 Art. 10 para. 2 of the Understanding on Rules and Procedures Governing the Settlement of Disputes, Marrakesh Agreement Establishing the World Trade Organization, Annex 2 (hereinafter DSU) of 15 April 1994, United Nations Treaty Series, Vol. 1869, 401.

only bring their insights to the attention of the panel or the Appellate Body in the form of *amicus curiae* briefs. At the outset, neither the panel nor the Appellate Body considered such submissions.[59] However, the Appellate Body adjusted its approach in *United States–Import Prohibition of Certain Shrimp and Shrimp Products (the Shrimp/Turtle Case)*.[60] In this case it was disputed whether the US import ban of shrimp coming from countries that did not use a specific turtle-friendly fishing technique could be justified under the GATT. The panel received two *amicus* briefs from environmental NGO's and considered those parts of the briefs that were explicitly endorsed by the US.[61]

The Appellate Body approved the panel's acceptance of *amicus curiae* briefs and formalized it in the case of *EC–Measures Affecting Asbestos and Products Containing Asbestos;* a dispute concerning the French import ban on asbestos and asbestos products for the protection of public health.[62] Because the WTO expected to receive a large number of *amicus* briefs on the public health issue, it disseminated procedural rules for *amicus curiae* seeking to participate in the dispute.[63] This formalization of the recognition of *amicus curiae* by the Appellate Body was much criticized by WTO members, who found that the Appellate Body had overstepped its authority, and is currently being discussed in the context of the DSU reform.[64] Although the formal acceptance of *amicus curiae* briefs may lead to the conclusion that the WTO's judicial bodies provide an opening for (common) interests other than those of the parties, the practice of both the panels and the Appellate Body paints a different picture altogether. In general, only those *amicus curiae* interventions that were added to or cited by one of the party submissions are considered. Because of this practice, there seems to be little added-value to the acceptance of *amicus curiae* briefs.[65] In conclusion it can be said that, by only allowing briefs that are endorsed by one of the parties, the WTO DSU strikes a balance between third party (civil society, businesses, industry)

---

59 WTO Appellate Body Report, *United States – Standards for Reformulated and Conventional Gasoline*, WT/DS2/AB/R (29 April 1996).

60 WTO Panel Report, *United States – Import Prohibition of Certain Shrimp and Shrimp Products*, WT/DS58/R (15 May 1998).

61 Ibid., para. 155.

62 WTO Appellate Body Report, *European Communities – Measures affecting Asbestos and Asbestos-containing Products*, WT/DS135/AB/R, (12 March 2001).

63 Ibid.

64 The WTO General Council discussed the additional procedures in a special session on 22 November 2000 (WTO Doc. WT/GC/M/60). The meeting concluded with a note of precaution to the Appellate Body, which subsequently decided to reject all requests for leave to submit an *amicus curiae* brief.

65 L. Johnson and E. Tuerk, 'CIEL's Experience in WTO Dispute Settlement: Challenges and Complexities from a Practical Point of View' in T. Treves (ed), *Civil Society, International Courts and Compliance Bodies*, Cambridge University Press, Cambridge 2005, p. 253.

concerns and the reluctance of member states to allow non-trade concerns to be deliberated in WTO proceedings.[66]

3.3.3. *ITLOS*

Like the procedural rules of the ICJ, Article 31 of the ITLOS Statute only grants the right to intervene to states that have a legal interest and the ITLOS rules explicitly allows *amicus curiae* interventions but limits it to states and IGO's.[67] Although the ITLOS does not accept *amicus curiae* briefs of non-governmental organisations in its contentious proceedings, the Seabed Disputes Chamber did give some recognition to such submissions in its 2011 *Advisory Opinion on Responsibilities and obligations of States sponsoring persons and entities with respect to activities in the Area.*[68] In this case two nongovernmental organizations, Greenpeace International and the World Wide Fund for Nature, filed an *amicus curiae* brief. While the Seabed Dispute Chamber did not make this submission part of the case file, it did link to it on the ITLOS website;[69] despite the fact that no treaty rule or internal ruling of the tribunal provides for such a procedure.[70]

3.4. CONSIDERATIONS ON THE MERITS

Because of the limited scope of this paper, the consideration of common interests in decisions on the merits will focus on one specific interest that has been considered by all three of the discussed judicial bodies, namely environmental protection and preservation.

3.4.1. *ICJ*

The first case in which the International Court of Justice was asked expressly to take the legal developments in international environmental law into consideration was its 1997 decision on the *Gabcikovo-Nagymaros Project (Hungary v. Slovakia).*[71]

---

66 N. Bernasconi-Osterwalder, D. B. Magraw, M. J. Oliva, M. Orellana and E. Tuerk, *Environment and Trade: A Guide to WTO Jurisprudence*, Earthscan, London 2006, p. 325.

67 Arts. 84 and 133 ITLOS Rules of the Tribunal of 17 March 2009, www.itlos.org.

68 ITLOS Seabed Disputes Chamber, Responsibilities and obligations of States sponsoring persons and entities with respect to activities in the Area, Advisory Opinion, Case No. 17 (1 February 2011).

69 See http://www.itlos.org/index.php?id=109 (last accessed 15 November 2013).

70 D. Anton, R. Makgill and C. Payne, 'Advisory opinion on responsibility and liability for international seabed mining (*ITLOS* Case No. 17): international environmental law in the seabed disputes chamber' (2011) 41 *Environmental Policy and Law*, 2, 60.

71 ICJ, *Gabcikovo-Nagymaros Project* (note 54); M.D. Evans, 'Case concerning the Gabcikovo-Nagymaros Project *(Hungary v. Slovakia)*' (1998) 47 *International & Comparative Law Quarterly*, 688. The court had itself already confirmed the importance of environmental protection in the ICJ, *Legality of the Threat or Use of Nuclear Weapons* (note 56).

This dispute concerned the termination, for environmental reasons, by Hungary of a 1977 treaty between the parties on the building of a system of dams. The court was asked to examine if international environmental law (IEL) prohibited the implementation of the treaty. Although Hungary brought detailed arguments of IEL before the court, the ICJ did not find IEL to justify Hungary's non-compliance with the bilateral treaty. Instead, the court chose to resort to a broad interpretation of the bilateral treaty. It interpreted the articles of the treaty that referred to the protection of the water quality, nature and fisheries as 'evolving provisions of environmental law' and thereby allowed itself to integrate modern concepts of common concern in the treaty.[72] By using this method, the court avoided to conclude that the treaty of 1977 could not be implemented but instead left it to the parties to reinterpret the treaty in accordance with international environmental law.

Environmental concerns also played an important role in the 2010 *Pulp Mills on the River Uruguay (Argentina v. Uruguay)* Case.[73] This dispute concerned the environmental authorizations unilaterally granted by Uruguay for the construction of pulp mills on the river Uruguay. Before the ICJ, Argentina argued that Uruguay's actions breached the obligation to prevent pollution and preserve the aquatic environment agreed upon in Article 41 of the bilateral 1975 statute on the use of the river Uruguay. Interestingly, the ICJ interpreted the obligation to prevent pollution and preserve the aquatic environment (Article 4 1 of the statute) to imply an obligation to carry out an environmental impact assessment (EIA) when transboundary harm could occur. The court considered this practice to be a requisite in general international law.[74] However, it also found that general international law does not specify the scope and content of an environmental impact assessment. While the consideration of alternative locations and a consultation of the affected populations may be included, it remains up to the state to determine the content of this obligation.[75] Because Uruguay had prepared an environmental impact assessment and no significant change had occurred in the aquatic environment since the pulp mills started functioning, the ICJ concluded that it could not find evidence that Uruguay had violated its obligation to perform an EIA nor its substantive obligation to preserve the environment.[76]

Two explanations have been put forward for the court's separation of the procedural obligations included in the statute and the substantive obligation to

---

72 E. Hey, 'International Water Law Placed in a Contemporary Environmental Context: The *Gabcikovo-Nagymaros* Case' (2000) 25 *Phys. Chem. Earth (B)* 3, 303.

73 ICJ, *Pulp Mills on the River Uruguay (Argentina v. Uruguay)* (Judgment), ICJ Reports 2010, p. 14.

74 Ibid., para. 204.

75 Ibid., para. 205.

76 Ibid., para. 219.

prevent environmental damage. The first explanation is that the court deems consultation and cooperation to be the best means to reach the parties' goal of 'achieving the optimum and rational utilization of the River Uruguay'. A second explanation is that in cases on environmental preservation it is extremely difficult for the applicant to prove its substantive claims and, therefore, the court focusses on procedural guarantees.[77] Whatever the reason, the court's judgment confirms that, despite its express recognition of environmental protection as a concern of humankind as a whole, it remains very cautious in its approach and prefers to focus on the cooperation of the parties rather than prioritizing environmental protection as a substantive obligation.

3.4.2. WTO

The most obvious illustration of the WTO's openness to environmental considerations can be found in its interpretation of Article XX of the GATT. This Article provides that state measures, which have been found inconsistent with one of the GATT rules, may still be justified if they are, inter alia, necessary to protect human, animal or plant life or health or relate to the conservation of exhaustible natural resources.[78] The Appellate Body has developed a two-tier test under Article XX which first assesses whether the design of the disputed measure falls within the scope of one of the interests protected by Article XX and then examines if the application of the measure does not constitute an 'arbitrary or unjustifiable discrimination' or a 'disguised restriction on international trade'.[79] Concerning the first question, the design of the measure, the Appellate Body emphasizes that the task of the WTO dispute settlement body is neither to examine the necessity of the protection of a public interest concern nor to establish the level of protection that should be pursued.[80] Its only task is to check if the measure falls within the scope of one of the interests listed in Article XX (a)-(j) and to verify that the measure is necessary to the protection of that interest.

Although Article XX provides only a limitative list of interests, the WTO bodies have interpreted these interests broadly. The earliest examples of this broad interpretation can be found in the WTO's case law on Article XX (g), which justifies measures relating to the protection of exhaustible natural resources. In the 1996 case of *US – Gasoline*, a case concerning the US Clean Air Act's discrimination of imported gasoline, the panel held that clean air is an exhaustible

77 J. Katz Cogan, 'The 2010 Judicial Activity of the International Court of Justice' (2011) 105 *American Journal of International Law*, 479.
78 Art. XX (b), (g) of the GATT.
79 WTO Appellate Body Report, *United States – Standards for Reformulated and Conventional Gasoline*, WT/DS2/AB/R (29 April 1996).
80 WTO Appellate Body Report, *European Communities – Measures affecting Asbestos and Asbestos-containing Products*, WT/DS135/AB/R, (12 March 2001), para. 168.

natural resource.[81] It did not consider it an objection that the resource, air, was renewable and defined by its quality.[82] An even more remarkable interpretation of the same subparagraph was put forward in *United States – Import Prohibition of Certain Shrimp and Shrimp Products (the Shrimp/Turtle* Case*).*[83] In this case the Appellate Body had to determine whether the US import ban of shrimp coming from countries that did not use a specific turtle-friendly fishing technique could be justified under Article XX (g). Despite a clear focus on mineral and non-living resources in the drafting history of Article XX (g), the Appellate Body held that the protection of sea turtles falls within the goal of conserving exhaustible natural resources.[84] The WTO thus accepts an evolutionary interpretation and reads the WTO agreements 'in the light of contemporary concerns of the community of nations about the protection and conservation of the environment'.[85] In justifying this approach, the Appellate Body explicitly referred to the 'acknowledgement by the international community of the importance of concerted bilateral or multilateral action to protect living natural resources'.[86]

To be justified under Article XX (b) a measure must not only be aimed at the protected interest, it must also be necessary to protect that interest. One of the factors used to establish this necessity is the material contribution of the contested measure to the objective. However, in the context of environmental protection the Appellate Body has recognized that this interest 'may be tackled only with a comprehensive policy' and therefore accepts that the defending party merely demonstrates that the measure is 'apt' to obtain the objective in the future.[87] That the Appellate Body accepts a qualitative link and does not require quantitative prove of the relationship between the measure and the policy goal, makes it much easier to justify inconsistencies on the basis of environmental protection.[88]

The second part of the Article XX test, focuses on the application of the disputed measure and was designed to prevent abuse of Article XX. The Appellate Body's application of this test was severely criticized after the *US-Shrimp/Turtle* Case.[89]

---

81 WTO Panel Report, *United States – Standards for Reformulated and Conventional Gasoline*, WT/DS2/R (29 January 1996), para. 6.37.

82 Ibid.

83 WTO Appellate Body Report, *United States – Import Prohibition of Certain Shrimp and Shrimp Products*, WT/DS58/AB/R (12 October 1998).

84 Ibid., para. 128.

85 Ibid., para. 129.

86 Ibid., para. 131.

87 WTO Appellate Body Report, *Brazil – Measures affecting Imports of Retreated Tyres*, WT/DS332/AB/R (3 December 2007), para. 151.

88 M. Matsushita, 'The Dispute Settlement Mechanism at the WTO: the Appellate Body – Assessment and Problems' in A. Narlikar, M. Daunton and R. M. Stern (eds), *The Oxford Handbook on the World Trade Organization*, Oxford University Press, Oxford 2012, p. 517.

89 WTO Appellate Body Report, *United States – Import Prohibition of Certain Shrimp and Shrimp Products*, WT/DS58/AB/R (12 October 1998).

In this case, the Appellate Body accepted that the US could ban the import of shrimp (products) caught without the use of TED's (Turtle Excluder Devices). Nevertheless, it found the US measure to be in violation of the GATT because the application of the ban was arbitrary. This assessment was based on the lack of transparency and due process in the US' certification process of importing states. This decision seemed to be a step back for the enforcement of environmental protection. However, once the US adapted its process, the measure was accepted by the WTO mechanism. Furthermore, by drawing attention to the importance of due process and negotiation, the Appellate Body indirectly enforced the duty to cooperate in environmental protection.

A similar conclusion was reached in the 2012 *US–Tuna/Dolphin III* Case concerning the TBT Agreement on technical regulations and standards.[90] This Agreement is of specific importance to common interests because it provides an opening for non-product related PPMs (process and production methods). In other words, measures that attempt to minimize the negative effects caused by the production or harvest of a certain product. In *US-Tuna/Dolphin III* Mexico challenged the United States' labelling scheme of dolphin-safe tuna because it allegedly discriminated against Mexican tuna products. Although the labelling scheme was found to be inconsistent with WTO law in the end, the Appellate Body confirmed that the US' objective of dolphin protection is a legitimate purpose for the enforcement of technical measures in the context of the TBT Agreement.[91]

3.4.3. ITLOS

The ITLOS has adopted a relatively progressive approach toward the consideration and enforcement of environmental protection by adopting the precautionary principle in its orders on provisional measures. The precautionary principle prescribes that scientific uncertainty on a serious risk of environmental harm should not preclude protective measures.[92] In the *Southern Bluefin Tuna* Case, the ITLOS held that 'the parties should in the circumstances act with prudence and caution to ensure that effective conservation measures are taken to prevent serious harm to the stock of Southern Bluefin Tuna'.[93] Although the *SBT* order avoids using the term, clear references to both the element of scientific uncertainty and serious risk to the environment can be found throughout the decision.[94] Thus,

---

90 WTO Appellate Body Report, *United States – Measures concerning the Importation, Marketing and Sale of Tuna and Tuna Products*, WT/DS381/AB/R (16 May 2012).

91 E. Trujillo, 'The Tuna-Dolphin Encore – WTO Rules on Environmental Labeling' (2012) 16 *Asil Insights*, 7, in conclusion.

92 Art. 15 of the Rio Declaration on Environment and Development (14 June 1992), UN Doc. A/CONF. 151/26.

93 ITLOS, *Southern Bluefin Tuna Case* (1999), para. 77.

94 Boyle (note 25), p. 373.

it could be assumed that the ITLOS adopted a precautionary reasoning.[95] This assumption was confirmed in the *Advisory Opinion on activities in the Area* where the Seabed Disputes Chamber stated that the precautionary approach was implicit in the Southern Bluefin Tuna Cases and that there is 'a trend towards making this approach part of customary international law'.[96] The Tribunal's use of the precautionary principle is interesting because it is not included in the UNCLOS and its meaning and status in general international law is at the least arguable.[97]

In the later *MOX Plant* Case on provisional measures, Ireland explicitly based its claim on the precautionary principle. In its order, the tribunal found the precautionary principle inapplicable because of the lack of proof delivered by Ireland on the risk of serious environmental harm.[98] Nevertheless, the ITLOS stated that '*prudence and caution*' require the parties to cooperate in the prevention of environmental harm.[99] It further established the duty of cooperation as a fundamental principle in the prevention of pollution of the maritime environment under UNCLOS and general international law.[100] This is in accordance with the view that the erga omnes nature of certain obligations entails a duty to cooperate.[101] The Tribunal interpreted the duty to cooperate to include an exchange of information, risk monitoring and preventive measures.[102] In his separate opinion, Judge Wolfrum stated that the duty to cooperate reflects a more general shift in international law from the bilateral to the consideration of common interests.

4. CONCLUSION

As stated in the introduction, the enforcement of common interests may be problematic in the context of an international judiciary that is functionally differentiated. The existence of a multitude of specialized international judicial bodies seems to encourage a judicial bias towards the constitutional values of the legal regime that provides jurisdiction. Even the ICJ, which has general jurisdiction, is often limited in its interpretation by the specific topic of the treaty that provides jurisdiction. Nevertheless, the present paper has established that international judicial bodies do leave room for the consideration of common interests both

95 Benzing (note 21), p. 392.
96 ITLOS Seabed Disputes Chamber, Responsibilities and obligations of States sponsoring persons and entities with respect to activities in the Area, Advisory Opinion, Case No. 17 (1 February 2011), para. 132.
97 P. Sands, *Principles of international environmental law*, Cambridge University Press, Cambridge/New York 2012.
98 ITLOS, *The MOX Plant* Case (2001), para. 75.
99 Ibid., para. 84.
100 Ibid., para. 82.
101 Shelton (note 5), p. 39.
102 ITLOS, *The MOX Plant* Case (2001), para. 89.

in their procedural and their substantive decisions. At the procedural level, two scenarios were identified in which a common interest is explicitly advanced by an international judicial body. In the first place, courts *proprio motu* align their decisions with common interests. An example of this scenario can be found in the orders on provisional measures of both the ICJ and the ITLOS. Secondly, courts allow states to enforce common interests, even if they have no direct interest in doing so. This is illustrated by the case law of all the examined bodies. They use a broad interpretation of standing in general, and 'legal interest' in particular, in cases that involve the enforcement of common interest issues. In contrast, judicial bodies show much more restraint in considering third party interventions on common interests. When considering the merits of the dispute, the studied judicial bodies approve and take account of common concerns. However, they all make sure to keep the focus of their decisions on the consent of the parties and the values protected in the treaty that grants jurisdiction. In this context, the duty to cooperate is often referred to when considering common interests. This reflects a more general, gentle, shift in international from the bilateral to the consideration of common interests. In the words of Judge Wolfrum, the duty to cooperate 'balances the principle of sovereignty of states and thus ensures that community interests are taken into account vis-à-vis individualistic state interests'.[103]

Although it is wise not to draw sweeping conclusions from the limited research presented here; the most remarkable observation in this paper is perhaps that international judicial bodies consider common interest in very similar ways. Despite their inherent bilateral nature, the examined judicial bodies have (re-) interpreted their procedural and substantive rules in light of common interest issues. The potential that these developments in the case law of the three examined bodies offer for the enforcement of common interests and international litigation in general, mainly comes from the methods that were developed to interpret international law in light of common interests while respecting the sovereignty of the state. On the one hand, the case law shows that the consideration of common concerns offers judicial bodies the opportunity to answer procedural questions, such as jurisdiction and standing, in a more flexible manner. On the other hand, the evolutionary interpretation of existing law by the examined bodies, adopted mainly for environmental purposes, may facilitate the introduction of a variety of common interests in specialized international regimes. Furthermore, the increasing level of consistency could suppress some of the negative effects that are often linked to the functional differentiation of international legal regimes. The risks of inconsistent and incoherent case law, and the connected risk of forum shopping, are reduced when the approach toward common interests is made more coherent through interpretation.

103 ITLOS, *Southern Bluefin Tuna* Case (1999), *Separate Opinion of Judge Wolfrum*, Case Nos. 3 and 4.

CHAPTER 5
COLLECTIVE SECURITY, THE COMMON INTEREST, AND THE RESPONSIBILITY TO PROTECT DOCTRINE

Vito Todeschini

1. INTRODUCTION

In 1945, the international society saw the birth of the United Nations (UN). The devastation brought about by the Second World War, as well as the failure of the League of Nations to prevent its outbreak, drove states to go beyond the mere establishment of another international organisation. They rather set up a complex system of rules, institutions and mechanisms aimed to pacify international relations to the maximum extent possible. The first paragraph of the preamble to the UN Charter clearly states the raison d'être of the Organisation: "to save succeeding generations from the scourge of war."[1] In this respect, it can be said that the UN serves an interest that all states share, a common interest of the international society.

Although the UN has been conceived as a multipurpose organisation,[2] its fundamental end is the maintenance of international peace and

1 Charter of the United Nations, 1 UNTS XVI (24 October 1945) (UN Charter), Preamble, para. 1.

2 See L.M. Goodrich, E. Hambro and A.P. Simons, *Charter of the United Nations. Commentary and Documents*, Columbia University Press, New York and London 1969, p. 25. The purposes of the UN are defined in Art. 1 of the Charter: "1. To maintain international peace and security, and to that end: to take effective collective measures for the prevention and removal of threats to the peace, and for the suppression of acts of aggression or other breaches of the peace, and to bring about by peaceful means, and in conformity with the principles of justice and international law, adjustment or settlement of international disputes or situations which might lead to a breach of the peace; 2. To develop friendly relations among nations based on respect for the principle of equal rights and self-determination of peoples, and to take other appropriate measures to strengthen universal peace; 3. To achieve international co-operation in solving international problems of an economic, social, cultural, or humanitarian character, and in promoting and encouraging respect for human rights and for fundamental freedoms for all without distinction as to race, sex, language, or religion; and 4. To be a centre for harmonizing the actions of nations in the attainment of these common ends."

security.[3] To this end, the UN Charter created the so-called system of collective security, the heart of which is the Security Council. This Organ is granted a high degree of flexibility in its action, which – unfortunately – too often tends to turn into selectivity. A way to address this issue seems to be offered by the Responsibility to Protect (R2P), a doctrine that is increasingly acquiring relevance in international rhetoric and policy.[4] One of the main objectives of R2P, indeed, is to guide the Security Council's action when dealing with gross human rights violations and serious violations of international humanitarian law (IHL), therefore attempting to impact on the maintenance of international peace and security.

The second section of this article deals with the meaning of the common interest under the UN Charter, and the factors hindering the pursuance thereof. The following sections examine the interplay between the R2P doctrine and the collective security system. While section three outlines the features of R2P and examines its normative status, section four attempts to evaluate whether and how this doctrine might positively affect the maintenance of international peace and security. The overall aim of the present article is to clarify the existing obstacles to the pursuit of the common interest, and the possible ways to overcome such obstacles.

2. THE COMMON INTEREST AND THE UN CHARTER

The Preamble to the Charter contains the following commitment:

> We the peoples of the United Nations determined: [...] to unite our strength to maintain international peace and security, and to ensure, by the acceptance of principles and the institution of methods, that armed force shall not be used, save in the common interest [...].[5]

In its sole reference to the common interest, the Charter unequivocally links this concept to the use of armed force. Considering the whole context, the notion of

3 Ibid., p. 26; R. Wolfrum, 'Article 1' in B. Simma, D.E. Khan, G. Nolte and A. Paulus (eds), *The Charter of the United Nations. A Commentary*, Vol. I, Oxford University Press, Oxford 2012, p. 109, para. 5. See also United Nations (UN), A/RES/25/2625, *Declaration on Principles of International Law concerning Friendly Relations and Co-operation among States in accordance with the Charter of the United Nations* (24 October 1970), Preamble, para. 1, in which it is reaffirmed that: "the maintenance of international peace and security [...] [is] among the fundamental purposes of the United Nations". Art. 1 of the Charter lists the maintenance of international peace and security as the first among the purposes of the UN. This is understandable considering the post-war context in which the Charter was drafted.

4 See sections 3 and 4.

5 UN Charter, Preamble, paras. 6 and 7 (emphasis added).

common interest is placed within the system of collective security,[6] the purpose of which is to maintain or restore international peace and security.[7] Within the UN Charter, the concepts of peace and security are intertwined and complementary. Whereas 'peace' may be construed as absence of armed conflict – so-called 'negative peace' –, the term 'security' generally encompasses "the activity which is necessary for maintaining the conditions of peace".[8] The comprehensive concept of international peace and security – or 'positive peace' – then gives expression to an overall purpose: the elimination of the causes and factors that lead or are likely to lead to war.[9]

For the purpose of maintaining international peace and security, the UN Charter establishes a set of norms and mechanisms that define the modern *jus ad bellum* – the rules governing the legality of the use of force in international law. On the one hand, the Charter prohibits the unilateral use of force by states,[10] except in cases of self-defence.[11] On the other hand, its Chapter VII creates the system of collective security.[12] In the words of Alexander Orakhelashvili:

> Collective security is premised on general interests shared by all states and aims to protect those interests by concentrating force. It is a public process involving the identification of a threat and the selection of a response by relying on normative

6 According to R. Wolfrum, these paragraphs must be read together with Arts. 1 (1) (2) and 2 (3) (4) (5) (6) (Purposes and principles), as well as Chapters IV (General Assembly), VI (Pacific settlement of disputes) and VII (Collective security) of the UN Charter. See R. Wolfrum, 'Preamble' in B. Simma et al. (eds), *The Charter of the United Nations*, p. 105, para. 12.

7 See UN Charter, Art. 1 (1).

8 Wolfrum (note 3), p. 109, para. 8.

9 See ibid., pp. 110–112, paras. 9–14. A wider concept is also reflected in: "The absence of war and military conflicts among states does not in itself ensure international peace and security. The non-military sources of instability in the economic, social, humanitarian and ecological fields have become threats to peace and security […]", see UN, S/23500, *Note by the President of the Security Council* (31 January 1992), para. 11. An even broader construction finds that: "The threats to peace and security in the twenty-first century include not just international war and conflict but civil violence, organized crime, terrorism and weapons of mass destruction. They also include poverty, deadly infectious disease and environmental degradation since these can have equally catastrophic consequences. All of these threats can cause death or lessen life chances on a large scale. All of them can undermine states as the basic unit of the international system", see UN, A/59/2005, *In larger freedom: towards development, security and human rights for all*, Report of the Secretary-General (21 March 2005), para. 78.

10 See UN Charter, Art. 2 (4): "All Members shall refrain in their international relations from the threat or use of force against the territorial integrity or political independence of any state, or in any other manner inconsistent with the Purposes of the United Nations." It is generally agreed that such a prohibition has developed into a norm of customary international law. See ICJ, *Military and Paramilitary Activities in and against Nicaragua (Nicaragua v. United States of America)* (Merits) (Judgment), ICJ Reports 1986, at 90, para. 190; *Legal Consequences of the Construction of a Wall in the Occupied Palestinian Territory*, Advisory Opinion, ICJ Reports 2004, at 39, para. 87; A. Randelzhofer and O. Dörr, 'Article 2 (4)' in B. Simma et al. (eds), *The Charter of the United Nations*, p. 203, paras. 1 and 64–66.

11 See UN Charter, Art. 51.

12 See UN Charter, Arts. 39–50.

> standards and transparent procedures, as opposed to mere political consensus within a selected group of states. Collective security is above all a matter of interpreting and applying a legal framework consisting of constituent treaties, summit communiqués and declarations, and institutional decisions of binding or recommendatory character.[13]

This system provides the Security Council with the power to adopt measures – from mediation and conflict prevention to economic and diplomatic sanctions to military intervention – in response to "any threat to the peace, breach of the peace, or act of aggression",[14] that is to say, any situation likely to or actually endangering international peace and security. Although the concept of collective security encompasses the mechanisms for the pacific settlement of disputes,[15] its distinctive character is to entrust a specific subject – the Security Council – with the monopoly on the use of force.[16] It is worth noting that the power to authorise the use of force set forth in Article 42[17] marks the most fundamental difference between the UN and the League of Nations, which envisaged no mechanisms of this kind.[18]

As the UN Charter makes clear, armed force can exclusively be used in the common interest. In this respect, the Preamble's reference to the maintenance of international peace and security puts the concept of the common interest in relation to the collective security system. That is to say, armed force is used in the common interest only when authorised by the Security Council.[19] It may be inferred that, according to the UN Charter, the maintenance of international

13 A. Orakhelashvili, *Collective Security*, Oxford University Press, New York 2011, p. 6.

14 UN Charter, Art. 39.

15 See UN Charter, Arts. 1 (1) and pp. 36 ff. See also Orakhelashvili (note 13), p. 15; Wolfrum (note 3), p. 113, para. 20.

16 See Y. Dinstein, *War, Aggression and Self-Defence*, Cambridge University Press, Cambridge 2011, p. 304, para. 808. Differently to collective self-defence – envisaged to face external aggression –, collective security is "basically 'introverted' in character (designed against a potential future aggressor from among the Contracting Parties) [...]", see ibid., p. 303, para. 806; see also Wolfrum (note 3), p. 112, para. 15.

17 See UN Charter, Art. 42: "Should the Security Council consider that measures provided for in Art. 41 [measures not involving the use of armed force] would be inadequate or have proved to be inadequate, it may take such action by air, sea, or land forces as may be necessary to maintain or restore international peace and security. Such action may include demonstrations, blockade, and other operations by air, sea, or land forces of Members of the United Nations."

18 Dinstein (note 16), pp. 303–304, para. 807.

19 Whereas cases of individual self-defence do not fall under the category of the maintenance of international peace and security, instances of collective self-defence possibly do. The collective reaction to an act of aggression against a single State may be interpreted as a response to what is collectively perceived as a wider threat to international peace and security. However, collective self-defence finds its rationale on the need for help of the attacked State, not on the maintenance or restoration of international peace and security. Hence, it is not inherently linked – even if it may virtually be – to the concept of the common interest. Dinstein (note 16), pp. 303, para. 806; Wolfrum (note 3), p. 112, para. 15.

peace and security conveys the content of the common interest. This conclusion seems to find support in two other provisions: Articles 2 (4) and 1 (4). Basically, the ban on unilateral use of force enshrined in the former constitutes the flipside of collective security. Hence, the Charter juxtaposes the prohibition to use force in self-interest with the principle of using force in the common interest. According to Article 1 (4), in turn, one of the purposes of the UN is: "To be a centre for harmonizing the actions of nations in the attainment of [...] common ends."[20] The common ends are those listed in the preceding three paragraphs of Article 1, inter alia and most notably the maintenance of international peace and security. The characterisation of the latter as a 'common end', coupled with the provisions on collective security, uphold the interpretation that under the Charter the conceptual meaning of common interest is the maintenance of international peace and security.

The Security Council enjoys broad discretion in the exercise of its prerogatives, that is, deciding whether to make a determination under Article 39 that a threat to or breach of the peace exist, and whether to act and which measures to adopt under Articles 40–42.[21] Drawing the exact boundaries of such discretion is difficult.[22] While some scholars deem the Council's action basically unbound,[23] others find a number of legal limits thereto.[24] Arguably, it is possible to assert that the Council cannot be considered totally free in exercising its powers.[25] Indeed, it is under an express obligation to comply with the 'Purposes and Principles' set forth in the Charter.[26] At the same time, the far-reaching scope of Articles 1 and 2 renders these provisions not apt to establish concrete limits to the Council's

---

20 See UN Charter, Art. 1 (4) (emphasis added).

21 See N. Krisch, 'Article 39' in B. Simma et al. (eds), *The Charter of the United Nations*, pp. 1275–1276, paras. 4–5; Goodrich (note 2), pp. 293 and 314–315.

22 See *infra* for the issue of the legal effects of customary international law on the Security Council's power.

23 Dinstein (note 16), pp. 308–309, paras. 8020–8022.

24 Orakhelashvili (note 13), pp. 150–151.

25 International Tribunal for the Former Yugoslavia (ICTY), *Prosecutor v. Duško Tadić*, Decision on the Defence Motion for Interlocutory Appeal on Jurisdiction, 2 October 1995, para. 28: "It is clear from [the] text [of Art. 39] that the Security Council plays a pivotal role and exercises a very wide discretion under this Article. But this does not mean that its powers are unlimited. The Security Council is an organ of an international organization, established by a treaty which serves as a constitutional framework for that organization. The Security Council is thus subjected to certain constitutional limitations, however broad its powers under the constitution may be. Those powers cannot, in any case, go beyond the limits of the jurisdiction of the Organization at large, not to mention other specific limitations or those which may derive from the internal division of power within the Organization. In any case, neither the text nor the spirit of the Charter conceives of the Security Council as *legibus solutus* (unbound by law)." See also Krisch (note 21), p. 1276, para. 6.

26 See UN Charter, Art. 24 (2): "In discharging these duties the Security Council shall act in accordance with the Purposes and Principles of the United Nations [...]." See also ICTY, *Prosecutor v. Duško Tadić*, para. 29.

action.[27] Actually, the Charter is designed to provide this Organ with the necessary flexibility to carry out its mandate.[28]

A central problem in this respect is that the practice of the Security Council proved to be quite incoherent, at times arbitrary.[29] Such inconsistency often results in a selective – not just flexible – application of Chapter VII.[30] Whereas a certain degree of flexibility is essential to the Council's action, selectivity – possibly entailing the use of double standards – seems at odds with the pursuit of the common interest. Selectivity may indeed put into question the very legitimacy of the Council's authority with respect to the use of force, as well as raise issues concerning its compliance with the UN Charter and with international law in general. In this respect, it is then worth paying attention to the R2P doctrine, which attempts to place the powers of the Security Council into a comprehensive framework for responsibility and intervention. R2P aims to take the Council's powers away from political bargaining in circumstances when gross human rights and serious IHL violations occur, making collective security work as an 'automatic' mechanism to cope with these situations.[31] Consequently, R2P intends to impose a duty to act on the Security Council, thus possibly impacting on the maintenance of international peace and security. The next sections examine the interplay between R2P and collective security, trying to understand whether and how the former may contribute to the pursuit of the common interest.

---

27 Krisch (note 21), p. 1256, para. 41.

28 Goodrich (note 2), p. 24; N. Krisch, 'Introduction to Chapter VII: The General Framework' in B. Simma et al. (eds), *The Charter of the United Nations*, pp. 1243–1245, paras. 12–16. An instance of the discretion the Council is provided with is its evolving interpretation of what constitutes a threat to international peace and security. Since the end of the Cold War, indeed, the Security Council has started to tackle not only inter-State conflict but also internal conflict and serious domestic crises. See N. Krisch, 'Introduction to Chapter VII', pp. 1241–1242, paras. 7–11.

29 See S. Chesterman, *Just War or Just Peace? Humanitarian Intervention and International Law*, Oxford University Press, Oxford 2002, pp. 160–162.

30 In this regard, the behaviour of the Security Council in the recent cases of Libya and Syria is significant. Whereas these situations present similarities as to the perpetration of gross violations of human rights, the Council has basically behaved in opposite manners, taking collective action in the former case and remaining almost inactive in the latter. Further, one could rightly add considerations on its substantial inaction with regard to the Palestinian question.

31 "The task is not to find alternatives to the Security Council as a source of authority, but to make the Security Council work much better than it has", see International Commission on Intervention and State Sovereignty (ICISS), *The responsibility to protect*, International Development Research Centre, Ottawa 2001, p. 49.

3. THE RESPONSIBILITY TO PROTECT DOCTRINE

R2P was originally conceived by the International Commission on Intervention and State Sovereignty (ICISS) as a way to reshape the concept of humanitarian intervention,[32] with a view – as some commentators noted – to finding "common ground for military intervention to support humanitarian objectives".[33] Basically, the ICISS changed the terms of the debate on humanitarian intervention from the 'right to intervene' to the 'responsibility to protect'.[34] Hinging on the conceptual shift from 'sovereignty as control' to 'sovereignty as responsibility', R2P stipulates that when gross violations of human rights and/or serious violations of IHL are occurring within a country, and the territorial state is unable or unwilling to stop these acts or is the perpetrator thereof, the international community bears a responsibility to step in. The doctrine essentially outlines a primary responsibility of the territorial state and a complementary responsibility of the international community to protect a population.[35] Additionally, this responsibility presents three dimensions: to prevent, to react, and to rebuild.[36]

In 2005, the UN General Assembly endorsed the doctrine in the World Summit Outcome (WSO) Document:

> Each individual State has the responsibility to protect its populations from genocide, war crimes, ethnic cleansing and crimes against humanity. This responsibility entails the prevention of such crimes, including their incitement, through appropriate and necessary means. We accept that responsibility and will act in accordance with it. [...] The international community, through the United Nations, also has the responsibility to use appropriate diplomatic, humanitarian and other peaceful means, in accordance with Chapters VI and VIII of the Charter, to help to protect populations from genocide, war crimes, ethnic

32 See ibid., p. vii. Humanitarian intervention may be defined as military action lacking authorisation from the Security Council undertaken to prevent or stop gross human rights violations.

33 R. Thakur and T.G. Weiss, 'R2P: From Idea to Norm and Action?' (2009) *Global Responsibility to Protect* 1, p. 35. The ICISS dedicated substantial part of its report to frame the criteria and conditions for undertaking legitimate humanitarian intervention. See ICISS, *The responsibility to protect*, pp. 31ff.

34 See ICISS, *The responsibility to protect*, p. 18.

35 See ibid., pp. 17–18.

36 See ibid., p. xi: "The responsibility to protect embraces three specific responsibilities: A. The responsibility to prevent: to address both the root causes and direct causes of internal conflict and other man-made crises putting populations at risk. B. The responsibility to react: to respond to situations of compelling human need with appropriate measures, which may include coercive measures like sanctions and international prosecution, and in extreme cases military intervention. C. The responsibility to rebuild: to provide, particularly after a military intervention, full assistance with recovery, reconstruction and reconciliation, addressing the causes of the harm the intervention was designed to halt or avert."

> cleansing and crimes against humanity. In this context, we are prepared to take collective action, in a timely and decisive manner, through the Security Council, in accordance with the Charter, including Chapter VII, on a case-by-case basis and in cooperation with relevant regional organizations as appropriate, should peaceful means be inadequate and national authorities are manifestly failing to protect their populations from genocide, war crimes, ethnic cleansing and crimes against humanity.[37]

On the one hand, the WSO Document narrowed the scope of R2P to the four specific crimes of genocide, war crimes, ethnic cleansing, and crimes against humanity. On the other hand, it acknowledged the possibility to take collective action through forcible means whenever diplomatic, humanitarian or other peaceful measures are inadequate to stop the commission of those crimes. Notably, the Document highlights the centrality of the collective security system with regard to the adoption of coercive measures. That is to say, it restates the exclusive authority of the Security Council concerning the authorisation to use armed force, therefore ruling out non-authorised military intervention.[38] In these terms, R2P appears in line with the collective security system, substantially adding nothing thereto.

In 2009, the UN Secretary-General put forward an R2P policy framework based on a 'deconstruction' of the WSO Document and resting on three pillars: protection responsibilities of the territorial state; international assistance and capacity-building; and, timely and decisive response by the international community.[39] In the Secretary-General's view, "All three [pillars] must be ready to be utilized at any point, as there is no set sequence for moving from one to another, especially in a strategy of early and flexible response".[40] This point was

---

37 UN, A/RES/60/1, *2005 World Summit Outcome* (24 October 2005), paras. 138–139.

38 See D. Akande, 'The Legality of Military Action in Syria: Humanitarian Intervention and Responsibility to Protect' *EJIL Talk!* (28 August 2013), http://www.ejiltalk.org/humanitarian-intervention-responsibility-to-protect-and-the-legality-of-military-action-in-syria/.

39 See UN, A/63/677, *Implementing the responsibility to* protect, Report of the Secretary-General (12 January 2009), para. 11: "[…] (a) Pillar one is the enduring responsibility of the State to protect its populations, whether nationals or not, from genocide, war crimes, ethnic cleansing and crimes against humanity, and from their incitement. The latter, I would underscore, is critical to effective and timely prevention strategies […]; (b) Pillar two is the commitment of the international community to assist states in meeting those obligations. It seeks to draw on the cooperation of Member States, regional and sub-regional arrangements, civil society and the private sector, as well as on the institutional strengths and comparative advantages of the United Nations system […]; (c) Pillar three is the responsibility of Member States to respond collectively in a timely and decisive manner when a State is manifestly failing to provide such protection. […] A reasoned, calibrated and timely response could involve any of the broad range of tools available to the United Nations and its partners. These would include pacific measures under Chapter VI of the Charter, coercive ones under Chapter VII and/or collaboration with regional and sub-regional arrangements under Chapter VIII […]."

40 UN, A/63/677, *Implementing the responsibility to protect*, para. 12.

reasserted in its 2012 report focusing on pillar three, namely, on the measures to address R2P situations in a timely and decisive manner. According to this report, the Security Council should preferably act under Chapter VI by resorting to peaceful measures such as "negotiation, enquiry, mediation, conciliation, arbitration, judicial settlement, resort to regional agencies or arrangements, or other peaceful means".[41] However, collective action may also require the use of coercive measures under Chapter VII, including military intervention.[42] In this perspective, although armed force should be a measure of last resort, military intervention may be undertaken whenever needed, that is, even if all peaceful means have not been exhausted beforehand.[43] This interpretation of R2P basically reaffirms the provisions of the UN Charter. In fact, the Security Council enjoys considerable discretion in deciding how to cope with threats to international peace and security. The yardstick in this respect is the adequacy of the measures to be adopted in response to a threat to or breach of the peace.[44] Accordingly, the Council may authorise the use of armed force without first exhausting all non-forcible tools at its disposal.[45] What matters, indeed, is the adoption of adequate and effective measures to address the situation at stake.[46]

However, it is worth highlighting that R2P seeks to go beyond this framework. Through the conceptualisation of the complementary responsibility of the international community, the doctrine's purpose is – inter alia – to guide the Security Council's action, trying to limit its discretion with respect to whether and how to act in R2P situations. It therefore aims to impact on the maintenance of international peace and security – hence, on the pursuit of the common interest – in a way that seeks to exclude any possibility for the Council not to act in cases of genocide, war crimes, ethnic cleansing, and crimes against humanity. In this respect, R2P intersects the issue of selectivity as an obstacle to the pursuit of the common interest, raising the question whether it could provide a way to overcome this problem. However, any attempt to prescribe new duties for the Council requires clarifying what the legal content of R2P is, namely, what legal obligations the latter might impose on the former.

Analysing the normative value of R2P firstly requires to draw a distinction between the primary responsibility of the territorial State and the complementary

---

41 UN, A/66/874, *Responsibility to protect: timely and decisive response*, Report of the Secretary-General (25 July 2012), paras. 22–29.
42 See ibid., paras. 31–32.
43 See ibid., para. 60.
44 See UN Charter, Art. 42.
45 See Goodrich (note 2), p. 314.
46 Notably, Krisch points out that "as Art. 42 seeks to limit the use of military force to exceptional cases, the Council's exercise of its discretion should be guided by the principle of proportionality", see N. Krisch, 'Article 42' in B. Simma et al. (eds.), *The Charter of the United Nations*, p. 1341, para. 19.

responsibility of the international community. The primary responsibility of a State to protect its population from genocide, war crimes, ethnic cleansing, and crimes against humanity is firmly grounded in international law.[47] Conversely, there exists no legal obligation connected to the complementary responsibility. Although R2P gained much support over time, it has not yet attracted enough *opinio juris sive necessitatis* to become a customary norm imposing new legal obligations.[48] Actually, the WSO Document contains a political commitment – not a duty – to undertake collective action in R2P situations, and no legal obligations may be derived from such document indeed.[49] Notably, the Security Council upheld this version of R2P,[50] without providing acknowledgement of the notion of complementary responsibility. Acting under Chapter VII, the Council has so far invoked R2P with exclusive reference to the primary responsibility of the territorial State to protect civilians, failing to mention the complementary responsibility of other international actors.[51] Generally speaking, complementary responsibility as a legal concept seems to be still contested.[52] This probably constitutes the main hindrance to the consolidation of R2P into a legal norm.

---

47 See UN, A/63/677, *Implementing the responsibility to protect*, paras. 3 and 18. The four R2P crimes are already prohibited under treaty-based and customary international law. With respect to genocide, see Art. I of the 1948 Convention on the Prevention and Punishment of the Crime of Genocide, Art. 4 of the Statute of the International Criminal Tribunal for the former Yugoslavia (ICTY Statute), Art. 2 of the International Criminal Tribunal for Rwanda (ICTR Statute), Art. 6 of the Rome Statute. With regard to war crimes, see Arts. 49, 51, 130, 147 of the 1949 Geneva Conventions I-IV (GCs) respectively, Art. 85 of the 1977 Additional Protocol I to the GCs, Art. 6 (b) of the London Charter of the International Military Tribunal (IMT Charter), Art. 3 of the ICTY Statute, Art. 4 of the ICTR Statute and Art. 8 of the Rome Statute. As to crimes against humanity, see Art. 6 (c) of the IMT Charter, Art. 5 of the ICTY Statute, Art. 3 of the ICTR Statute and Art. 7 of the Rome Statute. Ethnic cleansing has no specific international legal definition. It is generally considered a sub-category of the crime against humanity of persecution, for which see Art. 7 (1) (h)-2 (g) of the Rome Statute.

48 See A. Peters, 'The Security Council's Responsibility to Protect' (2011) 8 *International Organizations Law Review*, 12 "[…] I submit that R2P is an established hard norm with regard to the host state, and an emerging legal norm with regard to other states and the United Nations". See also N. Rao, 'The Choice to Protect: Rethinking Responsibility for Humanitarian Intervention' (2013) 3 *Columbia Human Rights Law Review* 44, 717–719. *Contra*, see L. Poli, 'R2p as an Emerging Rule of International Law and the *Opinio Necessitatis* of an Accountable International Community' (2010) LXV *La Comunità Internazionale*.

49 See M. Vashakmadze, 'Responsibility to Protect' in B. Simma et al. (eds), *The Charter of the United Nations*, p. 1209, para. 21.

50 See UN, S/RES/1674 (28 April 2006), operative paragraph (OP) 4.

51 See UN, S/RES/1970 (Libya) (26 February 2011), Preamble, para. 9; S/RES/1973 (Libya) (17 March 2011), Preamble, para. 4; S/RES/1975 (Côte d'Ivoire) (30 March 2011), Preamble, para. 9; S/RES/2085 (Mali) (20 December 2012), OP 9(d); S/RES/2098 (Democratic Republic of the Congo) (28 March 2013), Preamble, para. 24; S/RES/2100 (Mali) (25 April 2013), OP 16(c) (i) and 24. Recent UN Human Rights Council's resolutions on Syria have followed the same line. See UN, A/HRC/RES/23/26 (25 June 2013), OP 16; A/HRC/RES/23/1, 19 June 2013, OP 3; A/HRC/RES/22/24 (12 April 2013), OP 16.

52 See J. Welsh, 'Civilian Protection in Libya: Putting Coercion and Controversy Back into R2P' (2011) 3 *Ethics & International Affairs* 25, 255.

The attempt to place the Security Council's action into a comprehensive framework for tackling genocide, war crimes, ethnic cleansing, and crimes against humanity – to enhance the consistence of its practice in coping with these situations – arguably constitutes an added value of R2P. The very significance of the doctrine, actually, is to make inaction in face of the commission of these crimes definitely unjustifiable, as well as more compelling the need to take action by third states and by the Council in particular.[53] At present, the interaction between R2P and collective security is limited but not irrelevant. Although R2P does not alter the Charter's system – particularly the discretion of the Security Council and the framework on the use of force –, it could affect the way so-called mass atrocities are approached.[54] In spite of the fact that it does not pose any legal obligations, R2P increasingly stands "as a model for action or a principle containing guiding lines".[55] At the same time, given the remarkable relevance R2P has acquired in a relatively short period of time, it appears reasonable to consider the long-term possibility for it to become a hard legal norm of international law.[56] Thus, if that was the case, it should be clarified whether a development in its normative status could substantially effect on the Security Council's prerogatives. The next section will analyse the possible interplay between an R2P norm and collective security. In particular, it will evaluate whether and how, in perspective, R2P might contribute to the pursuit of the common interest of maintaining international peace and security.

4. THE COMMON INTEREST AND THE RESPONSIBILITY TO PROTECT

Anne Peters proposed an analysis of the obligations and effects that would stem from an R2P legal norm, intending to show that such a norm would impose a duty to take action on the Security Council as well as a number of limits on its discretionary powers. The author's basic premise is that, as an international organisation, the UN has legal personality and must abide by international

53 See S. Chesterman, 'Leading from Behind: The Responsibility to Protect, the Obama Doctrine, and Humanitarian Intervention After Libya' (2011) *New York University Public Law and Legal Theory Working Papers* 282, 7, http://lsr.nellco.org/nyu_plltwp/282; A. Peters, *The Security Council's Responsibility to Protect*, pp. 9–10.

54 Vashakmadze (note 49), p. 1210, para. 24: "It cannot be argued that the concept of the responsibility to protect has gained certain new characteristics and legal substance through this resolution practice [Security Council's resolutions concerning 'the protection of civilians in armed conflict']. However, a regular invocation of the responsibility to protect through the Security Council may have raised the pressure on the SC members to take action."

55 L. Poli, 'The Responsibility to Protect within the Security Council's Open Debates on the Protection of Civilians. A Growing Culture of Protection' in J. Hoffmann and A. Nollkaemper (eds), *Responsibility to Protect. From Principle to Practice*, Pallas Publications, Amsterdam 2012, p. 76.

56 Vashakmadze (note 49), pp. 1212–1213, paras. 27–28.

norms. The Council – as an organ thereof – must therefore exercise its powers in compliance with international law,[57] namely, its discretion in applying Chapter VII is broad but limited. In fact, the existence of limits is what distinguishes discretion from arbitrariness.[58] In Peter's view, an R2P norm would mainly have three legal effects on the Security Council's prerogatives. In the first place, inaction in R2P situations would be illegal. The author, in this regard, infers a possible Council's duty to act from states' positive obligations to protect human rights that are prescribed by international human rights law. Since the UN is bound by customary international law, Peters concludes that "the principles concerning protection developed for states can be transferred to the UN, acting through the Security Council".[59] In the second place, according to Peters, an R2P norm would narrow the Council's discretion when acting under Chapter VII, particularly when making a determination under Article 39 in regard to R2P situations. That is to say, it would not be allowed not to classify genocide, war crimes, ethnic cleansing, and crimes against humanity as constituting a threat to or breach of the peace. Following to this determination, additionally, the Council would be bound to act and it would not be totally free to decide which measures to adopt. For instance, was military intervention the only appropriate action to address a certain crisis, the Security Council could not adopt non-forcible measures.[60] In the third place, an R2P norm would affect the veto power. Peters highlights that the voting behaviour of the members of the Security Council, which act as delegates of all other UN members,[61] must not be arbitrary.[62] Limits to voting are especially relevant to the veto power, which the author considers as a procedural right that may be abused whenever the holder acts arbitrarily. As a result, the permanent five should use the veto in a non-abusive manner.[63] In Peters' view, as mentioned, an R2P norm would impose on the Council a legal obligation to act in the face of genocide, war crimes, ethnic cleansing, and crimes against humanity. Consequently, the permanent five would have the duty to vote positively in R2P situations; the use of the veto would amount to an abuse of right.[64] According

57 See A. Peters, 'The Responsibility to Protect and the Permanent Five' in J. Hoffmann and A. Nollkaemper (eds), *Responsibility to Protect*, p. 200.

58 Ibid.

59 Ibid., p. 201. Actually, it is surprising that Peters does not relate the states' duty to prevent R2P crimes to the obligation to prevent international crimes under customary law.

60 Ibid.

61 See UN Charter, Art. 24 (1): "In order to ensure prompt and effective action by the United Nations, its Members confer on the Security Council primary responsibility for the maintenance of international peace and security, and agree that in carrying out its duties under this responsibility the Security Council *acts on their behalf*" (emphasis added).

62 Peters (note 57), p. 203.

63 Ibid., p. 204: "An abuse of right is given when a state does not behave illegally as such, but exercises rights that are incumbent on it under international law in an arbitrary manner or in a way which impedes the enjoyment of other international legal subjects of their own rights." See also UN, A/63/677, *Implementing the responsibility to protect*, para. 61; A/RES/377(V)AA, *Uniting for peace* (3 November 1950), Preamble, para. 5.

64 Peters (note 57), p. 205.

to Peters, in conclusion, under an R2P legal regime both the exercise of the veto or inaction by the Security Council would constitute illegal acts.[65] Following this argument, the Council could in principle not act in a selective manner, being obliged to act whenever the scope of R2P is triggered. Not much space for discretionary choices would be left indeed.

Basically, Peters asserts that a number of legal effects would derive from a change in the normative status of R2P. Her analysis, however, encounters a number of problems pertaining to the very nature of the Security Council's powers and to the legal effects on the latter deriving from customary international law. In fact, it was the intention of the drafters of the UN Charter to grant this Organ a considerable discretion when dealing with situations endangering international peace and security.[66] Whereas the Council is arguably not totally unbound by law in exercising its powers,[67] the limits thereto are far from clear. Likely, constraints mainly concern the Council's action, that is to say, it is under an obligation not to breach certain norms of international law when acting pursuant to Chapter VII.[68] In the case of R2P, specifically considering Peters' arguments, it seems that the supposed obligations stemming therefrom would fundamentally concern the Council's inaction. Namely, an R2P norm would tell the Council what to do rather than what not to do. This stance raises a number of problems.

According to the broad language used in the UN Charter,[69] the Security Council's discretion encompasses both whether to take action at all in a given situation, and which type of measures to adopt.[70] There exists nothing in the Charter that obliges the Council to make a determination under Article 39. Furthermore, it is definitely problematic to state that a norm of customary international law – therefore, external to the Charter[71] – can trump the Council's discretion by imposing a positive duty to act. Scholars are divided on the issue of the subjection of the UN to customary law and ius cogens, especially when considering the effects of the latter on the Council's powers.[72] At any rate, even acknowledging

65 Ibid., p. 207.

66 See Krisch (note 21), pp. 1274–1275, para. 2.

67 See ICTY, *Prosecutor v. Duško Tadić*, paras. 28–29. In general, see *supra* section 2.

68 Krisch (note 21), p. 1276, para. 6. See also ICJ, *Application of the Convention on the Prevention and Punishment of the Crime of Genocide* (Provisional Measures) (Order), ICJ Reports 1993, p. 325, Separate Opinion of Judge Lauterpacht, p. 407, paras. 98–100.

69 See UN Charter, Arts. 1, 24 and 39.

70 Krisch (note 21), pp. 1275–1276, paras. 4–5; Goodrich (note 2), pp. 293 and 314–315. *Contra*, see Orakhelashvili (note 13), pp. 151–152.

71 In the maintenance of international peace and security – especially, with regard to action under Chapter VII – the Security Council is formally bound only by the 'Purposes and Principles' of the Charter, which in turn do not make reference to international law. The latter is solely mentioned in relation to Chapter VI. See UN Charter, Arts. 1 and 24.

72 For views in favour of the binding effect of customary international law and ius cogens on the Security Council, see ICJ, *Application of the Convention on the Prevention and Punishment of the Crime of Genocide* (note 68); Orakhelashvili (note 13), pp. 57–58; Peters (note 57),

that customary international law binds the Security Council, one thing is to say that the latter must not breach international norms when acting; another thing is to say that it is under a positive obligation to act in the maintenance of international peace and security. Differently to what Peters asserts, thus, it appears extremely problematic to state that an R2P norm could bind the Security Council to take action and to act in a given manner. Additionally, setting limits to the use of the veto power is unfortunately questionable. It is reasonable to argue that in principle the permanent five should not abuse this right. However, there is no provision in the Charter setting specific limits thereto. The exercise of the veto must arguably be in compliance with Article 1; yet, for the reasons mentioned above, seeking to limit the veto power through positive obligations deriving from customary international law appears to be extremely problematic.[73] To recap, even if R2P developed into a norm of customary law, its binding effect on the Security Council's prerogatives is highly debatable given the broad discretion such organ enjoys. The only explicit limitations thereto are to be found in Articles 1 and 2 of the UN Charter stating the Purposes and Principles of the Organisation. This may appear as a rather formalistic reading of the role of the Council; nevertheless, it is the reality of the UN and the collective security system.[74]

Although R2P might not have a significant impact on the normative level, it might still contribute to the maintenance of international peace and security at an operational level. First of all, the strength of the doctrine lies on its rhetoric effect and capacity of mobilisation.[75] Even if R2P has not created new legal obligations yet, it is now part of the UN's vocabulary and constitutes a working concept within UN practice.[76] Moreover, the added value of the doctrine is to provide political tools in the field of prevention of mass atrocities. In this respect, it is worth mentioning the efforts made by the UN Secretary-General concerning the operationalization of the commitment contained in the WSO Document.[77] The core of such process is the mandate and mission of the Special Adviser on the Prevention of Genocide and the Special Adviser on the Responsibility to Protect. Indeed, these Offices focus on "alerting relevant actors to the risk of genocide, war

p. 200. For views against such effect, see N. Krisch, 'Introduction to Chapter VII', pp. 1257, para. 41 and pp. 1259–1260, paras. 45–46; Dinstein (note 16), pp. 348–349, paras. 926–932.

73 See A. Zimmerman, 'Article 27' in B. Simma et al. (eds), *The Charter of the United Nations*, p. 928, para. 252; Vashakmadze (note 49), pp. 1232–1233, paras. 73–74.

74 For a critical analysis of the historical and normative development of international institutions in the domain of the maintenance of peace, see D. Zolo, *Cosmopolis. Prospects for World Government*, Polity Press, Cambridge 1997.

75 In relation to the Case of Libya, see Vashakmadze (note 49), p. 1230, para. 68.

76 For a survey of the use of R2P by the UN, see Vashakmadze (note 49), pp. 1213–1221, paras. 29–49.

77 See UN Secretary-General Reports, A/63/677, *Implementing the responsibility to protect*; A/64/864, *Early warning, assessment, and the responsibility to protect*, 14 July 2010; A/65/877, *The role of regional and sub-regional arrangements in implementing the responsibility to protect*, 28 June 2011; A/66/874, *Responsibility to protect: timely and decisive response*.

crimes, ethnic cleansing and crimes against humanity, enhancing the capacity of the United Nations to prevent these crimes, [...] and working [...] to develop more effective means of response when they do occur".[78] The Special Adviser on R2P, in particular, works for the improvement of an early warning and assessment mechanism.[79] That is, a system designed to enhance the UN's capacity to prevent the occurrence of genocide, war crimes, ethnic cleansing, and crimes against humanity, as well as to analyse information concerning these crimes in order for the Organisation to respond in an adequate manner.[80] Fairness and accuracy of factual assessment are of utmost relevance in respect to whether a certain humanitarian crisis actually amounts to an R2P situation.[81] A wrongful or ill-informed factual assessment is always possible indeed.[82] It is necessary to take into account how misrepresentation of the facts on the ground – and misinformation thereabout – might affect the decision-making process, potentially misleading the members of the Security Council in their decisions.[83] In general, the early warning and assessment mechanisms that have been and are being developed under the aegis of R2P may assist the Council in its determinations concerning threats to and breaches of the peace.[84] At the end of the day, the preventive dimension appears to be the very asset brought about by the doctrine.

---

78 See http://www.un.org/en/preventgenocide/adviser/ (accessed on 29 November 2013).

79 This is part of the commitment included in the WSO Document, in which it is affirmed that: "Each individual State has the responsibility to protect its populations from genocide, war crimes, ethnic cleansing and crimes against humanity. This responsibility entails the prevention of such crimes, including their incitement, through appropriate and necessary means. [...] The international community should, as appropriate, encourage and help states to exercise this responsibility and support the United Nations in establishing an early warning capability", see UN, A/RES/60/1, *2005 World Summit Outcome*, para. 138.

80 See in general UN, A/63/677, *Implementing the responsibility to protect*, Annex, A/64/864, *Early warning, assessment, and the responsibility to protect.*

81 See UN, A/66/874, *Responsibility to protect: timely and decisive response*, para. 19.

82 The Case of Libya is telling in this respect. In such instance, the Security Council acted on the basis of contrasting information about what was happening in the country. During the early phase of the protests, news that the Libyan government was committing large-scale human rights violations – chiefly, that it was air-bombing peaceful demonstrations – was spread. See Al Jazeera, 'Fresh violence rages in Libya' (22 February 2011), http://www.aljazeera.com/news/africa/2011/02/201122261251456133.html (accessed on 13 September 2013). This information influenced the Security Council in its action. Later on, such reports were called into question. See Russia Today, '"Airstrikes in Libya did not take place" – Russian military' (1 March 2011), http://rt.com/news/airstrikes-libya-russian-military/ (accessed on 13 September 2013).

83 UN, A/66/874, *Responsibility to protect: timely and decisive response*, para. 51: "At every stage of the implementation process, from identification and assessment to policy formulation and action, international actors need to act responsibly. *Faulty or ill-informed analysis at an early stage could set international decision makers on the wrong path, leading to overreaction or under-reaction.* [A] pattern of false alarms or, worse, selective reporting could also damage the credibility of the [UN]. It is therefore important that early warning and assessment be conducted fairly, prudently and professionally, without political interference or double standards [...]" (emphasis added).

84 See Vashakmadze (note 49) p. 1230, paras. 69 and 71. R2P might also give new strength and meaning to Art. 34 of the Charter concerning the investigative powers of the Security Council, which reads: "The Security Council may investigate any dispute, or any situation which might lead to international friction or give rise to a dispute, in order to determine

5. CONCLUSION

In the context of the UN Charter, maintaining international peace and security means to act in the common interest. To this purpose, armed force may be used within the boundaries of collective security, that is, only pursuant to an authorisation by the Security Council. The practice of the latter, in this respect, is unfortunately marked by a considerable degree of inconsistency, which often results in a selective rather than flexible application of Chapter VII. The Council may indeed not address certain humanitarian situations possibly amounting to a threat to or breach of the peace because its members – especially the permanent five – are not able to reach an agreement thereupon. Actually, the prevalence of political bargaining on law is a consequence of the very nature of this body as envisaged by the Charter. However, the outcome of such reality may run contrary to the pursuit of the common interest.

R2P constitutes an attempt to overcome this issue by establishing a duty to act on relevant international actors. Accordingly, whenever genocide, war crimes, ethnic cleansing, and crimes against humanity occur, the Security Council would be obliged to take action using all adequate means, including military intervention. Although R2P may provide the Council's practice with more consistency in the maintenance of international peace and security, the doctrine does not substantially solve the issue of selective authorisation to use force, a major problem within the collective security system. In fact, R2P has not consolidated into a legal norm yet, and many obstacles stand on the way to reach that point. Additionally, even if R2P finally developed into a norm of customary international law, it is unlikely it could affect the Security Council's discretion in the exercise of its powers. The possibility to limiting the latter through positive obligations deriving from customary law is still a highly debated issue. Therefore, as long as the collective security system is so designed, R2P has little or no contribution to give on the normative level. Rather, the doctrine may indirectly contribute to the maintenance of international peace and security through its preventive dimension. Especially, R2P may contribute to the operationalization of an effective early warning and assessment mechanism that could assist the Security Council in making determinations and adopting measures to address threats to and breaches of the peace. Although the doctrine does not overcome the core problems of the collective security system, it may still help to correct the practice of the Council in a manner more consistent with the pursuit of the common interest of maintaining international peace and security.

---

whether the continuance of the dispute or situation is likely to endanger the maintenance of international peace and security." For an analysis of the relationship between Arts. 34 and 39, see Orakhelashvili (note 13), pp. 163–164.

CHAPTER 6

PROTECTING THE COMMUNITY INTEREST IN A STATE CENTRIC LEGAL SYSTEM: THE UN CHARTER AND CERTAIN NORMS OF 'SPECIAL STANDING'

Jure Vidmar

1. INTRODUCTION

In 1970, the International Court of Justice (ICJ) stated in the well-known *obiter dictum* in the *Barcelona Traction* case that certain obligations are "the concern of all states. In view of the importance of the rights involved, all states can be held to have a legal interest in their protection; they are obligations erga omnes".[1] Following this logic, when certain norms are breached, it is not a single state but the international community as a whole who is injured. This is well-illustrated in the position of the Study Group of the International Law Commission on Fragmentation of International Law: "If a State is responsible for torturing its own citizens, no single State suffers any direct harm ... such action violates some values or interests of all, or ... [of] the international community as a whole."[2] It is also notable that the Study Group referred to the 'international community'; and not to the 'international community *of states*'. This indicates that in contemporary international law the community interest is not an interest of states.

While contemporary international law indeed knows of concepts which look beyond the interest of states, many of its rules and procedures remain state-centric. There may exist a 'minimum threshold of the community values'[3] but due to state-

1 ICJ, *Barcelona Traction, Light and Power Company Limited (Belgium v. Spain)* (New Application: 1962) (2nd phase) (Judgment), ICJ Reports 1970, p. 3, para. 33.

2 UN Doc. A/CN.4/L.682, para. 393.

3 See, e.g., S. Sivakumaran, 'Impact on the Structure of International Obligations' in M. Kamminga and M. Scheinin (eds), *The Impact of Human Rights Law on General International Law*, Oxford University Press, Oxford 2009, p. 146.

centric procedures, the enforcement of these values still crucially depends on states and their willingness to accept certain international obligations. This paper will identify the concepts in international law that indicate the existence of the community interest and define the notion of the 'community values'. Subsequently it will demonstrate that despite the move away from states, they remain in the background of international activity and enforcement of the community interest. Very instructive in this regard is the preambular reference in the UN Charter, that "armed force shall not be used, save in the common interest".[4] Since justified use of force in the UN Charter is regulated by Chapter VII, this indicates that collective enforcement of the international peace and security is a prime example of the common interest which overrides some classical tenets of international law. With reference to ius cogens and obligations erga omnes, it will be argued that the notion of the common interest is broader than Chapter VII powers of the Security Council, yet the common interest often remains unenforceable beyond the Charter provisions.

2. THE INTERNATIONAL COMMUNITY (OF STATES) AS A WHOLE

The phrase 'international community as a whole' came to international legal parlance with the *Barcelona Traction* dictum.[5] It follows from this dictum that the obligations erga omnes have a special standing in international law due to their community-oriented nature. This section will argue that such a nature derives from the concept's strong ethical underpinning. However, the erga omnes character does not imply a special hierarchical standing of these obligations. Consequently, their practical effect remains questionable. The international community interest is also reflected in ius cogens norms, but not even this concept can serve as an enforcement mechanism of the community values.

2.1. THE INTERNATIONAL COMMUNITY AND OBLIGATIONS ERGA OMNES

In the *Barcelona Traction obiter dictum*, the ICJ confirmed the existence of certain obligations which do not operate solely on the basis of reciprocity. When they are breached, it is the international community of *states* as whole who is injured, not only a specific state. This effect is further explained in the Report of the Study Group of the International Law Commission on Fragmentation of International

4 UN Charter, preamble.
5 ICJ, *Barcelona Traction* (note 1).

Law.[6] Some difficult issues arise at this point. Namely, it is unclear how *obligations erga omnes are identified, what their legal effects are and, ultimately, is the international community to be understood as an international community of states or more broadly than that?*

In one explanation, all non-bilateral obligations have an erga omnes character.[7] This view is problematic as it ignores the ICJ's reference to the "importance of the rights involved", contained in the *Barcelona Traction* dictum.[8] The 'importance' is a substantive issue and can only be defined by the special character of the obligations at stake. Maurizio Ragazzi argues that the obligations of this character have two components: "the moral content" and the "required degree of support by the international community".[9] The concept of obligations erga omnes thus reflects the notion of a value loaded international community interest. However, when establishing importance for the international community as a whole, the ICJ has only given circular references and rather generally invoked norms and principles of international law. In *East Timor*, the court accepted the erga omnes character of the right of self-determination by arguing that self-determination was "one of the essential principles of contemporary international law".[10] *East Timor* thus defines 'importance' identified in *Barcelona Traction* as something which is 'essential'. Such twists are of little help when one needs to explain which norms are the concern of the 'international community as a whole', why that is so, and why other norms do not have such a strong standing.

The ICJ has also been unable to identify obligations erga omnes, their content and underpinnings, on the basis of the formal sources of law alone. As Ragazzi has put it, obligations erga omnes reflect "an exceptionless [sic] moral norm (or moral absolute) prohibiting an act which, in moral terms, is intrinsically evil *(malum in se)*".[11] According to Ragazzi, obligations erga omnes are binding not only because states agree that they are, but even more importantly, "because nobody can claim exceptions from moral absolutes".[12] The second claim, that 'moral absolute' operates as a direct source of international law, remains debatable. But it is undisputed that the concept of obligations erga omnes nevertheless has its underpinnings in strong moral values and it is these underpinnings that shape international law making.

---

6 UN Doc. A/CN.4/L.682, para. 393.

7 C. Annacker, 'The Legal Regime of *Erga Omnes* Obligations in International Law' (1993) 46 *Österreichische Zeitschrift für öffentliches Recht und Völkerrecht*, 131, 136.

8 ICJ, *Barcelona Traction* (note 1).

9 M. Ragazzi, *The Concept of International Obligations Erga Omnes*, Clarendon, Oxford 1997, p. 163.

10 ICJ, *East Timor, Portugal v. Australia* (Jurisdiction) (Judgment), ICJ Reports 1995, p. 90, para. 29.

11 Ragazzi (note 9), p. 183.

12 Ibid.

Although the concept of obligations erga omnes is value loaded, it is not seen as a hierarchically superior international law. The Report of the Study Group of the International Law Commission on Fragmentation of International Law defines the concept along the following lines:

> A norm which is creative of obligations erga omnes is owed to the 'international community as a whole' and all states – irrespective of their particular interest in the matter – are entitled to invoke State responsibility in case of breach. The erga omnes nature of an obligation, however, indicates no clear superiority of that obligation over other obligations. Although in practice norms recognized as having an erga omnes validity set up undoubtedly important obligations, this importance does not translate into a hierarchical superiority ...[13]

Analysing the ICJ's approach to obligations erga omnes, Karl Zemanek similarly concludes: "While one observes ... a certain evolution in the thinking of the court in respect of erga omnes obligations, this evolution has not yet reached a point where the court could be relied on to accept claims to performance by parties which have a specific legal interest but are not directly affected."[14] Obligations erga omnes may thus be seen as legal manifestation of the international community interest. The concept encompasses 'moral absolutes'. But it does not take hierarchical precedence over other norms of international law. The legal effects of these obligations remain unclear. It thus also remains unclear how the international community interest is enforced within the international legal system.

The concept further remains somewhat ambiguous, as no single authoritative list exists of erga omnes obligations. Some guidelines follow from subsidiary sources of international law, in particular ICJ's decisions and academic writings. For a long time the ICJ had been reluctant to employ the term ius cogens and was referring to an erga omnes character as virtually a synonym for ius cogens.[15] But the ICJ has not explored the content of obligations erga omnes beyond the overlap

---

13 UN Doc. A/CN.4/L.682, para. 380.

14 K. Zemanek, New Trends in the Enforcement of erga omnes Obligations (2000) 4 *Max Planck Yearbook of United Nations Law* 1, p. 11.

15 For more on the relationship between ius cogens and obligations erga omnes see C. Tams, *Enforcing Obligations Erga Omnes in International Law*, Cambridge University Press, Cambridge 2005, p. 157; E. de Wet, 'The International Constitutional Order' (2006) 55 *International and Comparative Law Quarterly*, 51, 57; S. Kadelbach, '*Jus Cogens*, Obligations *Erga Omnes* and other Rules – The Identification of Fundamental Norms' in C. Tomuschat and J.M. Thouvenin (eds), *The Fundamental Norms of the International Legal Order: Jus Cogens and Obligations Erga Omnes*, Nijhoff, Leiden 2006, pp. 21–26; M. Byers, 'Conceptualising the Relationship Between *Jus Cogens* and *Erga Omnes Rules*' (1997) 66 *Nordic Journal of International Law*, 211, 213–219.

with ius cogens, which is itself a somewhat mysterious concept.[16] It is in the nature of ius cogens norms that they have an erga omnes effect,[17] but not all obligations erga omnes are to be found on the flipside of ius cogens.[18] Which obligations have an erga omnes but not ius cogens character remains unclear. Christian Tams concludes that "[e]rga omnes outside ius cogens is likely to remain uncharted territory until states begin to invoke the concept more commonly in formalised proceedings".[19]

Importantly, obligations erga omnes under general international law need to be distinguished from the concept of obligations erga omnes partes where obligations are mutually owed between parties to a certain multilateral treaty. As the ICJ put it in *Belgium v. Senegal*: "It follows that any State party to the Convention [against Torture] may invoke the responsibility of another state party with a view to ascertaining the alleged failure to comply with its obligations erga omnes partes ... and to bring that failure to an end."[20] The court continued: "These obligations may be defined as 'obligations erga omnes partes' in the sense that each state party has an interest in compliance with them in any given case."[21] In this particular case, violations of the Convention against Torture were at stake. But this is different than drawing legal consequences outside of the treaty framework. The concept of obligations erga omnes partes merely specifies that violations of treaty provisions by one state injures every state party to that treaty. To the extent that such a treaty foresees international judicial settlement of disputes in the framework of that treaty, the violation can even have a procedural remedy. But such remedies are not available for violations of obligations erga omnes under general international law and outside of the context of treaty relations. Obligations erga omnes partes thus regulate the functioning of the nexus of obligations arising under multilateral treaties and should not be conflated for the effects of obligations erga omnes under general international law.

Obligations erga omnes may be seen as a legal manifestation of the international community interest. To the extent of their overlap with norms ius cogens, they may also be seen as an enforcement mechanism of the latter. But it is wrong to see obligations erga omnes as hierarchically superior law. This may be different, at least theoretically, with the concept of ius cogens.

---

16 For a survey of obligations for which the ICJ has established that they are of erga omnes character see C. Tams, *Enforcing Obligations Erga Omnes in International Law*, Cambridge University Press, Cambridge 2005, pp. 117–118.

17 De Wet (note 15), p. 61.

18 Ibid.

19 Tams (note 15), p. 157.

20 ICJ, *Questions Relating to the Obligation to Prosecute or Extradite (Belgium v. Senegal)* (Judgment), ICJ Reports 2012, p. 422, para. 68.

21 Ibid., para. 69.

2.2. THE COMMUNITY INTEREST AND IUS COGENS

In the 1969 Vienna Convention on the Law of Treaties (VCLT), the concept of ius cogens was for the first time unequivocally mentioned in international treaty law.[22] But even in this instance it was only given a rather narrow power to void treaties. The Convention also remained silent on the content of the concept. Article 53 of the VCLT, inter alia, provides that "a peremptory norm of general international law is a norm accepted and recognized by the international community of states as a whole".[23] The concept of peremptory norms thus also rests on the presumption of the existence of an international community of states with a shared interest. It is notable, however, that the VCLT qualified the notion of the international community with states, while the ICJ a year later, defined obligations erga omnes as "obligations of a State towards the international community as a whole",[24] thus omitting 'states'. The court known for its conservative approach to international law certainly did not drop 'states' accidentally.

In the Article 53 definition, a peremptory norm is subject to acceptance – by the international community of states as a whole – of the normative content as well as its peremptory character. It is, however, erroneous to see *ius cogens* as an inherently treaty law concept. Indeed, the concept predates the 1969 VCLT and was invoked by writers even in the pre-Second World War era.[25] At the time, it was unclear whether or not it was a concept generally operating in international law. This has now been generally accepted.[26] Even the VCLT reference to 'general international law' suggests that ius cogens is a concept of customary international law. Any norm of customary international law requires its acceptance by states through state practice and opinio juris. However, the acceptance of the special peremptory character, not only normative content, by 'the international community of states as a whole' points to the strong ethical underpinning of these norms.[27] Sandesh Sivakumaran argues that ius cogens represents a minimum threshold of the international value system.[28]

22 Vienna Convention on the Law of Treaties (1969), UNTS 1155, 331 (VCLT), Art. 53.

23 Ibid.

24 ICJ, *Barcelona Traction* (note 1).

25 For a detailed account on the early writings on ius cogens, see D. Shelton, 'Normative Hierarchy in International Law' (2006) 100 *American Journal of International Law*, 291, 297–299.

26 There are currently 111 state parties to the Vienna Convention. Many of its provisions are nevertheless binding on non-parties to the convention via customary international law. Although some states have refrained from ratification precisely because of Art. 53, there is little doubt that the article has customary international law status. Indeed, the status of permanent objector to ius cogens has not been accepted by the international community of states.

27 De Wet (note 15), p. 57.

28 Sivakumaran (note 3), p. 146.

The strong community-oriented ethical underpinning of ius cogens norms has implications for the law-making. International law is, in principle, a consensus-based legal system. States create treaty obligations for themselves and at free will. It is *state* practice and *opinio juris* which leads to the emergence of customary norms of international law, from which states again have an escape route through the concept of a persistent objector. In principle, it is only new states which become automatically bound by pre-existing customary law and even automatically accede to certain treaties previously governing their territory (e.g. human rights treaties).[29] Yet the peremptory status of certain norms, encompassing the minimum threshold of the international value system, also overrides some fundamental tenets of a consensus-based international law making.

The ethical underpinning of the peremptory norms can compensate for deficiencies in universal acceptance of these norms. In this context three examples appear to be particularly instructive: (1) the right to the freedom from torture is supported by very strong *opinio juris*, yet state practice is rather weak. There is nevertheless little doubt that the freedom from torture has a ius cogens status.[30] (2) Apartheid South Africa claimed that it was a persistent objector to the prohibition of racial discrimination. This claim was universally rejected on the basis that unlike ordinary customary law, peremptory law does not allow for the persistent objector's status.[31] (3) France used to claim that it had never consented to the concept of ius cogens as such.[32] This argument was rejected and now even France has accepted the binding nature of these norms in terms of both content and character.[33]

These examples reveal that with regard to the peremptory norms, international law-making works differently than otherwise. As McCorquodale argues, "some human rights create legal obligations on a state irrespective of whether it has ratified a particular treaty, either because the human right is part of customary international law and so binding on all states or by virtue of a rule of ius cogens,

29 See A. Rasulov, 'Revisiting State Succession to Humanitarian Treaties: Is There a Case for Automaticity?' (2003) 14 *European Journal of International Law*, 141.

30 See R. Garnett, 'The Defence of State Immunity for Acts of Torture' (1997) 18 *Australian Yearbook of International Law*, 97, making the following argument: 'It may be argued … that the absolute nature of the conventional prohibitions, when coupled with the near universal *opinion juris* amongst states as to the illegality of the practice, may be a sufficient basis for concluding that torture is prohibited as a peremptory norm.'

31 Byers (note 15), p. 222.

32 Ibid., p. 229. See also Shelton (note 25), p. 166.

33 See A. Pellet, 'Comments in Response to Christine Chinkin and in Defense of *Jus Cogens* as the Best Bastion against the Excesses of Fragmentation' (2006) 27 *Finnish Yearbook of International Law*, 83, 85. Arguing: 'Several decades have […] been needed for the general acceptation of this concept [ius cogens] – and, among the pockets of resistance was […] France but also, less anecdotally, the ICJ itself (both not being without any link […]). Now the way has been cleared: Asterix has stopped its rearguard action against the notion.'

which no state can derogate from or evade by contrary practice".[34] Moreover, in *Furundzija*, the International Criminal Tribunal for the former Yugoslavia (ICTY) reasoned: "Because of the importance of the values [which the prohibition of torture] protects, this principle has evolved into a peremptory norm of ius cogens, that is a norm that enjoys a higher rank in the international hierarchy than treaty law and even 'ordinary' customary rules."[35]

Hierarchical superiority of ius cogens remains a contested issue, particularly so after the ICJ's *Germany v. Italy* decision on jurisdictional immunities.[36] Despite these conceptual problems, the concept of ius cogens nevertheless reflects community values which override state centrism and certain classical tenets of international law-making. The concept changes the traditional paradigm of international law as voluntary law and introduces a set of norms which can be legally binding on states even in the absence of their consent. It thus manifests a strong sense of the international community interest which prevails over the will of individual states. However, these effects should not be conflated for hierarchical superiority and enforcement mechanism. When ius cogens norms are breached, the concept does not create remedies that would trump other international legal obligations.[37] In this sense international law remains state centric and dependant on the will of states to provide remedies for gross violations of human rights within their own jurisdictions.

3. THE COMMUNITY INTEREST AND THE UN SYSTEM

The aftermath of the Second World War modified the structure of the international legal system. As Nigel White put it: "If we move from the post-1919 world order to the post-1945 order, the picture … is one of societal values shaping, informing and regulating the operation of a complex set of institutions,

34 R. McCorquodale, 'An Inclusive International Legal System' (2004) 17 *Leiden Journal of International Law*, 477, 486.

35 *Prosecutor v. Anto Furundzija*, Case No. IT-95-7/1, Trial Chamber II, at 260, para. 153 (10 December 1998).

36 ICJ, *Jurisdictional Immunities of the State* (*Germany v. Italy*, Greece intervening) (Judgment), ICJ Reports 2012, p. 99. Consider para. 93, where the ICJ provided the following reasoning with regard to the question of whether ius cogens takes precedence over immunities because of its special character. The ICJ noted that "[t]his argument […] depends upon the existence of a conflict between a rule, or rules, of ius cogens, and the rule of customary law which requires one State to accord immunity to another". The ICJ found that "no such conflict exists". This is so because "[t]he two sets of rules address different matters. The rules of State immunity are procedural in character and are confined to determining whether or not the courts of one State may exercise jurisdiction in respect of another State. They do not bear upon the question whether or not the conduct in respect of which the proceedings are brought was lawful or unlawful".

37 Ibid.

within a system framed by legal instruments of foundational significance."[38] While the structure and procedures of international law remained state-centric, mechanisms were developed which constrained the powers of states domestically and internationally. The constraints on the powers of states were imposed in the interest of the international community.

At least in the building period of the UN system, the 'international community' remained understood as the international community of *states*. However, as Dino Kritsiotis notes, this is also an era "of determining whether [the international community] knows of values other than the sovereign identities of its individual members [states]".[39] In this section it will be argued that the system of the UN Charter adopted the idea of an international community interest which extends beyond a state-centric community definition and acknowledged the existence of the common community values.

3.1. THE UN CHARTER AND THE INTERNATIONAL COMMUNITY INTEREST

The UN Charter's opening words are "we the peoples".[40] Although symbolic, this announced a shift away from the traditional structure of international law which would more appropriately read as 'we the states'.[41] The preamble also includes references to 'mankind' and a commitment to prevent suffering as experienced in the Second World War.[42] Apart from these symbolic preambular references, the interest of the international community was 'given teeth' through the institutional design of the post-Second World War international (legal) order. Robert McCorquodale argues that "the UN Charter is the centre of an international 'constitutional order'".[43] In a formalistic sense, the UN Charter is an international treaty. However, it is a treaty which creates the core international institutions of the post-Second World War international order and provides for the mechanism of enforcement of the community interest reflected in the Charter. In this regard Erika de Wet argues that "[t]he international value system is closely linked to the UN Charter, as the latter's connecting role is not only structural but also substantive in nature. In addition to providing a structural linkage of the different communities through universal State membership, the UN Charter

38 N. White, 'The United Nations System: Conference, Contract of Constitutional Order?' (2000) 4 *Singapore Journal of International and Comparative Law*, 281, 290.

39 D. Kritsiotis, 'Imagining the International Community' (2002) 13 *European Journal of International Law*, 961, 967.

40 UN Charter, preamble.

41 After all, the UN Charter is an international treaty concluded by states which makes UN membership open only to states.

42 UN Charter, preamble, para. 1.

43 McCorquodale (note 34), p. 478.

also inspires those norms that articulate fundamental values of the international community".[44]

This proposition links the international community interest with a shared international value system which is manifested in and enforceable through the UN Charter. The argument will now turn to the concepts of Chapter VII powers and Article 103. It will be argued in what sense they manifest and enforce the community interest.

3.2. THE COMMUNITY INTEREST AND CHAPTER VII POWERS

By virtue of Chapter VII, the Security Council is empowered to "determine the existence of any threat to the peace, breach of the peace, or act of aggression"[45] and, in order to bring such a situation to an end, take measures which are legally binding on all states. The preserving of international peace and security considered to be of such importance that the Security Council, acting on behalf of the entire international community, can authorise an exception to the prohibition on the use of force contained in Article 2 (4) of the UN Charter.[46] Chapter VII of the UN Charter thus allows the Security Council to override some of the classical tenets of international law in the interests of the international community and its fundamental values.

The concept of international peace and security has become interpreted widely in practice. Not only have traditional threats to use force or actual use of force in *international relations* fallen within this category, but also gross and systematic human rights violations internally.[47] The concept of international peace and security from the UN Charter has been used to protect groups and individuals against their own states and limit governmental abusiveness internally. A good recent example is that of Libya. In the binding Security Council resolutions 1970 and 1973, the Security Council identified the existence of a threat to international peace and security and drew a number of legal consequences, such as: travel ban,[48] asset freezing,[49] referral to the International Criminal Tribunal,[50] and arms embargo.[51] In order to protect civilians, the Security Council authorised the use of *all necessary means*, which can be seen as a deliberate ambiguity that authorises

44 De Wet (note 15), p. 57.
45 UN Charter, Art. 39.
46 UN Charter, Art. 42.
47 De Wet (note 15), p. 64.
48 SC Res. 1970 (26 February 2011), para. 15.
49 Ibid., paras. 17–21.
50 Ibid., paras. 4–8.
51 Ibid., paras. 9–14.

the use of force.[52] However, in so doing the Council specifically excluded "a foreign occupation force of any form on any part of Libyan territory".[53] The Resolutions are not concerned with the choice of a political system. Resolution 1970, for example, urged the Libyan authorities to: "Act with the utmost restraint, respect human rights and international humanitarian law, and allow immediate access for international human rights monitors."[54] Resolution 1973 condemned "the gross and systematic violation of human rights, including arbitrary detentions, enforced disappearances, torture and summary executions".[55]

Notably, the situation in Libya led to such a response through Chapter VII despite the absence of a trans-boundary element and in what appears to be a purely internal situation. In contemporary interpretation, gross and systematic violations of human rights can constitute a threat to the international peace and security. In this vein, the Security Council acted under Chapter VII also in respect of the Taliban government of Afghanistan and invoked, inter alia, the inequality of women as one of the reasons for establishing the existence of a threat to international peace and security.[56] The response shows that severe inequality of women is incompatible with community values.

The Security Council has also developed practices which either indirectly or directly limit the rights of groups and individuals, whereby the interest of the international community not only overrides the sovereignty of states but also the rights of individuals.[57] The Security Council, thus, has powers to limit the rights of groups or individuals for the benefit of the international community as a whole. In so doing, the Security Council needs to strike a balance between the interests of international peace and security (which is understood broadly) and human rights. This is where the contribution turns next.

---

52 See C. Henderson, 'International Measures for the Protection of Civilians in Libya and Cote D'Ivoire' (2011) 60 *International and Comparative Law Quarterly*, 767, 770–771.

53 SC Res. 1973 (17 March 2011), para. 4.

54 SC Res. 1970, para. 2(a).

55 SC Res. 1973, preamble para. 4.

56 See SC Res. 1267 (15 October 1999), preamble, where the Security Council, when acting under Chapter VII, expressed 'deep concern over the continuing violations of international humanitarian law and of human rights, particularly discrimination against women and girls'.

57 See A. Tzanakopoulos, 'Human Rights and United Nations Security Council Measures' in E. de Wet and J. Vidmar (eds), *Hierarchy in International Law: The Place of Human Rights*, Oxford University Press, Oxford 2012, pp. 51–52.

3.3. THE BOUNDARIES OF ARTICLE 103 AND THE COMMUNITY INTEREST

In principle, obligations created by the Security Council under Chapter VII need to be implemented regardless of any other international obligation. This is because Chapter VII resolutions draw their binding force from the UN Charter which contains a supremacy clause elaborated in Article 103: "In the event of a conflict between the obligations of the members of the United Nations under the present Charter and their obligations under any other international agreement, their obligations under the present Charter shall prevail."[58] This provision elevates the UN Charter to the status of a superior international treaty.

The reference to 'any other agreement' and the drafting history of the Charter suggest that its superiority is limited to treaty law; however, international law has evolved since then and nowadays Article 103 should be understood as prevailing over any other international legal obligation, treaty-based or customary.[59] Indeed, many obligations arising under multilateral treaties are also reflected in customary law. Article 103 would remain somewhat toothless if it only prevailed over a treaty provision *sensu stricto* and could not bite against a 'treaty reflection' in customary law. In many instances states could then invoke customary law in order to get out of the Charter obligations. Article 103 does not void an obligation that contravenes the Charter, but rather suspends the duty of a state to fulfil such an obligation. In the words of the Study Group of the International Law Commission (ILC) on Fragmentation of International Law, Article 103 is a "means for securing that Charter obligations can be performed effectively and not [a means for] abolishing other treaty regimes".[60] This means that Article 103 is a rule of precedence rather than a value-underpinned hierarchical relationship with other norms of international law.[61]

Nevertheless, the House of Lords adopted a somewhat different approach in *Al-Jedda*. Lord Bingham of Cornhill reasoned that in the context of Chapter VII of the UN Charter, "Article 103 should not ... be given a narrow, contract-based, meaning. The importance of maintaining peace and security in the world can scarcely be exaggerated".[62] Lord Bingham thereby suggested that Article 103, in combination with Article 25[63] and Chapter VII, also has an important substantive

58 UN Charter, Art. 103.

59 See M. Milanovic, 'Norm Conflict in International Law: Whither Human Rights?' (2009) 20 *Duke Journal of Comparative and International Law*, 69, 78–79.

60 UN Doc. A/CN.4/L.68.

61 Tzanakopoulos (note 57), pp. 98–103.

62 *R (on the application of Al-Jedda) (FC) (Appellant) v. Secretary of State for Defence (Respondent)* [2007] UKHL 58 (2008); 1 AC 332; ILDC 832 (UK 2007), para. 34.

63 Art. 25 of the UN Charter provides: 'The Members of the United Nations agree to accept and carry out the decisions of the Security Council in accordance with the present Charter.'

value, as it intends to promote and enforce the international peace and security, a value in the interest of everyone in the international community. This reasoning goes back to the view that the UN Charter itself expresses fundamental (constitutional) values of the international community.[64] Article 103 makes these values effective and upgrades them above any other international obligation. The rule of precedence may thus not only be of institutional treaty nature but a substantive tool for enforcing the international community interest.[65] The exact effects of Article 103 have recently attracted notable judicial scrutiny.

In *Nada*, the Swiss Federal Supreme Court had to resolve a conflict between an obligation arising under the UN Security Council's Chapter VII resolution and an obligation arising under the European Convention of Human Rights (ECHR). The Swiss Court established a primacy of the Chapter VII resolution as an effect of Article 103. The court ascribed this to the "effect of normative hierarchy in international law".[66] The remark on normative hierarchy is probably no more than an *obiter dictum*. The end effect is more important here and this is that the court was willing to accept that Article 103 automatically trumps all other international legal obligations. This may be seen as a principled upholding of the UN Charter obligations and the community interest. However, the Swiss Court's approach of accepting absolutely and unqualifiedly the primacy of Article 103 appears to be wrong. Certain limits on Article 103 do exist. As one commentator noted:

> By declaring that the Security Council was only bound by *ius cogens* and that, by virtue of Article 103 of the UN Charter, obligations under the UN Charter, including binding Security Council resolutions, prevailed over all other rules of national and international law, the Federal Supreme Court imputed an enormous abundance of power to the Security Council which could hardly be justified. This result is even less appropriate as the role of the Security Council at present is not the same as it was when the UN Charter was drafted. The Security Council is no longer merely reacting to certain situations concerning mainly states or regions, but is evolving into a world legislator. This new role necessitates corresponding control mechanisms.[67]

---

64 McCorquodale (note 34), p. 116.

65 In this respect see also D. Shelton, 'International Law and "Relative Normativity"' in M. Evans, *International Law*, Oxford University Press, Oxford 2009, pp.159–185, 178, arguing that Art. 103 may be seen as a 'supremacy clause' which 'has been taken to suggest that the aims and purposes of the United Nations – maintenance of peace and security and protection of human rights – constitute an international public order to which other treaty regimes and the international organizations giving effect to them must conform'.

66 *Youssef Nada v. State Secretariat for Economic Affairs and Federal Department of Economic Affairs*, Administrative Appeal Judgment, BGE 133 II 450, 1A 45/2007; ILDC 461 (CH 2007), 14 November 2007, para. 6.2.

67 Oxford Reports on International Law, International Law in Domestic Courts, the *Nada* Case, Analysis, para. 3.

One should not presume *prima facie* that Chapter VII would, via Article 103, enforce any 'community interest'. After all, the Security Council is a political body and its decisions need to be subjected to some scrutiny which reveals what precisely Article 103 would be enforcing.

In *Al-Jedda*, the House of Lords adopted a milder approach with respect to Article 103. Lord Brown of Eaton-Under-Heywood still upheld the primacy of an obligation created under the UN Charter over Article 5(1) of the ECHR (the right to liberty and security of person). However, he also noted that "[no] such reasoning, of course, would apply in the case of capital punishment".[68] It is not universally accepted by the international community of states as a whole that the prohibition of the death penalty has a ius cogens status. But the prohibition nevertheless reflects a strong regional value in some parts of the world, including Europe. The prohibition of capital punishment is thus a particularly strong value in a part of the international community and could be used to escape an obligation to follow Article 103. Since a court making such a decision would be imposing a strong value-based community interest, this seems to me more acceptable than a priori adherence to Article 103, regardless of the circumstances.

When *Nada* reached Strasbourg, the European Court of Human Rights (ECtHR) reasoned that the Security Council "must have regard to the purposes for which the United Nations was created".[69] The court resorted here to its reasoning in *Al-Jedda* that "there must be a presumption that the Security Council does not intend to impose any obligation on member states to breach fundamental principles of human rights".[70] The court did not specify that only ius cogens would be relevant for these purposes, but human rights in general. Nevertheless, in *Nada* the ECtHR did not go as far as claiming that Article 103 did not need to be followed. Instead, the ECtHR criticised the Swiss Court for not using the space for manoeuvring which was available due to the very specific circumstances of the case.[71] Indeed, the applicant with severe health problems lived in an Italian enclave surrounded by Swiss territory. Since he was not allowed to enter Switzerland, he could not reach other areas of Italy – the state of his citizenship – and seek medical attention there.[72] These are very peculiar circumstances and the ECtHR used them to confine its decision to the facts of this case. Judge Maliverni took up this issue and argued that on the basis of the UN Charter and recent jurisprudence "[o]ne does not need to be a genius to conclude ... that the Security Council itself

68 *R (on the application of Al-Jedda)* (2007), 58, (2008) 1 AC 332; ILDC 832 (UK 2007), para. 152.
69 ECHR, Case of *Nada v. Switzerland*, Application No. 10593/08 (Judgment), ECHR Reports 2012, para. 171.
70 Case of *Al-Jedda v. United Kingdom* (2011) EHRR 1092, para. 102.
71 The *Nada* Case (note 69), para. 180.
72 Ibid., paras. 195–198.

must also respect human rights, even when acting in its peace-keeping role" and criticised the ECtHR for not saying this directly.[73]

Although the ECtHR remained somewhat elusive, its reasoning affirmed at least that the effects of Article 103 can be subject to interpretation and reconciled with human rights obligations. As De Wet argues:

> The line of reasoning introduced by the ECtHR in Al-Jedda and continued in Nada, reflects that ECHR member states are under an obligation to show that it has done as much as possible to prevent a disproportionate limitation of ECHR standards by a particular UN SC Resolution … [T]he *Nada* Decision of the ECtHR has indicated that even where the language of a UN SC Resolution leaves no apparent scope for interpretation, states remain under an obligation to find a way to give some effect to international human rights standards. The presumption that the UN SC did not intend to deviate from human rights standards seems to be almost irrebuttable, even where it would amount to a distortion of the text of a UN SC decision.[74]

In effect, this exercise is not about human rights trumping Article 103. It is rather about systemic integration whereby Security Council measures should be interpreted with the presumption that the Council did not intend to violate human rights.

It is accepted that when acting under Chapter VII, the Security Council must not act *ultra vires*.[75] In his separate opinion in the provisional measures phase of *Bosnia Genocide*, Judge ad hoc Elihu Lauterpacht argued that the ICJ, "as the principal judicial organ of the United Nations, is entitled, indeed bound, to ensure the rule of law within the United Nations system and, in cases properly brought before it, to insist on adherence by all United Nations organs to the rules governing their operation".[76] Judge ad hoc Lauterpacht then developed an argument that the Security Council cannot demand a violation of ius cogens:

> The concept of ius cogens operates as a concept superior to both customary international law and treaty. The relief which Article 103 of the charter may give the Security Council in case of conflict between one of its decisions and an operative treaty obligation cannot – as a matter of simple hierarchy of norms – extend to a

73 Ibid. Concurring Opinion of Judge Maliverni, para. 15.
74 E. de Wet, 'From Kadi to Nada: Judicial Techniques Favouring Human Rights Over United Nations Security Council Sanctions' (2013) 12 *Chinese Journal of International Law* 4, 787.
75 J. Pauwelyn, *Conflict of Norms in Public International Law: How WTO Law Relates to Other Rules of International Law*, Cambridge University Press, Cambridge 2003, pp. 285–290.
76 ICJ, *Application of the Convention on the Prevention and Punishment of the Crime of Genocide (Bosnia and Herzegovina v. Yugoslavia* ('*Bosnia Genocide* Case') (Request for the Indication of Provisional Measures), ICJ Reports 1993, p. 325, Separate Opinion of Judge *ad hoc* Lauterpacht, para. 99.

> conflict between a Security Council resolution and ius cogens. Indeed, one only has to state the opposite proposition thus – that a Security Council resolution may even require participation in genocide – for its unacceptability to be apparent.[77]

This may be another potential effect of ius cogens in international law, although it is quite unlikely the Security Council would ever directly demand its violation. It is notable, however, that Judge ad hoc Lauterpacht here argued in favour of reviewability of Security Council resolutions where these obviously do not serve the community interest. Article 103 is, therefore, not an absolute rule of precedence and needs to be weighed against other community-oriented obligations in international law.

While judge ad hoc Lauterpacht made his argument in the context of the function of the ICJ, even domestic courts have effectively performed judicial review of Security Council resolution or, better, domestic measures for their implementation.[78] The boundaries of Article 103 have become better defined by *Kadi*. The complex story of this case has been examined in detail elsewhere.[79] For the purposes of this contribution it should be noted that the then EU Court of First Instance (CFI), on the basis of Article 103, refused to review measures against individuals taken by the Security Council.[80] However, the European Court of Justice (ECJ) subsequently overruled this view and adopted the so-called *Solange* argument.

This doctrine originates with the German Federal Constitutional Court. As Antonios Tzanakopoulos argues: "In the two relevant decisions, the German Court successively asserted its power to review decisions of an international organisation for compliance with fundamental rights guaranteed under the German Constitution, and then decided to defer to the international organisation when it was satisfied that an equivalent level of protection was available within the international organisation's framework."[81] In *Kadi* this meant that Security Council resolutions are to be respected only as long as they respect human rights.[82] The rights involved here were not of a *ius cogens* character.

---

77 Ibid., para. 100.

78 Tzanakopoulos (note 57), pp. 54–61.

79 See, e.g. E. de Wet, 'Holding the United Nations Security Council Accountable for Human Rights Violations through Domestic and Regional Courts: a case of "Be Careful what You Wish For"?' in J. Farrall and K. Rubenstein (eds), *Sanctions Accountability and Governance in a Globalised World*, Cambridge University Press, Cambridge 2009, pp. 143–168. E. De Wet and J. Vidmar, 'Conflicts between International Paradigms: Hierarchy versus Systemic Integration' (2013) 2 *Global Constitutionalism*, 196, 208.

80 Tzanakopoulos (note 57), p. 54.

81 A. Tzanakopoulos, 'Judicial Dialogue in Multilevel Governance: The Impact of the *Solange* Argument', in O.K. Fauchald and A. Nollkaemper (eds), *The Practice of International and National Courts and (De)Fragmentation of International Law*, Hart, Oxford 2012, p. 188.

82 Ibid., pp. 204–206.

Another instalment of the case followed in *Kadi II*.[83] The court reasoned:

> When the European Union implements Security Council resolutions adopted under Chapter VII of the Charter of the United Nations, on the basis of a Common Position or a joint action adopted by the member states pursuant to the provisions of the EU Treaty relating to the common foreign and security policy, the competent European Union authority must take due account of the terms and objectives of the resolution concerned and of the relevant obligations under that Charter relating to such implementation.[84]

After *Kadi*, it would still be too simplistic to claim that human rights obligations prevail over Security Council measures.[85] As De Wet points out, the CJEU's decision is only binding on EU organs and does not bind the Security Council or any other UN organ. Indeed, "[t]he EU courts do not have the judicial competence to order the UN SC or its sanctions committees to de-list any particular individual, nor to introduce effective judicial protection at the international level".[86] *Kadi II* also creates legal uncertainty as its reasoning is grounded on EU rather than international human rights law.[87] Domestic courts outside of the EU might still give precedence to Security Council measures. Nevertheless, the approach of giving Article 103 an automatic and absolute precedence is obviously incorrect. Much attention has been given to the purpose of Chapter VII, that is, maintenance of the international peace and security. This is one of the fundamental values of the international community. But so is human rights protection. Article 103 is therefore not a blank cheque. Its measures need to be implemented carefully when they interfere with human rights and the balance will continue to remain subject to academic and judicial scrutiny.[88]

4. CONCLUSIONS

Contemporary international law acknowledges the existence of at least a minimum threshold of community values which attempt to protect groups and

83 Court of Justice of the European Union, *Commission and Others v. Kadi*, C-584/10 P, Judgment of 18 July 2013.

84 Ibid., para. 106.

85 See E. de Wet and J. Vidmar, 'Conclusion' in E. De Wet and J. Vidmar, *Hierarchy in International Law: The Place of Human Rights*, Oxford University Press, Oxford 2012, pp. 300–303.

86 De Wet (note 74), p. 12.

87 Ibid.

88 For a thorough analysis see A. Tzanakopoulos, 'Domestic Court Reactions to UN Security Council Sanctions' in A. Reinisch (ed), *Challenging Acts of International Organizations Before National Courts*, Oxford University Press, Oxford 2010, p. 54. See also E. de Wet and A. Nollkaemper, 'Review of the Security Council Decisions by National Courts' (2002) 45 *German Yearbook of International Law*, 166, 171.

individuals *against* states and abuses of their sovereign powers. International law-making and law-breaking is thus no longer a matter of inter-state relations only and exclusively. Contemporary international law aims to protect the interest of an international community of more than just states.

In particular, the UN Charter period has seen rise of human rights and the creation of legal regimes as well as institutions for their protection. For the protection of the international peace and security, the Security Council can, in the interest of the international community, override some classical tenets of international law and act collectively against a particular state. Practice of the Security Council shows that the concept of international peace and security is interpreted widely. Indeed, not only traditional threats to or actual use of force in international relations have fallen within this category, but also gross and systematic human rights violations within one state's borders. However, not even the Security Council is unchecked in its actions. Where its decisions could lead to denial of fundamental human rights, the Security Council's measures may be perceived as being *ultra vires*. This standard has been developed from below, that is, by domestic courts. It can be concluded that in the interest of the international community, the Security Council can take measures against states and individuals. But the implementation of these measures needs to take place within the parameters of fundamental human rights.

International law also knows of concepts of particularly strong, ethically-underpinned, community-oriented obligations which are not a matter of reciprocal relationship between states and are binding even if a particular state has explicitly *not* accepted them as such. However, one should not overstretch the effect of these norms. Despite their special value-based standing, they do not operate as hierarchically superior law. Although reflecting a strong sense of international community and its values, the enforceability of these norms is thus still lacking.

The post-Second World War era has seen a notable turn to a community-oriented international legal system as well as a shift from an international community of states toward an international community full stop. Yet UN membership is only open to states, as are the ICJ proceedings; states continue to enjoy sovereign immunity and participate in the international law-making process. The enforcement of the community interest thus still, for a great part, runs through state-centric procedures and within a state-centric international structure.

CHAPTER 7

HUMAN RIGHTS AND CLIMATE CHANGE: EXTENDING THE EXTRATERRITORIAL DIMENSION VIA THE COMMON CONCERN

Werner Scholtz

1. INTRODUCTION: HUMAN RIGHTS AND CLIMATE CHANGE

The recognition of the linkages between human rights and climate change has steadily gained momentum in international law.[1] This acknowledgment is affirmed in Resolution 7/23 of the United Nations Human Rights Council (UNHRC) ("Human Rights and the Environment"), which inter alia requested the United Nations High Commissioner for Human Rights to conduct an analytical study on this relationship. This study was submitted to the tenth session of the UNHRC in 2009. Accordingly, Resolution 10/4 of the UNHRC ("Human Rights and Climate Change") takes cognisance of the fact that climate change-related impacts have implications for the effective enjoyment of human rights, such as the rights to

[1] Various authoritative texts have dealt with the legal interface between human rights law and the impacts of climate change. See, for instance, J. Knox, 'Climate Change and Human Rights Law' (2009) 50 *Virgina Journal of International Law*, 164; S. McInerney-Lankford, M. Darrow and L. Rajamani, *Human Rights and Climate Change: A Review of the International Legal Dimensions*, World Bank, Washington 2011; D. Bodansky, 'Climate Change and Human Rights. Unpacking the Issues' (2010) 38 *Georgia Journal of International and Comparative Law*, 51–524; E. Cameron and M. Limon, 'Restoring the Climate by Realizing Rights: The Role of the International Human Rights System' (2012) 21 *RECIEL*, 204. See also A. Boyle, 'Human Rights and the Environment: Where Next?' (2013) 23 *European Journal of International Law*, 613.

life, adequate food, water, health, adequate housing and self-determination. This Resolution recognises that human rights obligations have the potential to inform and strengthen international and national climate change policy-making. In terms of this Resolution, the Council accordingly decides to hold a panel discussion on the relationship between climate change and human rights. Furthermore, the mandate of the recently appointed independent expert on the issue of human rights, obligations relating to a safe, clean, healthy and sustainable environment, includes the identification, promotion and exchange of views concerning the use of human rights obligations and commitments to "inform, support and strengthen environmental policymaking".[2] The furtherance of the human rights approach to climate change will therefore also be part of his mandate. Moreover, the Cancun Agreements adopted at the sixteenth Conference of the Parties (COP) of the United Nations Framework Convention on Climate Change (UNFCCC) clearly recognises the link between climate change and human rights.[3]

Although it is evident that the human rights approach has penetrated the sphere of the international climate change regime, it is important to clarify the human rights obligations of states in the context of climate change. According to Cameron and Limon it is "Only by addressing and generating greater understanding about these central questions will vulnerable states and international human rights mechanisms be able to more effectively leverage international human rights law as an effective additional means (outside the UNFCCC) of responding to climate change".[4] In this regard, "For human rights law to require states to address the entire range of harms caused by climate change, it must impose duties on states with respect to those living outside their territory".[5] Hence, the extraterritorial dimension of human rights remains the central issue in the discourse on human rights and climate change.[6] The Analytical Study on the Relationship between

2 J. Knox was appointed in terms of Res. 19/10 of 2012.

3 Decision 1/CP.16 takes note of Res. 10/4 and para. 8 emphasises that "parties should in all climate change related actions, fully respect human rights". Appendix I to Decision 1/CP.16 includes a series of safeguards on Reducing Emissions from Deforestation and Forest Degradation in Developing countries (REDD). The safeguards require that REDD actions "complement or are consistent with the objectives of national forest programmes and relevant international conventions and agreements." (Para. 2 (a)). The safeguards include elements in human rights instruments, such as "respect for the knowledge and rights of indigenous peoples and members of local communities, by taking into account relevant international obligations, national circumstances and laws, and noting that the United Nations General Assembly has adopted the United Nations Declaration on the Rights of Indigenous Peoples". See para. 2(c) and (d). For a discussion on the linkages between REDD and human rights: A. Savaresi, 'The Human Rights Dimension of REDD' (2012) 21 *RECIEL*, 102–113.

4 Cameron and Limon (note 1), p. 209.

5 Knox (note 1), p. 200.

6 Cameron and Limon (note 1), p. 212.

Human Rights and the Environment of the UNHCHR[7] under the section on the "extraterritorial dimensions of human rights and the environment"[8] stresses that that this issue provides "fertile ground for further inquiry"[9] in relation to global environmental issues, such as climate change.[10]

Accordingly this chapter investigates the potential development of the extraterritorial dimension of human rights in the context of the consequences of climate change. This chapter does not intent to revisit the discourse on the pros and cons of the human rights approach to climate change.[11] It also does not assume that climate change should be viewed predominantly from a human rights approach. Rather, the point of departure of this chapter is that the human rights approach has important insights and cannot be ignored in relation to the consequences of climate change.[12] Irrespective of the critique against the human rights approach to climate change, this approach can play an important role and "it behooves us to better understand the interrelationship between the two".[13] This contribution is an attempt to address the most central issue of the relationship between human rights and climate change, which is the extraterritorial dimension thereof. I shall therefore analyse two proposed approaches to the development, which are: the establishment of extraterritorial human rights obligations and the duty of cooperation. My analysis of the aforementioned proposals leads me to suggest a third conceptual approach. I indicate that the common concern of humankind, which is a facet of common interest, may constitute a suitable basis for the extension of the extraterritorial dimension of human rights obligations. I conclude the article with remarks.

7 UN Doc. A/HRC/19/34 of 16 December 2011 (the Analytical Study). Human Rights Council Res. 16/11 of 12 April 2011 requested the OHCHR to conduct a detailed analytical study on the relationship between human rights and environmental law.

8 See section IX.

9 Para. 64.

10 Para. 66.

11 Bodansky (note 1).

12 See in this regard S. Caney, 'Climate Change, Human Rights and Moral Thresholds', pp. 163–177 in S. Gardiner, S. Caney, D. Jamieson, H. Shue and R.K. Pachauri (eds), *Climate Ethics*, Oxford University Press, Oxford 2010.

13 Bodansky (note 1), p. 524.

2. THE EXTRATERRITORIAL DIMENSION OF HUMAN RIGHTS

"Extraterritorial human rights obligations"[14] has been the source of comprehensive scholarship[15] and the focal point of jurisprudence. The extraterritorial dimension of the two most prominent human rights treaties is contested. Article 2 (1) of the International Covenant on Civil and Political Rights (ICCPR) requires its parties "to respect and to ensure to all individuals within its territory and subject to its jurisdiction the rights recognized in the present Covenant".[16] This provision has been interpreted to restrict state's duties to individuals or territory where states have "effective control".[17] Until now, no adjudicative body has addressed this issue in relation to climate change. It might be difficult to satisfy the effective control test in instances of climate change.[18]

---

14 Several other terms have been used, such as 'international', 'transborder', 'transboundary' or 'transnational'. See M.K. Gibney, K. Tomasevski and J. Vedsted-Hansen, 'Transnational State Responsibility for Violations of Human Rights' (1999) 12 *Harvard Human Rights Journal*, 267. Gibney rejects the usage of notions with the prefix "trans-" or "cross-" due to the suggestion of geographic proximity which does not accord with the issue at hand. Gibney, for instance, also does not support "global obligations" due to the fact that all actors are responsible for everything (and accordingly nothing). He prefers extraterritorial obligations, but recognises the shortcoming of this term. The acceptance of this term may create the impression that human rights obligations are in principal territorial. M. Gibney, 'On Terminology: Extraterritorial Obligations', p. 32–47 in M. Langford, W. Vandenhole, M. Scheinin and W. van Genugten (eds), *Global Justice, State Duties: The Extraterritorial Scope of Economic, Social and Cultural Rights in International Law*, Cambridge University Press, Cambridge 2013. I shall use the term "extraterritorial obligations" for purposes of consistency, but my understanding is influenced by para. 8 of the Maastricht Principles on Extraterritorial Obligations of states in the Area of Economic, Social and Cultural Rights. The Maastricht Principles divides ETOs in "obligations relating to the acts and omissions of a State" that have extraterritorial implications and "obligations of a global character". The extraterritorial human rights obligations to protect and to fulfil are still viewed as part of *lex ferenda*, whereas the obligation to respect constitutes *lex lata*. See S. Skogly, *Beyond National Borders: States' Human Rights Obligations in International Cooperation*, Intersentia, Antwerp 2006, p. 66 et seq. Scholars have indicated a need for the development of the obligations to fulfil and protect in an era of globalisation and interdependence. See F. Coomans, 'Application of the International Covenant on Economic, Social and Cultural Rights in the Framework of International Organisations' (2007) 11 *Max Planck United Nations Yearbook*, 390 and F. Coomans, 'Some Remarks on the Extraterritorial Application of the International Covenant on Economic, Social and Cultural Rights' in F. Coomans and M.T. Kamminga (eds), *Extraterritorial Application of Human Rights Treaties*, Intersentia, Antwerp 2004, pp. 183–199.

15 See, for instance, Skogly (note 14); M. Gibney and S. Skogly, *Universal Human Rights and Extraterritorial Obligations*, University of Pennsylvania Press, Philadelphia 2010.

16 For an overview, see D. McGoldrick, 'Extraterritorial Application of the International Covenant on Civil and Political Rights' in Coomans et al. (eds) (note 14), pp. 41–81.

17 See para. 8 of General Comment 31 of the United Nations Human Rights Committee, *The Nature of the Legal Obligations Imposed on States Parties to the Covenant*, CCPR/C/21/Rev.1/Add. 13, 26 May 2004. The word "and" should be read disjunctively. See also para. 111 of the *Wall* Case (ICJ, *Legal Consequences of the Construction of a Wall in the Occupied Palestinian Territory* (Advisory Opinion), ICJ Reports 2004, 136).

18 The European Court of Human Rights adopted a controversial restrictive approach in the *Bankovic* Case in the interpretation of the jurisdictional clause in Art. 1 of the European Convention on Human Rights. It rejected the argument that the NATO bombing of Serbia

The Analytical study on the discussion of extraterritorial obligations affirms that the extraterritorial economic, social and cultural rights (ESCRs) are of particular importance in relation to environmental degradation.[19] Article 2(1) of the International Covenant on Economic, Social and Cultural Rights (ICESCR) contains the undertaking by each Party "to take steps, individually and through international assistance and co-operation, especially economic and technical, to the maximum of its available resources, with a view to achieving progressively the full realisation of the rights recognised in the present Covenant". Hence, the ICESCR contains a clearer extraterritorial dimension since it does not contain a territorial limitation similar to that of the ICCPR and it explicitly requires parties to cooperate and provide assistance.[20] The Analytical Study on the Relationship between Human Rights and the Environment of the UNHCHR affirms that "the key question with regard to the extraterritorial dimension of human rights and environment is the spatial scope of the application of human rights law instruments". Subsequently, it refers to the absence of a jurisdiction clause in the African Charter on Human and People's Rights (Banjul Charter).[21] This seems to suggest that the absence of a jurisdiction clause may provide a legal base

---

constituted effective control of the areas bombed (*Bankovic v. Belgium* et al., Application 52207/99, Admissibility Decision (12 November 2001)). See for critique of the decision M. Gondek, 'Extraterritorial Application of the European Convention on Human Rights: Territorial Focus in the Age of Globalisation?' (2005) 52 *Netherlands International Law Review*, 349–387. Subsequently the Court followed a more articulated interpretation of Art. 1 in *Öcalan* (*Öcalan v. Turkey* (Merits), Application 46221/99, Chamber Judgment (12 March 2003)) and *Issa* (*Issa v. Turkey*, Application 31821/96, ECtHR Judgment (16 November 2004)). See also K. Da Costa, *The Extraterritorial Application of Selected Human Rights Treaties*, Martinus Nijhoff, Leiden 2013, pp. 93–253.

19 Para. 68.

20 See the discussion of Skogly (note 14), p. 98. Developed countries have, however, resisted the proposition that this provision imposes duties on them to assist other states to meet their obligations under the Covenant. Several substantive provisions include obligations concerning international assistance and cooperation. In relation to the right to an adequate standard of living, Art. 11 (1) states that "parties will take appropriate steps to ensure the realisation of this right, recognising to this effect the essential importance of international co-operation". Art. 11 (2), which pertains to the right of everyone to be free from hunger, reads that parties "shall take, individually and through international co-operation, the measures, including specific programmes, which are needed". Art. 15 (4) also underscores the importance of international cooperation as it reads that "the States Parties to the present Covenant recognise the benefits to be derived from the encouragement and development of international contacts and co-operation in the scientific and cultural fields". The International Court of Justice, however, remarked that the absence of a jurisdictional provision might be due to "the fact that this Covenant guarantees rights which are essentially territorial", para. 112 of the *Wall* Case. The Court confirmed that the International Covenant on Economic, Social and Cultural Rights applies to the territories under its occupation and Israel is under an obligation "not to raise any obstacle to the exercise of such rights in the fields where competence has been transferred to Palestinian authorities". See para. 112.

21 Art. 1, para. 69 of the Charter merely states that: "The Member States of the Organisation of African Unity, parties to the present Charter shall recognise the rights, duties and freedoms enshrined in the Charter and shall undertake to adopt legislative or other measures to give effect to them."

for the extraterritorial dimension of human rights[22] (in Africa)[23] in the Banjul Charter. Several substantive provisions on international cooperation support the extraterritorial dimension of human rights in the Banjul Charter.[24] Article 22 is one such an example since subsection 2 reads that "States shall have the duty, individually or collectively, to ensure the exercise of the right to development".[25]

Furthermore, various General Comments of the Committee on Economic, Social and Cultural Rights have interpreted references to international assistance and co-operation as an indication of extraterritorial obligations.[26] The exact content of these obligations is, however, still unclear.

Several impediments exist concerning the development of the extraterritorial dimension of human rights in the context of climate change.[27] Apart from the opposition of developed states to such an extension, jurisdiction[28] may impede the development of extraterritorial ESCRs to fulfil. A further problem with the development of the extraterritorial dimension of human rights is that it would

---

22 Craven opines that the decision in the *Bosnia* Case that "the obligation each State thus has to prevent and to punish the crime of genocide is not territorially limited by the Convention" raises the possibility that in the absence of a jurisdictional clause, human rights treaty obligations may generally be regarded as "extending to all acts of state irrespective of where they may be taken as having effect". M. Craven, 'Human Rights in the Realm of Order: Sanctions and Extraterritoriality' in in Coomans et al. (eds) (note 14), p. 251.

23 The Charter is a regional instrument which applies to the African continent.

24 For instance, Art. 21 (3) states that "the free disposal of wealth and natural resources shall be exercised without prejudice to the obligation of promoting international economic cooperation based on mutual respect, equitable exchange and the principles of international law".

25 Para. 4 of the Preamble furthermore reaffirms "the pledge ... to coordinate and intensify their cooperation and efforts to achieve a better life for the peoples of Africa and to promote international cooperation having due regard to the Charter of the United Nations and the Universal Declaration of Human Rights" and para. 6 recognises that "fundamental human rights stem from the attributes of human beings which justifies their national and international protection".

26 The CESCR has identified obligations of cooperation and assistance, which depends on the availability of resources and ability. See, for instance, General Comment 14, *The Right to the Highest Attainable Standard of Health*, E/C.12/2000/4, 11 August 2000, paras. 45 and 39. For a discussion of the comments by the Committee on Economic, Social and Cultural Rights, see also R. Künnemann, 'Extraterritorial Application of the International Covenant on Economic, Social and Cultural Rights' in F. Coomans and M.T. Kamminga (eds), *Extraterritorial Application of Human Rights Treaties*, Intersentia, Antwerp 2004, pp. 208–211. See also the approach of the Office of the United Nations High Commissioner for Human Rights, *Report of the Office of the United Nations High Commissioner for Human Rights on the Relationship between Climate Change and Human Rights*, A/HRC/10/61, 15 January 2009, paras. 84–86.

27 Knox (note 1), p. 210. See for a discussion on ETOs in relation to the environment F. Coomans and R. Künnemann, *Cases and Concept on Extraterritorial Obligations in the Area of Economic, Social and Cultural Rights*, Intersentia, Antwerp 2012, pp. 103–143.

28 See, for a discussion on the meaning of jurisdiction in Human Rights Law M. den Heijer and R. Lawson, 'Extraterritorial Human Rights and the Concept of Jurisdiction' in M. Langford, W. Vandenhole, M. Scheinin and W. van Genugten (eds), *Global Justice, State Duties: The Extraterritorial Scope of Economic, Social and Cultural Rights in International Law*, Cambridge University Press, Cambridge 2013, p. 158 *et seq.*

result in the treatment of climate change as a "series of individual transboundary harms" and a "state-by-state consideration of extraterritorial effects of domestic actions", which is not suitable for the global nature and effects of climate change.[29] The plight of (Environmentally Displaced Persons) EDPs[30] may provide a concrete example of the current deficiencies of the application of the human rights framework to the consequences of climate change. EDPs may not successfully claim the fulfilment of ESCRs from third states for having contributed to climate change through the emission of greenhouse gas emissions due to the absence of a jurisdictional link.[31]

It is my opinion that climate change indeed requires the "international community to act as a single polity".[32] Thus, the solution to the problem cannot be found in a (bilateral) state centric[33] approach. A shift from bilateralism[34] to community interests and the emergence of an international community has been observed in international law.[35] Knox accordingly proposes that the duty of cooperation presents a more suitable base for the extension of human rights

29 Knox (note 1), p. 211.

30 See D. Zartner Falstrom, 'Stemming the Flow of Environmental Displacement: Creating a Convention to Protect Persons and Preserve the Environment' (2001–2002) 13 *Colorado Journal International Environmental Law and Policy*, 15.

31 U. Beyerlin, 'Environmental Migration and International Law' in H.P. Hestermeyer et al. (eds), *Coexistence, Cooperation and Solidarity Liber Amicorum Rüdiger Wolfrum Volume I*, Martinus Nijhoff, Leiden 2011, p. 328.

32 Knox (note 1), p. 212.

33 See further C. Schreuer, 'The Waning of the Sovereign State: Towards a New Paradigm for International Law' (1993) 4 *European Journal of International Law*, 447.

34 See, however, for a discussion concerning a new wave of bilateralism in international environmental law E. Morgera, 'Bilateralism at the Service of Community Interests? Non-judicial Enforcement of Global Public Goods in the Context of Global Environmental Law' (2012) 23 *European Journal of International Law*, 743–767.

35 See B. Simma and A.L. Paulus, 'The International Community: Facing the Challenge of Globalisation' (1998) 9 *European Journal of International Law*, 268. B. Simma, 'From Bilateralism to Community Interest in International Law' (1994) VI *Recueil Des Cours*, 217. For an extensive analysis see A.L. Paulus, *Die Internationale Gemeinschaft im Völkerrecht*, C.H. Beck, Munich 2001. Hermann Mosler has referred to the existence of an international legal community during his Hague lectures. See H. Mosler, 'The International Society as a Legal Community' (1974) IV *Recueil Des Cours*, 140. See also C. Tomuschat, 'Obligations for States Without or Against Their Will' (1993) IV *Recueil Des Cours*, 199. See also the discussion of J.A. Frowein, 'Das Staatengemeinschaftsinteresse – Probleme bei Formulierung und Durchsetzung' in K. Hailbronner et al. (eds), *Festschrift für Karl Doehring*, Springer, Berlin 1989, p. 219. Several scholars have, however, advocated the existence of functional networks instead of an international community. See, for instance, A. Slaughter, *A New World Order*, Princeton University Press, Princeton 2004, p. 131 et seq. The emergence of an international community is an aspirational and progressive development. The existence of concepts such as erga omnes and ius cogens supports this view, since these concepts allow the international community to pursue community interests. The shift towards the pursuit of community interest has, for instance, not resulted in an amendment to the ICJ Statute, which determines that the jurisdiction thereof is based on the consent of parties and that "peremptory norms represent the normative formalisation of the highest social aspirations of the international community, whose normative realisation remains no less uncertain than that of ordinary rules". As Kritsiotis remarks: "Our international community is 'deep' enough to have conceived of the

law to climate change.[36] The problem with this proposal is that it does not go far enough in order to ensure that the international community as a whole (as a single polity) addresses the global climate change challenge. The duty of cooperation is grounded in Article 2 (1) of the ICESCR and Articles 55 and 56 of the UN Charter,[37] which relates to state actors and the UN. Hence, the proposal of Knox focuses on an isolated component of the international community and is overtly state-centric. The international community does not consist of states only.[38] Unfortunately, individual states are ill-equipped to address global problems and realise the common interests of humanity.[39] The solution does not suit the nature of the problem. The emission of greenhouse gases results in an increase in the concentration of global greenhouse gases, which in turn affects the global climate. In order to address the consequences of climate change, human rights protection must transcend territorial borders.

3. EXTENSION OF EXTRATERRITORIAL HUMAN RIGHTS VIA THE COMMON CONCERN

The preamble of the United Nations Framework Convention on Climate Change of 1992 (UNFCCC) acknowledges "that change in the Earth's climate and its adverse effects are a common concern of humankind". It is my opinion that the common concern of humankind provides a point of departure for the development of the extraterritorial dimension of human rights obligations in relation to climate change. In terms of the Preamble of the UNFCCC climate change and the consequential non-observance of human rights, in particular ESCRs, may be seen as a common concern.

The common concern of humankind (CCH) is a facet of "common interest", which induces the development of rules.[40] Common interest is conducive to the

idea of *jus cogens* but not deep enough to know what to do with it". D. Kritsiotis, 'Imagining the International Community' (2002) 14 *European Journal of International Law*, 990.

36 Knox (note 1), p. 212.

37 Art. 55 (c) requires the promotion of "universal respect for, and observance of, human rights and fundamental freedoms for all without distinction as to race, sex, language, or religion" and Art. 56 affirms that "[a]ll Members pledge themselves to take joint and separate action, in cooperation with the Organisation, for the achievement of the purposes set forth in Art. 55."

38 See E. de Wet, 'The International Constitutional Order' (2006) 55 *International & Comparative Law Quarterly*, 56.

39 P. Allott, *Eunomia: New Order for a New World*, Oxford University Press, Oxford 1990, p. 249.

40 See J. Brunnée, 'The Global Climate Regime: Wither Common Concern?' in H.P. Hestermeyer et al. (eds), *Coexistence, Cooperation and Solidarity Liber Amicorum Rüdiger Wolfrum Volume I*, Martinus Nijhoff, Leiden 2011, pp. 721–736; J. Brunnée, '"Common Interest" – Echoes from an Empty Shell? Some Thoughts on Common Interest and International Environmental Law' (1989) 37 *Zeitschrift für ausländisches öffentliches Recht und Völkerrecht*, 791–808. However,

cooperation of states based on their realisation of interdependence.[41] The existence of a common concern is not dependant on the explicit reference of this notion in a treaty. The Convention for the Protection of the World Cultural and Natural Heritage of 1972 and the Montreal Protocol on Substances that Deplete the Ozone Layer of 1987 follow the common concern regime without making any reference to this concept.[42] Furthermore, it is worth noting that the "concern" element does not carry with it any proprietary meaning, but relates to the causes as well as the responses[43] to common concerns. The UNFCCC recognises the consequences of climate change, such as environmental displacement, as a common concern. Hence, the response measures (the fulfilment of particularly ESCRs) is a common interest of the international community. This proposal adheres to the Vienna Declaration that affirms that the promotion and protection of human rights is a legitimate concern of the international community.[44]

The common concern does not pertain exclusively to states, but refers to mankind. Mankind includes all of the members of the human species as a whole and encompasses present and future generations, and as such invokes intergenerational and intragenerational equity.[45] It has been suggested that the inclusion of this notion in several international instruments implies that "mankind" is an emerging subject of international law.[46] It is, however, difficult to consider future generations as (partial or full) subjects of current international law with the capacity to possess international rights and/or duties.[47] This,

common interest is the product of the coinciding individual state interests, which implies that it is characterised by egocentric (anthropocentric) rather than altruistic features.

41 W. Scholtz, 'Collective (Environmental) Security: the Yeast for the Refinement of International Law' (2008) 19 *Yearbook of International Environmental Law*, 150. I use the term "interdependence" to refer to the instances where the solution to a problem can be addressed only by the concerted actions of states. Climate change presents a good example of ecological interdependence. The existence of factual interdependence does not mean that states will indeed cooperate in order to solve an issue. See in this regard D. Greig, 'International Community, Interdependence and All That … Rhetorical Correctness?' in G. Kreijen et al. (eds), *State, Sovereignty and International Governance*, Oxford University Press, Oxford 2002, p. 569. The existence of interdependence amongst many states may even hinder a solution. Once again climate change is illustrative of the truth of this statement.

42 See J. Brunnée, 'Common Areas, Common Heritage and Common Concern' in D. Bodansky et al. (eds), *The Oxford Handbook of International Environmental Law*, Oxford University Press, Oxford 2007, p. 565.

43 The Convention on Biological Diversity (CBD) of 1992 affirms that "the conservation of biological diversity is a common concern of humankind".

44 UNHCR, The Vienna Declaration and Programme of Action, UN Doc. A/CONF.157/23, para. 4 (1993).

45 A.A.C. Trindade, *International Law of Mankind Towards a New Jus Gentium*, Martinus Nijhoff, Leiden 2010, p. 281. Art. 3 (1) of the UNFCCC includes intragenerational and intergenerational equity as one of the guiding principles.

46 Trindade (note 45), p. 281 et seq.

47 See A. Malhotra, 'A Commentary on the Status of Future Generations as a Subject of International Law' in E. Agius et al. (eds), *Future Generations and International Law*, Earthscan, London 1998, pp. 39–49.

however, does not mean that such a development in future is unthinkable and that this notion does not have the potential to expand the recognition of the international legal personality of participants of international law.[48] The concept and meaning of international legal personality has undergone various changes, the number of recognised subjects of international law has been expanded,[49] and it is not impossible to establish among the living some form of representation for mankind.[50] For instance, the position of the individual in international law has seen some remarkable changes with the advent of international criminal law, humanitarian law and human rights law. The recognition of the status of certain non-state actors, such as non-governmental organisations, is a topical debate in international law.[51] It must be borne in mind that non-state actors play an important role in various aspects of international law[52] Human rights and international environmental law are the two fields where NGO participation is the most frequent.

Thus, the notion of the common concern of humankind may serve as a catalyst for the further expansion of legal subjects in international law. This is possible since the concern of mankind may give rise to legal obligations and rights that apply not only to states but also to non-state actors, and which fulfil an important role concerning the pursuit of the common interest of constituents of mankind. The latter statement does not mean that states have become irrelevant. States still have an important role to play in international law and they will most probably remain the primary actors of international law. The expansion of legal personality does not alter this position, but rather envisages a complementary role for other actors and as such ensures that all actors of the international community as a whole may cooperate in order to promote ESCRs.

Furthermore, CCH provides the international community with a legitimate interest in global environmental resources and a common responsibility of

48 The ICJ has established the possibility that non-state entities may also be subjects of international law. See ICJ, *Reparations for Injuries Suffered in the Service of the United Nations* (Advisory Opinion), ICJ Reports 1949, p. 174. This decision also provides for full and partial legal personality for subjects. Only states have full legal personality.

49 For a comprehensive overview of the topic, see R. Portmann, *Legal Personality in International Law*, Cambridge University Press, Cambridge 2010.

50 See *Minors Oposa v. Secretary of the Department of Environmental and Natural Resources* (1993) 33 ILM 173 (1994).

51 See in general, J. Klabbers, '(I Can't Get No) Recognition: Subjects Doctrine and the Emergence of Non-State Actors' in J. Petman et al. (eds), *Nordic Cosmopolitanism: Essays in International Law for Martti Koskenniemi*, Martinus Nijhoff, Leiden 2003, pp. 351–370.

52 See, for an overview, P. Alston et al. (eds), *Non-State Actors and Human Rights*, Oxford University Press, Oxford 2005. It is of particular interest to observe the rise of international NGOs. K. Martens, 'Examining the (Non-)Status of NGOs in international Law' (2003) 10 *Indiana Journal of Global Legal Studies*, 1, 4. See F. Yamin, 'NGOs and International Environmental Law: A Critical Evaluation of their Roles and Responsibilities' (2001) 10 *Review of European Community and International Environmental Law*, 149.

assistance to ensure the sustainable development thereof.[53] Thus, states exercise functional powers[54] in relation to global environmental resources, which mean that states are restricted in their actions by the legitimate interests of mankind. Accordingly, common concern also has important consequences for state sovereignty.[55] CCH introduces a custodial element to sovereignty. States act as custodians for the well-being of individuals.[56] Custodial sovereignty recognises the internal and external rights and obligations of states. Thus, the internal obligations of a state relates primarily to the inhabitants of a custodial state and the external to the international community. However, it is also true that the internal responsibility of states is also of concern for the international community since it relates to the promotion and protection of the common interest. This implies that the international community of states also incurs a legitimate interest in relation to the internal responsibilities of states. Thus, sovereignty has a relational or interactive nature. The internal element of sovereignty is therefore primarily exercised for the benefit of the inhabitants of the state, and the State has the primary responsibility for the promotion of the welfare of its inhabitants through domestic structures.

Hence, global responsibilities in terms of CCH may constitute erga omnes[57] obligations. Consequently, Sands and Peel therefore opine that an actio popularis may be applied to environmental obligations associated with inter alia the common concern or in respect of environmental matters which are associated with human rights obligations.[58] In casu, this implies that the CCH in relation to human rights and climate change may give rise to the enforcement of the common interest by individual states on behalf of the international community.

---

53 P. Birnie, A.E. Boyle and C. Redgwell, *International Law and the Environment*, Oxford University Press, Oxford 2009, p. 128. The existence of such an interest does not depend on the presence of transboundary harm.

54 See for the distinction between discretionary and functional powers, R-J. Dupuy, 'Humanity and the Environment' (1991) *Colorado Journal of International Law and Policy*, 203.

55 W. Scholtz, 'Custodial Sovereignty: Reconciliation of Sovereignty and Global Environmental Challenges amongst the Vestiges of Colonialism' (2008) 55 *Netherlands International Law Review*, 323.

56 For a discussion W. Scholtz, 'The Reconciliation of Transnational Economic, Social and Cultural Human Rights *via* the Common Interest' (2013) 37 *South African Yearbook of International Law*, 232–248.

57 ICJ, *Case concerning the Barcelona Traction, Light and Power Company, Limited (Belgium v. Spain) (New Application: 1962)* (2nd Phase) (Judgment), ICJ Reports 1970, p. 3. For a discussion C.J. Tams, *Enforcing Obligations Erga Omnes in International Law*, Cambridge University Press, Cambridge 2005.

58 P. Sands and J. Peel, *Principles of International Environmental Law*, Cambridge University Press, Cambridge 2012, p. 146–150. Sands, however, bemoans the reluctance of states to act on behalf of the international community. Art. 48 of the ILC Articles on State Responsibility for Internationally Wrongful Acts of 2001 recognises that any state may bring an international claim in respect of the breach of an obligation owed to the international community of states. For a discussion Birnie et al. (note 53), p. 131.

CCH also results in differential burden-sharing. According to the Hague Recommendations on International Environmental Law "costs should be shared equitably among states, taking into account historic responsibilities and present technical and financial capabilities".[59] Hence, CCH lays a foundation for a shared responsibility on the basis of differential treatment[60] concerning the promotion of human rights in the context of climate change. The emerging international moral principle of solidarity[61] constitutes a basis for differential treatment provisions.[62] It is important to clarify the division of responsibility in the instance of the extension of the extraterritorial dimension of human rights in order to ensure that states do not escape their primary responsibility towards their inhabitants.[63]

Common concern may imply a progression towards a departure from an overly inter-state centred international law to a structure that accommodates the proliferation of other participants, which may ultimately promote the well-being of mankind. This viewpoint takes cognisance of the artificial construct of state borders and reflects the interconnected nature of all human beings in the shared biosphere. The aforementioned discussion does not imply that the common concern has already transformed inter-state law towards an international order that serves the well-being of individuals.[64] The common concern, however, has sparked this potential development in that it caters for a more "universalist

59 Para. 3 of 'The Hague Recommendations on International Environmental Law of 16 Augustus 1991' in S. Bilderbeek (ed), *Biodiversity and International Law: The Effectiveness of International Environmental Law*, IOS Press, Washington 1992, pp. 194–202.

60 L. Rajamani, *Differential Treatment in International Environmental Law*, Oxford University Press, Oxford 2006. See also J. Pauwelyn, 'The End of Differential Treatment for Developing Countries? Lessons from the Trade and Climate Change Regimes' (2013) 22 *Review of European Community and International Environmental Law*, 29–41.

61 See P. Dann, 'Solidarity and the Law of Development' in R. Wolfrum and C. Kojima (eds), *Solidarity: A Structural Principle of International Law*, Springer, Berlin 2010, pp. 55–77.

62 In terms of solidarity states have to be made responsible for the external effects of their policies. This implies that states should conduct their policies in a manner that takes cognisance of the interests of the international community. Solidarity also entails positive action since a state should also undertake (jointly or separately) positive measures to the benefit of the community. Para. 6 of the UN Millennium Declaration (General Assembly Res. A/55/L.2 of 18 September 2000) affirms that solidarity is one of the "fundamental values to be essential to international relations in the twenty-first century". This paragraph also defines solidarity in terms of burden-sharing. See R.S.J. Macdonald, 'Solidarity in the Practice and Discourse of Public International Law' (1996) 8 *Public Interest Law Reporter*, p. 259. R. Wolfrum, 'Solidarity amongst States: An Emerging Structural Principle of International Law' in P. Dupuy et al. (eds), *Völkerrecht als Wertordnung, Festschrift für Chrstian Tomuschat*, Engel, Kehl 1995, p. 1087 et seq. International environmental law contains various examples of the influence of solidarity. See C.L. Riemer, *Staatengemeinschaftliche Solidarität in der Völkerrechtsordnung*, Riemer, Düsseldorf 2003, p. 160.

63 See M. Gibney, *International Human Rights Law Returning to Universal Principles*, Rowman & Littlefield, London 2008, p. 3. For a discussion Scholtz (note 56), p.243.

64 A. Clapham, 'The Role of the Individual in International Law' (2010) 21 *European Journal of International Law*, 25–30.

outlook",[65] which is concerned with the well-being of mankind through the universal promotion of ESCRs in an interdependent world faced by global challenges. This aspect of the common concern exhibits an aspiration towards cosmopolitan ideals.[66]

A regional treaty which provides an example of the potential extension of the jurisdiction through common interest is the Banjul Charter. Article 27 states that: "The rights and freedoms of each individual shall be exercised with due regard to the rights of others, collective security, morality and common interest." The inclusion of common interest should be read in conjunction with Article 23 which states that "The principles of solidarity and friendly relations shall govern relations between states". The consequences of climate change will have dire consequences for human rights on the African continent.[67] The international climate change regime takes cognisance of the specific position of Africa.[68] The African Commission on Human and People's rights has also taken note of the relationship between human rights and climate change in Africa through

---

65 This is reflected in an Advisory Opinion of the Inter-American court on Human Rights, which emphasised that "modern human rights treaties in general, and the American Convention in particular, are not multilateral treaties of the traditional type concluded to accomplish the reciprocal exchange of rights for the mutual benefit of the contracting states. Their object and purpose is the protection of the basic rights of individual human beings irrespective of their nationality, both against the State of their nationality and all other contracting states. In concluding these human rights treaties, the states can be deemed to submit themselves to a legal order within which they, for the common good, assume various obligations, not in relation to other states, but towards all individuals within their jurisdiction". See The Effect of Reservations on the Entry Into Force of the American Convention on Human Rights (Arts. 74 and 75), Advisory Opinion, OC-2/82, 24 September 1982, Inter-Am. Ct. H.R. (Ser. A) No. 2 (1982).

66 See R. Pierik, et al. (eds), *Cosmopolitanism in Context*, Cambridge University Press, Cambridge, 2010. Fassbender presents evidence which indicates that that the UN Charter "has left behind the traditional state-centric view of international law, by gearing its rules to the ultimate goal of the general welfare of peoples and individual beings". B. Fassbender, *The United Nations Charter as the Constitution of the International Community*, Brill, Leiden 2009, p. 102.

67 The Intergovernmental Panel on Climate Change (IPCC) Fourth Assessment Working Group II Report describes Africa as one of the most vulnerable continents to the consequences of climate change. IPCC Fourth Assessment Working Group II Report, Chapter 4, http://www.ipcc.ch/publications_and_data/ar4/wg2/en/contents.html.

68 Para. 3 of Decision 2/CP.15, in Report of the Conference of Parties on its fifteenth session held in Copenhagen from 7 to 19 December 2009, Addendum, Part Two: Action taken by the Conference of the Parties at its fifteenth session, FCCC/CP/2009/11/Add.1 (30 March 2010), para. 95 of Decision 1/CP.16, 'The Cancun Agreements: Outcome of the work of the Ad Hoc Working Group on Long-term Cooperative Action under the Convention', FCCC/CP/2010/7/Add.1 (15 March 2011) [hereinafter The Cancun Agreements (LCA)] and the Preamble of Decision 1/CMP.6, 'The Cancun Agreements: Outcome of the work of the Ad Hoc Working Group on Further Commitments for Annex I Parties under the Kyoto Protocol at its fifteenth session', FCCC/KP/CMP/2010/12/Add.1 (15 March 2011). See W. Scholtz, 'African Vulnerability: Recognition Through a Principle in the International Climate Change Regime' (2011) *South African Yearbook of International Law*, 201–208.

the adoption of Resolution 153.[69] The Preamble of the Resolution "considers" Articles 22 and 24 of the Banjul Charter and accordingly expresses the concern of the Commission that the omission of human rights safeguards in the draft texts of conventions at international climate change negotiations may lead to several negative results for vulnerable people.[70] Articles 22[71] and 24[72] of the Banjul Charter respectively represent the only international binding right to development and the first right to a generally satisfactory environment. This regional African human rights treaty, which reflects the African conception of human rights and takes into account the specific needs of Africa and also includes an array of first (civil and political), second (cultural and social) as well as third (solidarity) generation rights which may be affected by the consequences of climate change.[73]

The extraterritorial dimension of the Banjul Charter may, for example, be conducive to the protection of the human rights of EDPs in Africa. It must be borne in mind that already in 1990 the Intergovernmental Panel on Climate Change has projected that climate change is likely to result in the forced migration of vulnerable people throughout Africa and this may exacerbate the existing dire situation on the African continent, which hosts a large number of refugees and internally displaced persons.[74] The African Union Convention for the Protection and Assistance of Internally Displaced Persons in Africa of

---

69 Resolution on Human Rights and Climate Change and the Need to Study its Impact in Africa, The African Commission on Human Rights and Peoples' Rights, (African Commission), meeting at its 46th Ordinary Session held from 11 to 25 November 2009 in Banjul, The Gambia, http://www.achpr.org/sessions/46th/resolutions/153/.

70 This Resolution was adopted prior to COP 15. This objective of the Commission has not been achieved.

71 This provision reads that "All peoples shall have the right to their economic, social and cultural development with due regard to their freedom and identity and in the equal enjoyment of the common heritage of mankind". The African Commission on Human and People's Rights pronounced on this provision in *Centre for Minority Rights Development (Kenya) and Minority Rights Group International on behalf of Endorois Welfare Council v. Kenya*, Communication 276/2003.

72 This provision states that "All peoples shall have the right to a general satisfactory environment favourable to their development". See Communication 155/96, *Social and Economic Rights Action Centre and another v. Nigeria* (2001) AHRLR 60 (ACHPR 2001) (15th Annual Activity Report), hereafter the *SERAC* Case. See D. Shelton, *Decision Regarding Communication 155/96* (2002) 96 *American Journal of International Law*, 937–943.

73 The tripartite division has become less accepted during the late eighties. The African Commission on Human and People's Rights (ACHPR) has also introduced the conceptualisation of obligations to "promote", "respect", "protect"and "fulfil"in the *SERAC* case. Examples of relevant rights include: the right to life (Art. 4), the right to property (Art. 14), the right to work under equitable and satisfactory conditions (Art. 15) and the right to enjoy the best attainable state of physical and mental health (Art. 16). See for an authoritative discussion on the African human rights system, F. Viljoen, *International Human Rights Law in Africa*, Oxford University Press, Oxford 2012.

74 Africa hosts more than double the number of refugees protected in Europe, North America and Oceania combined. J.C. Hathaway, 'Preface: Can International Refugee Law be made Relevant Again?' in J.C. Hathaway (ed), *Reconceiving International Refugee Law*, Martinus Nijhoff, Leiden 1997, p. xxi.

2009 (Kampala Convention) restricts State Parties' obligation to people that are internally displaced due to climate change.[75] This means that the Kampala Convention does not address trans-border forced migration. The extraterritorial dimension of the Banjul Charter implies that African states need to cooperate in order to jointly realise the human rights of the vulnerable. EDPs are entitled to the right to a satisfactory environment and the right to development irrespective of the fact that they have migrated in order to escape the effects of climate change. Does this mean that African states are responsible for the observance of ESCRs of EDPs all over Africa? Such a construct does not seem to be possible and financial constraints may make it impractical. The extraterritorial dimension of the Banjul Charter may imply that more powerful and industrialised states, such as South Africa may inter alia have a duty of assistance and cooperation towards other African states for the realisation of the right to a satisfactory environment and development. These suggestions may be resisted by states, such as South Africa. However, it is not unthinkable that the African Commission on Human and Peoples Rights[76] may in future be confronted with the alleged breach of the extraterritorial dimension of a solidarity right in the Banjul Charter. This will present an opportunity for the African Commission to engage in a global judicial dialogue[77] in order to contribute to the discourse on human rights and the environment in a progressive manner.

4. CONCLUDING REMARKS

It is important to develop the extraterritorial dimension of human rights in order to ensure that human rights may play an important role in responding to the consequences of global environmental degradation. This contribution deals primarily with the profound challenges concerning the linkages between climate change and the human rights framework.[78] The extraterritorial dimension of economic, social and cultural rights (ESCRs) is of particular importance in this regard. The absence of a jurisdiction clause and provisions concerning international assistance and cooperation in the International Covenant on Economic, Social and Cultural Rights (ICESCR) presents fertile ground for the development of the extraterritorial dimension of ESCRs. I have, however, indicated that this

75 Art. 5 (4) of the Kampala Convention.

76 Part II, Chapter I of the Charter establishes the Organisation of the African Commission on Human and People's Rights (ACHPR) in order to safeguard the protection of human and people's rights in Africa.

77 A-M. Slaughter, 'A Typology of Transjudicial Communication' (1994–1995) 29 *University of Richmond Law Review*, 99.

78 The inclusion of the common concern in the Convention on Biological Diversity implies that this contribution is also of relevance for the relationship between other forms of global environmental degradation and the extension of the extraterritorial dimension of human rights.

development faces several challenges. The major problem is that extraterritorial human rights obligations are not an optimal fit to respond to the complex global nature of climate change since these results in a state-by-state consideration of the extraterritorial effects of state actions. I have therefore analysed the proposal to base the extraterritorial dimension of human rights on the international duty of cooperation. This proposal is also not suitable since it is constrained by the overtly state centric nation thereof. Thus, I have proposed that the Preamble of the UNFCCC may present a point of departure for a solution, which transcends state borders. The Preamble acknowledges "that change in the Earth's climate and its adverse effects are a common concern of humankind". The impact of climate change on the observance of human rights and subsequent response measures may be seen as a common concern, which may induce the development of normative measures in response to the common concern. Common concern is a comprehensive notion which includes current and future state and non-state actors of the international community. The reference to mankind makes provision for a holistic, comprehensive approach that acknowledges the vulnerability of individuals, societies and states. Furthermore, the CCH may contribute to the expansion of legal subjects in international law. As the only full subjects, states are still the most important participants in international law and they are primarily responsible for the well-being of mankind. Common concern also provides for a shared responsibility concerning the observance of human rights. This is in line with the need for collective action to address climate change.[79] Ultimately, CCH may introduce a departure from an overtly state centric approach in order to facilitate the cooperation of the constituents of the international community which could address the dire consequences of global climate change. It is only in this manner that human rights may find universal application pursuant to the well-being of current and future generations of the world.

[79] The failure of the human rights approach to take account of the need for collective action is a major concern of scholars. See, for instance, BODANSKY (note 1), p. 524.

CHAPTER 8

SHAPING THE COMMON INTEREST IN GLOBAL DEVELOPMENT: THE WORLD BANK AND ITS MEMBER STATES AS RESPONSIBLE ACTORS

Ana Sofia Barros*

1. INTRODUCTION

The World Bank's (hereinafter WB) main purpose, as currently defined, is to achieve poverty alleviation through the promotion of economic growth and social equity, all of which entail important human rights dimensions. With a mandate necessarily linked to the pursuit of global sustainable development,[1] the WB can thus be said to contribute to the realization of an interest that is generally perceived as being common to the international community.[2] The concrete human rights obligations governing WB operations – and the attendant international responsibility regime – remain, however, ill-defined. This holds

* Research for this chapter was undertaken with the support of an exchange grant provided by the European Science Foundation (ESF) for a research visit at the University of Helsinki. The author would like to thank Jan Klabbers for useful comments on earlier versions of this text. The present chapter contains elements of a publication co-authored by the present author and C. Ryngaert entitled 'The Position of Member States in (Autonomous) Institutional Decision-Making: Implications for the Establishment of Responsibility' (2014) 11 *International Organizations Law Review* 1 (forthcoming).

1 The notion of development is currently understood as a necessarily sustainable process, including social justice and environmental protection as its core integral components. See inter alia N. Schrijver, The Evolution of Sustainable Development in International Law: Inception, Meaning and Status, Martinus Nijhoff Publishers, Leiden 2008, pp. 64–101, 162–220; C. Voigt, *Sustainable Development as a Principle of International Law: Resolving Conflicts between Climate Measures and WTO Law*, Martinus Nijhoff Publishers, Leiden/Boston 2009, pp. 3–6, 11–55, 160–186.

2 See outcome document of the United Nations Conference on Sustainable Development, 'The future we want', annexed to Resolution adopted by the General Assembly on 27 July 2012, Doc. A/RES/66/288, referring to sustainable development as being a key element among global matters of concern to the international community (paras. 80 and 81) and to the urgent need to address today's global challenges of sustainable development (para. 77).

true for both the Bank and its member states when acting within its framework. Such legal vacuum is quite problematic considering the adverse human rights and environmental impacts that have been, in the last decades, associated with the WB's lending practices, particularly those relating to large infrastructure projects.[3] Current responsibility gaps thus merit careful consideration, as the way in which responsibility is delineated (in a legal regime) and established (through national and international adjudication) is also an important component of the global governance structure through which international organisations and their members contribute to the attainment of the common interest.[4]

The present chapter is based on the premise that a clear international responsibility framework, while accounting for the injurious (human rights) impacts of the WB's sustainable development endeavours, furthers the protection of the common interest. It therefore attempts to conjecture the contours of a legal regime covering the conduct of both the WB and its member states, for responsibility purposes.[5] To that end, sustainable development prescriptions will be explored through the lens of international human rights law, in particular socio-economic and participation rights, in consideration of the fundamental social justice dimension informing the concept of development.[6] As will be shown, the confluence of human rights and development has direct implications on how to interpret the international obligations of both actors and judge their performance. Sustainable development is thus used as a normative concept and an analytical tool, inasmuch as its social justice dimension places respect for the rights of individuals at the centre of development processes – which also entails providing individuals with the means to invoke international responsibility whenever wrongful acts occur in the context of WB operations.

Before discussing the international responsibility of the WB and its member states, the opening section reflects upon their relationship and the roles they

[3] For an overview of well documented negative human rights and environmental impacts see: Human Rights Watch, 'Abuse-Free Development: How the World Bank Should Safeguard Against Human Rights Violations', July 2013, pp. 10 and 30–44.

[4] A. Nollkaemper, 'International adjudication of global public goods: the intersection of substance and procedure' (2012) 23 *European Journal of International Law* 3, 769, 770.

[5] Importantly, the responsibility of both actors emerges as a complement to the responsibility of the borrowing country in the implementation of WB supported projects.

[6] Inasmuch as the present chapter focuses on the impacts of WB operations upon the rights of individuals, it will not directly address the economic, environmental and poverty reduction dimensions of sustainable development, nor the legal framework on which they are underpinned, albeit acknowledging that, from a common interest perspective, a consistent delineation of the responsibility framework governing WB activities would have to thoroughly address such dimensions as well. Given the chapter's purpose of advancing legal arguments towards the invocation, by alleged victims, of WB and member State responsibility, the human rights regime will be emphasized in that it encompasses the main set of international legal procedures through which individuals may seek redress – even where solely environmental harm is at stake, in view of the environmental dimension of human rights.

play as autonomous legal persons in shaping global development – for in order to attribute conduct to one or the other, or both, and thereby determine who is responsible for what, it is first necessary to grasp how their legal distinctness comes about. The human rights responsibilities of both actors are explored in the following sections, by testing them against the general international duty of due diligence. Implying a specific standard of care, due diligence adds an important procedural dimension to the human rights regime, which is particularly relevant in the context of WB development activities. Sections 2 and 3 present a similar structure, by which the general principles of international law for apportioning responsibility are applied to the WB and to its members. Accordingly, the first part of sections 2 and 3 explores the human rights obligations of each development actor, while the second part of both sections investigates attribution criteria. Notwithstanding the interconnectedness of the WB and its member states, implying that one may be held responsible for/in connection with the acts of the other, section 3.2. attempts to show that member state participation in WB undertakings, particularly in its decision-making processes, may, in its own right, entail legal consequences, thereby giving rise to independent state responsibility within the institutional setting offered by the Bank.

2. CONSTRUCTING THE COMMON INTEREST WITHIN THE FRAMEWORK OF THE WORLD BANK

The post-war period witnessed an exponential growth in the creation of international organisations. Various reasons may explain this phenomenon,[7] however, an underlying factor will surely relate to the existence of an interest that is shared by the creators of the organisation and is perceived as being best attained collectively. Accordingly, to carry out tasks that states individually cannot, international institutions are equipped with mechanisms that (purportedly) allow them to pursue their goals with autonomy, and express a 'distinct will' from their members. As international legal persons, organisations (rather than their members) may thus incur responsibility for any wrongful acts attributable to them (see below).

Established in 1944, the WB has become a major actor in economic globalisation, with a mandate that has evolved towards shaping the contours of the fight against poverty and the promotion of sustainable development. To pursue its tasks,

[7] For an account of what motivates states to create international organisations, see K. Abbott and D. Snidal, 'Why States Act through Formal International Organizations' (1998) 42 *Journal of Conflict Resolution* 1, 3–32.

the WB was vested with 'full juridical personality'[8] and created as a corporate-like structure, whereby management is assumed by a president and a large internationally recruited staff, and decisions are made by a collective body in accordance with agreed decision-making rules.[9] Authority is concentrated at the highest level in a Board of Governors (usually composed of finance ministers or heads of the central banks of the member states), whose power can be largely delegated to the Board of Executive Directors.[10]

The Bank's bureaucracy plays a non-negligible role in shaping its development practice:[11] officers prepare the project-related reports on the basis of which the Board makes its loan decisions, establish priorities in project implementation and mobilise resources on the ground. Moreover, they are granted a wide margin to interpret and apply international law norms and principles in the course of the implementation of Bank policies.[12] These decisions may then be reviewed by the Inspection Panel, which assesses the WB's compliance with its operational policies and reports its findings to the Board of Executive Directors.[13] The existence of such an internal accountability mechanism further enhances the authority of the WB as an independent actor on the international scene. Importantly, managerial decisions and Panel reports constitute precedents of how the WB interprets and applies international legal rules and standards in specific cases,[14] thereby contributing to the evolution of international law with regard to complex development issues which range from environmental risk assessment to the rights of indigenous peoples. Hence, the WB can be said to play a significant role in shaping the meaning of global sustainable development.

8 Articles of Agreement of the International Bank for Reconstruction and Development (hereinafter IBRD Articles of Agreement), 2 UNTS 134, 27 December 1945, Art. VII, Section 2. Similarly, Articles of Agreement of the International Development Association, 439 UNTS 249, 24 September 1960, Art. VIII, Section 2; Articles of Agreement of the International Finance Corporation, 264 UNTS 117, 20 July 1956, Art. VI, Section 2; Convention Establishing the Multilateral Investment Guarantee Agency (1988), 1508 UNTS 99, Art. 1 (b).

9 For example, IBRD Articles of Agreement, Art. V.

10 Ibid.

11 As noted by Reinalda and Verbeek, bureaucrats that staff international organisations may have significant influencing power due to their capacity to mobilise technical expertise and raise public awareness, their leadership role in negotiations and agenda-setting capacity. See B. Reinalda and B. Verbeek, 'Policy autonomy of intergovernmental organizations: A challenge to international relations theory?' in R. Collins and N. White (eds), *International Organizations and the Idea of Autonomy: Institutional Independence in the International Legal Order*, Routledge,New York 2011, pp. 95, 96.

12 D. Bradlow, *The Reform of the Governance of the IFIs: A Critical Assessment*, The World Bank Legal Review: International Financial Institutions and Global Legal Governance, 2012, pp. 53 and 54.

13 See Res. IBRD 93-10 and IDA 93-6, from 22 September 1993, establishing the World Bank Inspection Panel, in particular paras. 12 and 22.

14 Bradlow (note 12).

The extent to which an international organisation such as the WB is able to develop policy preferences of its own regarding a particular interest constitutes an important factor for determining its autonomy.[15] In any case, an international organisation can only genuinely act in the *common* interest of all its members – which may coincide with the common interest of the international community as a whole – if it is perceived by the latter as a neutral actor (with regard to individual national interests) and is not subjected to their control.[16] In this light, whilst the international organisation is under an obligation to fulfil its attributed functions, its member states are bound to respect the autonomous performance of such functions and, generically, to act in accordance with the purposes set out in the organisation's constituent instrument.[17] States, *qua* members of the organisation, are thus required to act in good faith so that the 'primacy of common aims over manifestations of excessive individualism by states which are incompatible with them' is guaranteed.[18]

The relationship between the WB (and any international organisation) and its members is not, however, as linear as it would seem. The ambiguous nature of member state participation is mainly owed to the dual capacity with which state representatives, such as the Executive Directors of international financial institutions, act in an institutional setting: on the one hand, they play the role of functionnaries of these organisations and, on the other hand, they represent the interests of their states. That the position of Executive Directors is dichotomous can be concluded from a report prepared by the Independent Evaluation Office of the IMF in 2008, according to which: "[m]ore than half of Board members reported that they occasionally face a conflict between their role as representatives of their authorities and their role in upholding the Fund's institutional interests [...] while in practice all Directors clearly understand their representational role, their status as officers of the Fund is less clear."[19]

---

15 On the autonomy of international organisations see, generally R. Collins and N. White (eds), *International Organizations and the Idea of Autonomy: Institutional Independence in the International Legal Order*, Routledge, London 2011.

16 Haftel and Thompson indicate the concepts of autonomy, neutrality (of interests with respect to other political actors, such as states) and delegation (of authority) as tree key elements in the conceptualization of institutional independence. See Y. Haftel and A. Thompson, 'The Independence of International Organizations: concept and applications' (2006) 50 *The Journal of Conflict Resolution* 2, 255–257.

17 N. White, 'Decision-making', in J. Klabbers and A. Wallendahl (eds), *Research Handbook on the Law of International Organizations*, Edward Elgar, London 2011, pp. 243–245. See also N. Blokker, 'International Organizations and their Members' (2004) 1 *International Organizations Law Review*, 147 and 148.

18 R. Kolb, 'Article 2 (2)', in B. Simma, D. Khan, G. Nolte and A. Paulus (eds), *The Charter of the United Nations: A Commentary*, 3rd ed, Oxford University Press, New York 2012, p. 174, with regard to the obligation of good faith in the framework of the UN Charter.

19 See Independent Evaluation Office Report, 'Governance of the IMF: An Evaluation' (2008), p. 16, http://www.ieo-imf.org/ieo/pages/ CompletedEvaluation110.aspx.

As has been reported, (major) 'shareholders' of the WB seem to sometimes *bypass* the *common* interest and use Bank financing decisions to further their national geo-strategic or commercial objectives instead of basing their choices on development needs or the criteria that is officially declared by the WB.[20] As the WB's shareholders are typically represented by high ranking government officials, the space is there for the pursuit of national preferences to occur within the Bank. While various elements (such as a powerful secretariat) help shape and influence member State behaviour, and while the institution is structured to operate autonomously, there is still a significant leeway for member states to act in accordance with their own preferences.

This goes on to show that the 'institutionalisation' of the common interest in global sustainable development through WB operations cannot be understood without simultaneously accepting the prominence of (its member) states, not only as creators of the organisation,[21] but also as drivers and participants in institutional undertakings. In this light, responsibility issues must be solved by inquiring beyond the 'legal trope'[22] of the Bank's legal personality. As will be seen in section 3, looking underneath the veil of institutional decisions may be required in some instances, in order for the acts of states, as international legal subjects, to be directly assessed on the basis of international (human rights) law.

---

20 A. Clapham, *Human Rights Obligations of Non-State Actors*, Oxford University Press, Oxford 2010, pp. 140–142; C. Tan, 'Mandating Rights and Limiting Mission Creep: Holding the World Bank and the International Monetary Fund Accountable for Human Rights Violations' (2008) *Human Rights and International Legal Discourse*, 79–116, 93. Also, empirical research from 2004 brings to light significant precedents regarding the lending patterns of the financial institutions, concluding that these are influenced by the economic and political interests of their larger shareholders. See R. Faini and E. Grilli, 'Who Runs the IFIs?', Centro Studi Luca D'Agliano, Development Studies Working Papers, No. 191, 2004.

21 As explained by Mikesell, in the course of the Bretton Woods debates, the US pushed for an institutional design whereby it would be able to heavily influence the operations of the financial institutions and thus promote its economic objectives within those frameworks. See R. Mikesel, 'The Bretton Woods Debates: A Memoir', Princeton 1994, as quoted in M. Fratianni and J. Pattison, 'Governance and Conflicts of Interest in International Financial Institutions' in M. Fratianni, P. Savona and J. Kirton (eds), *Corporate, Public and Global Governance: The G8 Contribution*, Ashgate, London 2007, p. 132.

22 D. Bederman 'The Souls of International Organizations: Legal Personality and the Lighthouse at Cape Spartel' (1996) 36 *Virginia Journal of International Law*, 331.

3. THE HUMAN RIGHTS RESPONSIBILITY OF THE WORLD BANK AS A DEVELOPMENT ACTOR

3.1. LEGAL AND POLICY FRAMEWORK

As subjects of international law, international organisations are recognised the capacity to hold rights and duties within the international legal system.[23] These may be identified by resorting to general rules of international law, the treaties to which the organisation has acceded and its constituent instrument.[24] The scope and extent of such rights and obligations is determined on the basis of the specific purposes and competencies expressly or implicitly attributed to the organisation.[25]

In this light, human rights law can be said to apply to the WB, provided that it has obtained the status of custom and general principles of law, and where it can be derived from the interpretation of the Bank's Articles of Agreement. As a specialised agency of the UN, which has entered into relationship agreements with the Economic and Social Council in accordance with Articles 63 and 57 of the UN Charter,[26] the WB is moreover bound to respect the principles and objectives of the UN, where human rights occupy a central character.[27] Importantly, it should be kept in mind that the WB's lending operations are designed to serve a public purpose – and in such exercise of sovereign powers (delegated to the Bank by its founders), the Bank can be said to be subjected to human rights law imperatives.[28]

With respect to the interpretation of the WB's Articles of Agreement, although the aims of the Bank are not expressed in human rights terms, it can be stated that respect for human rights constitutes an integral part of its development objectives and competences.[29] References to the prohibition of both the provision of loans

---

23 ICJ, *Reparation for Injuries Suffered in the Service of the United Nations* (Advisory Opinion), ICJ Reports 1949, p. 174, pp. 178, 179.

24 ICJ, *Interpretation of the Agreement of 25 March 1951 between the WHO and Egypt* (Advisory Opinion), ICJ Reports 1980, p. 73, pp. 89–90.

25 ICJ, *Effects of Awards of Compensation made by the United Nations Administrative* Tribunal (Advisory Opinion), ICJ Reports 1954, p. 47.

26 Agreement Between the United Nations and the International Bank for Reconstruction and Development, 16 UNTS 346 (1948).

27 See Arts. 1, 55 and 56 of the UN Charter. It can be stated that the WB is required to interpret its Articles of Agreement in a manner that is consistent with the human rights provisions contained in the UN Charter, further elaborated by the International Bill of Rights.

28 R. McCorquodale, 'International Organisations and International Human Rights Law: One Giant Leap for Humankind' in K. H. Kaikobad and M. Bohlander (eds), *International Law and Power: Perspectives on Legal Order and Justice*, Martinus Nijhoff, Leiden 2009, pp. 157–160.

29 The consistency of human rights with the WB's mandate has been upheld, albeit cautiously, by different Bank officials in the last decade. See R. Daniño, 'The Legal Aspects of the World Bank's Work on Human Rights: Some Preliminary Thoughts', Human Rights and Development: Towards Mutual Reinforcement, Oxford University Press, Oxford 2005 and

based on considerations other than "economic" ones[30] and the interference in the "political affairs" of states[31] do not invalidate such statement, as they allow for a human-rights oriented interpretation to be made.[32] As a dynamic and living instrument,[33] the Articles of Agreement of the WB should therefore be interpreted in a broad sense, permeable to current perceptions of what the concept of development means and implies. As mentioned above, development is understood as a necessarily sustainable process, which brings with it a core social justice (and thus, human rights) component.

Although, with few exceptions, the policies guiding WB operations do not refer to human rights standards,[34] they can still be read in light of a human rights-based approach to development.[35] Indeed, the Bank's Safeguard Policies include areas such as involuntary resettlement, indigenous peoples and environmental assessment which present a clear human rights dimension, and increasingly emphasise public participation in policy-making.[36] While the human rights-based approach has been developed further at a programmatic level, it is pertinent

A. Palacio, 'The Way Forward: Human Rights and the World Bank', World Bank Special Report, 2006.

30 IBRD Articles of Agreement, Art. III, Section 5(b); IDA Articles of Agreement, Art. V, Section 1(g) and IFC Articles of Agreement, Art. III, Section 9.

31 IBRD Articles of Agreement, Art. IV, Section 10 and IDA Articles of Agreement, Art. V, Section 6.

32 Firstly, human rights considerations fall within the Bank's remit, in that they may have economic effects and therefore impact on its economic decisions. Secondly, the inclusion of the "political prohibition" was aimed at responding to the Bank's need to ensure impartiality in its external policy prescriptions, without prejudice to human rights obligations, as explained in H. Cissé, 'Should the Political Prohibition in Charters of International Financial Institutions Be Revisited? The Case of the World Bank' (2012) 3 *The World Bank Legal Review: International Financial Institutions and Global Legal Governance*, 59 and 60.

33 M. Darrow, *Between Light and Shadow: The World Bank, the International Monetary Fund and International Human Rights Law*, Hart Publishing, Oxford/Portland Oregon 2003, pp. 116–118.

34 The policy on Indigenous Peoples does state that it is aimed at ensuring that the development process fully respects, among others, the human rights of Indigenous Peoples. It includes various provisions whereby this group's rights to land are provided recognition and protection, and processing requirements such as social assessment, consultation and disclosure are envisaged (see OP 4.10, adopted in 2005 and revised in 2013, in particular, paras. 1 and 9–11).

35 For an overview of donor policies embracing a human rights-based approach to development see S. McInerney-Lankford, 'Human Rights and Development: a Comment on Challenges and Opportunities from a Legal Perspective' (2009) 1 *Journal of Human Rights Practice* 1, 62–66. Much has been written about the confluence of human rights and development, and, in particular, the potential of a human rights-based approach to development. See, inter alia OECD/WB, 'Integrating Human Rights into Development: Donor Approaches, Experiences, and Challenges', 2nd ed, 2013; M. Darrow, 'The Millennium Development Goals: Milestones or Millstones? Human Rights Priorities for the Post-2015 Development Agenda' (2012) *Yale Human Rights and Development Law Journal*, 55–127.

36 Respectively, Operational Policies 4.12 on Involuntary Resettlement, 4.10 on Indigenous Peoples (in particular paras. 9–11), 4.01 on Environmental Assessment (in particular para. 14, read in conjunction with para. 8 (a) (b)) and 4.36 on Forestry. See also 'World Bank Policy on Access to Information', from 1 July 2010.

to emphasise its legal dimension: it brings with it the critical notion of duty (and, therefrom, of responsibility), and thus, its specific contribution lies in making development 'good practice and principles *a matter of obligation*'.[37]

The human rights obligations of the WB must therefore be translated in its own practice. At a minimum, the WB has a 'do no harm' duty to ensure that through its loan decisions, development projects, programmes or policy advice it will not negatively interfere with the enjoyment of human rights in borrowing countries, nor undermine the ability of the latter to comply with their human rights obligations.[38] These concerns are, to some extent, already accounted for in the environmental domain: the WB's operational policies on environmental assessment (OP. 4.01) specifically refer to the need to consider the borrower's obligations 'pertaining to project activities, under relevant international environmental treaties and agreements'[39] and determine that the Bank will not finance 'project activities that would contravene such country obligations'.[40] Such systematic approach could therefore inspire any reform towards enhancing the Bank's human rights performance.

The international duty of due diligence merits particular consideration in this context as it introduces a general normative framework with significance for the identification and screening, preparation and appraisal phases of projects and programmes. Aimed at preventing harm, it imposes the identification and assessment of human rights and environmental risks through the systematic use of impact assessments[41] – with particular attention being paid to the needs of

37 McInerney-Lankford (note 35), p. 70.

38 See, for example, the Committee on Economic, Social and Cultural Rights' General Comment No. 18 on the Right to Work, UN Doc. E/C.12/GC/18 (2005), para. 53 and General Comment No. 15 on the Right to Water, UN Doc. E/C.12/2002/11 (2002), para. 60.

39 Operational Policy 4.01 in Environmental Assessment, para. 3.

40 Ibid. For a more detailed account of the WB's approach see: Environment Department of the World Bank, 'International Agreements on Environment and Natural Resources: Relevance and Application in Environmental Assessment', Environmental Assessment Sourcebook and Updates, No. 10, 1996.

41 In the 2010 *ICJ Pulp Mills* Case, the Court asserted that the practice of carrying out environmental impact assessments has in recent years 'gained so much acceptance among states that it may now be considered a requirement under general international law', provided that the activity at stake presents a risk of producing significant adverse environmental impacts. The ICJ moreover asserted that the failure to do so would constitute a violation of 'due diligence, and the duty of vigilance and prevention which it implies'. See Case concerning *Pulp Mills on the River Uruguay (Argentina v. Uruguay)*, (Judgment), ICJ Reports 2010, p. 14, para. 204. While it is true that human rights impact assessments are less well-established, it is noteworthy that in recent years a growing interest in their use has emerged within various UN human rights mechanisms, such as the Committee on the Rights of the Child, the Committee on Economic, Social and Cultural Rights and several UN Special Rapporteurs, as described in a report of the Nordic Trust Fund – the World Bank, 'Study on Human Rights Impact Assessments: A Review of the Literature, Differences with other Forms of Assessments and Relevance for Development', 2013, pp. 4–6.

the most marginalised and vulnerable groups, such as people with disabilities or children.[42] Human rights due diligence requires, as well, a collaborative relationship with the communities affected by WB operations, and meaningful public consultation processes at the stage of standard-setting and project design.[43]

Finally, throughout the implementation phase, due diligence entails constant monitoring tasks by the Bank, so that adverse human rights effects are prevented or at least mitigated. Under such duty, the WB is required to ensure that sub-contractors or consultants responsible for the implementation of projects/programmes do not negatively impact upon the rights of individuals, where it is able to exercise *control* over their actions. Whilst following-up on the borrower's obligations under loan agreements through the supervision of project implementation, the WB must respond to issues of policy compliance as they arise.[44]

Crucially, judicial and non-judicial mechanisms must be set in place to ensure that individuals are able to invoke the WB's failure to comply with its legal and policy framework,[45] as interpreted in light of human rights prescriptions.[46] For remedial action against the WB to be meaningful, individuals should be recognized such entitlement not only on the basis of harm suffered, but also as interested parties in how the achievement of the common interest of sustainable development is being impacted upon by the Bank in a given operation.[47]

42 See UN Committee on the Rights of the Child's General Comment No. 16 on State obligations regarding the impact of the business sector on children's rights, UN Doc. CRC/C/GC/16 (2013), para. 48.

43 A. Ebrahim and S. Herz, 'The World Bank and democratic accountability: the role of civil society' in J. A. Scholte (ed), *Building Global Democracy? Civil Society and Accountable Global Governance*, Cambridge University Press, Cambridge 2011, p. 63.

44 As the Inspection Panel has held, 'the Bank is responsible for putting into place adequate legal covenants in project documents to ensure that all relevant policy requirements will be met, to advise the borrower, and to ensure policy compliance, and in the case of project implementation, to take the necessary steps required by the Bank Policy on Supervision'. See World Bank Inspection Panel, 'Accountability at the World Bank. The World Bank Inspection Panel at 15 Years', 2009, p. 17.

45 See ILA Final Report, 'Accountability of International Organisations', adopted at the Berlin Conference, 2004, at 32–49.

46 The WB's Inspection Panel neither applies human rights law nor is it competent to establish human rights violations. It is thus far from being a human rights accountability mechanism. However, individual claims of human rights violations can still be subjected to its appraisal. For instance, in the Chad-Cameroon pipeline investigation (from 2002), the Panel explicitly considered whether the human rights context in Chad would impede the implementation of the project in a manner consistent with Bank policies, particularly those regarding informed and open consultations (see World Bank Inspection Panel, 'Accountability at the World Bank: The Inspection Panel at 15 Years', 2009, p. 50).

47 This is of course problematic in human rights regimes where the focus of human rights adjudication lies on the rights of victims of a violation. Illustrative of such individualistic perspective is the environmental litigation before the European Court of Human Rights, which has proved ill-suited to deal with the diffused repercussions that harm to the

3.2. ESTABLISHING RESPONSIBILITY

The international legal personality of the WB entails that it may incur responsibility for any wrongful acts attributable to it.[48] The circumstances determining the establishment of responsibility have been laid down in the International Law Commission's (hereinafter ILC) Articles on the Responsibility of International Organizations (hereinafter ARIO).[49] The basic attribution principle is that the acts of the organisations' organs and agents are attributable to it. Where such organs or agents are not connected to the organisation through a formal organic link, acts may still be attributed to the latter if said organs or agents are under its control.[50]

The human rights responsibility of an international organisation may also arise where it aids or assists (Article 14) or directs and controls (Article 15) a State (or another international organisation) in the commission of a wrongful act. 'Aid or assistance' becomes particularly prominent in the context of WB operations, even if it only materialises in a financial way. A typical example of this would be a Bank's lending operation involving a loan for a project where human rights risks had been previously identified and not accounted for, thereby contributing to the commission of human rights violations by the borrowing State.[51] Here, the Bank's responsibility can be invoked for complicity in facilitating projects that violate human rights norms, provided the criteria established in Article 14 are met: the injurious impacts were *known* by the Bank; in using the aid received, the borrower State allowed human rights violations to occur; and the WB was bound by human rights obligations closely akin to the borrower State.

Not surprisingly, such an interpretation of Article 14 ignited considerable concern among international financial institutions. As remarked by the WB in its observations to the ARIO as adopted on first reading in 2009, the provision was 'worrisome' and could 'create a dangerous chilling effect for any international

---

environment has on the collective life of the people living in and around injured areas. See inter alia F. Francioni, 'International Human Rights in an Environmental Horizon' (2010) 21 *The European Journal of International Law* 1, 48–52, providing an overview of case-law in the European and African human rights regimes.

48 See ICJ Reparation for *Injuries* Case (mentioned above, note 23), where the concept of international legal personality was given a central role in the determination of whether or not an international organisation possesses certain rights or responsibilities.

49 Articles on the Responsibility of International Organizations, with commentaries, in Report of the International Law Commission on the Work of its Sixty-Third Session, UNGAOR, 66th Session, Supplement 10, UN. Doc. A/66/10, 2011.

50 See Arts. 6 and 7 of the ARIO.

51 Special Rapporteur Gaja referred to such an example in its 'Eighth report on responsibility of international organizations', Sixty-third session, UN Doc. A/CN.4/640, 2011, p. 17.

financial institution providing economic assistance'.[52] Possibly in order to reduce the risk of the responsibility of these institutions being invoked,[53] the final draft of the commentaries to the ARIO included a reference to the requirement of *intent*, in keeping with the commentaries to the articles on State responsibility (hereinafter ASR).[54] It should however be noted that in the ICJ 2007 *Genocide* case[55] the Court asserted that for complicity to be established, it would have to be proved that the accomplice 'acted knowingly', i.e., 'was aware of the specific intent *(dolus specialis)* of the principal perpetrator', and gave 'support in perpetrating the [wrongful act] with full knowledge of the facts',[56] without however requiring that the *intention* of the principal perpetrator was shared by the accomplice.[57]

The commentaries to Article 14 moreover require that the aid or assistance contribute *significantly* to the commission of the wrongful act,[58] despite ILC Special Rapporteur Gaja's acknowledgment that 'it may be considered as incoherent from a policy perspective'.[59] Indeed, as rightly observed by Reinisch, such a prerequisite is highly undetermined[60] and, in any case, it should not matter whether the aid or assistance is big or small, or whether the violation at stake is one of human rights or of a mere technical rule, as long as there is knowledge of the circumstances of the internationally wrongful act.[61]

52 ILC, Sixty-third session, 'Responsibility of international organizations: Comments and observations received from international organizations', UN Doc. A/CN.4/637, 2011, p. 27.

53 It should be noted that the WB asked the ILC to 'consider expressly indicating, in its commentary to draft Art. [14], that organizations providing financial assistance do not, as a rule, assume the risk that assistance will be used to carry out an international wrong', ibid., p. 28.

54 See the current version of para. (4) of the commentary to Art. 14 ARIO, where reference is made to the commentary to Art. 16 of the Articles on Responsibility of States for Internationally Wrongful Acts, Report of the International Law Commission on the Work of Its Fifty-third Session, UNGAOR, 56th Session, Supplement 10 (A/56/10), 2001.

55 ICJ, *Application of the Convention on the Prevention and Punishment of the Crime of Genocide (Bosnia and Herzegovina v. Serbia and Montenegro),* (Judgment), ICJ Reports 2007, p. 43.

56 Ibid., paras. 421 and 432, respectively.

57 For this reason, Corten and Klein deem the requirement of intent as not adequately reflecting the state of the law. See O. Corten and P. Klein, 'The Limits of Complicity as a Ground for Responsibility: Lessons Learned from the *Corfu Channel* Case' in K. Bannelier, T. Christakis and S. Heathcote (eds), *The ICJ and the Evolution of International Law: The Enduring Impact of the Corfu Channel Case*, Routledge, Abingdon 2012, pp. 329, 330.

58 Para. (4) of the commentary to Art. 14 ARIO.

59 G. Gaja, Special Rapporteur, Eight Report (mentioned note 51), p. 16.

60 Reinisch notes that measuring significance in terms of financing percentages, for example, may not be accurate in that a WB credit may only constitute a small portion in a co-financed project and nevertheless become significant for responsibility purposes in view of the 'seal of approval' often linked to WB financing, triggering financing by other official or private lenders. A. Reinisch, 'Aid or Assistance and Direction and Control between States and International Organizations in the Commission of Internationally Wrongful Acts' (2010) 7 *International Organizations Law Review*, 71.

61 Ibid.

The choices of the ILC undeniably run afoul of the protection of individuals harmed by the activities of international organisations. By introducing a requirement of intent, the ILC opted to set a standard of proof which is unlikely to be met, and particularly questionable when the provision of a good pertaining to the realm of common interests is at stake.[62]

When considering the impacts of WB activities, the determination of wrongfulness should also encompass cases where a subjective-psychological element is not required, and thus, where a breach of an objective standard of behaviour suffices for the establishment of responsibility. Beyond the ARIO framework, the Bank's due diligence obligations referred to above must therefore be recalled. In light of these, harmful conduct perpetrated by private entities responsible for project/programme implementation may also involve the Bank's responsibility for the lack of positive action in preventing or responding to such violations.[63] On the basis of the ICJ decisions in both the *Genocide* case referred above and the earlier *Corfu Channel* case,[64] known as an authority for its interpretation of the due diligence obligation, it is possible to conclude that establishing responsibility for failure to exercise due diligence (see below section 3.2.) is an appropriate avenue to explore as an alternative to resorting to the notion of complicity.[65]

Enforcement of the WB's compliance with its responsibilities raises, of course, major problems: on the one hand, internal accountability mechanisms such as the Inspection Panel or the Compliance Advisor and Ombudsman established by the IFC and the MIGA only have recommendatory powers; on the other hand, external mechanisms, i.e. domestic courts, cannot but grapple with issues of immunity. It is however noteworthy that, contrary to most international organisations which usually enjoy 'full' functional immunity or other extended grants of immunity, the WB's Articles of Agreement envisage the amenability of the WB to suit in national courts.[66] In practice, the scope of immunity depends on how national courts interpret functional immunity – and these, as noted by Reinisch and Wurm, tend to interpret broadly the 'remaining' immunity in order to abstain from adjudicating a certain dispute.[67]

---

62 See Nolkaemper (note 4), pp. 778, 779, stating that procedural rules should arguably operate in more flexible terms when the protection of public goods is at stake.

63 McCorquodale (note 28), p. 158. The due diligence duty will be further explored in the following section concerning member state responsibility.

64 ICJ, *Corfu Channel Case (United Kingdom of Great Britain and Northern Ireland v. Albania)* (Merits), ICJ Reports 1949, p. 4.

65 See the analysis of both cases in Corten and Klein (note 57).

66 See Art. VII, Section 3 of the IBRD Articles of Agreement, Art. VI, Section 3 of the IFC Articles of Agreement and Art. 44 of the MIGA Convention.

67 A. Reinisch and J. Wurm, 'International Financial Institutions before National Courts' in D. Bradlow and D. Hunter (eds), *International Financial Institutions and International Law*, Wolters Kluwer, Austin 2010, pp. 103–135.

The immunity of international organisations should be weighed against the right of individuals of access to justice. According to the jurisprudence that has been developed so far by the European Court of Human Rights (hereinafter ECtHR), waiving the immunity of international organisations might indeed be required in light of the right of access to courts.[68] Noting, however, the inherent jurisdictional limitations of domestic courts under international law, some authors rather emphasise other dispute settlement mechanisms, such as arbitration.[69]

Be it as it may, it is essential to recall that the 'question of immunity from legal process is distinct from the issue of compensation for any damages incurred', as asserted by the ICJ with respect to UN operations.[70] And, in fact, the UN, as well as NATO, have already proved to endorse this understanding, by accepting responsibility for harm caused to individuals in the context of military interventions.[71] The WB should follow suit, when the circumstances so demand – and its image as a responsible actor in shaping the common interest in global sustainable development could only gain in credibility and legitimacy.

4. THE HUMAN RIGHTS RESPONSIBILITY OF MEMBERS IN THE CONTEXT OF WORLD BANK OPERATIONS

4.1. LEGAL FRAMEWORK

When acting within the framework of the WB, lending member states may affect the enjoyment of human rights in borrowing states. Determining the responsibility of the former in such contexts implies that their human rights

[68] See ECHR, *Waite and Kennedy v. Germany*, Application No. 26083/94, ECHR Reports 1999-I, para. 67, where the ECtHR held that: 'where states establish international organisations in order to pursue or strengthen their cooperation in certain fields of activities, and where they attribute to these organisations certain competences and accord them immunities, there may be implications as to the protection of fundamental rights … It should be recalled that the Convention is intended to guarantee not theoretical or illusory rights, but rights that are practical and effective. This is particularly true for the right of access to the courts.' (emphasis added).

[69] R. Martha, 'International Financial Institutions and Claims of Private Parties: Immunity Obliges' in *The World Bank Legal Review: International Financial Institutions and Global Legal Governance* 2012, 92–131.

[70] ICJ, *Difference Relating to Immunity from Legal Process of a Special Rapporteur of the Commission on Human Rights* (Advisory Opinion), ICJ Reports 1999, p. 62, para. 66.

[71] The UN has for example accepted legal liability for its activities in the Congo, as mentioned in the commentary to Art. 36 of the ARIO (note 49). See also C. F. Amerasinghe, *Principles of the Institutional Law of International Organizations*, Cambridge University Press, 2005, pp. 399–402. With regard to NATO, in 2000 it paid compensation to a Bulgarian family for damage to their property by a deflected missile during its military operations against Yugolsavia. See H. Schermers and N. Blokker, *International Institutional Law: Unity Within Diversity*, Martinus Nijhoff Publishers, Leiden 2011, p. 1013.

obligations have an extraterritorial scope of application. This does not mean, however, that any individual wherever in the world somehow impacted upon by State conduct will automatically fall within its jurisdiction. Certain links must therefore be established.

Human rights bodies have mostly dealt with this issue in circumstances of occupation, and military and administrative control over territory or persons abroad. In such instances, where civil and political rights are usually at stake, the existence of (effective) State control has been used as a critical test for the extraterritorial application of human rights obligations.[72] The doctrine of State control may however be too restrictive a test to apply in the framework of economic, social and cultural rights.[73] Indeed, it can hardly be asserted that through their participation in the WB, member states were able to exercise control over, say, indigenous communities that have been forcibly displaced to make way for the construction of a dam. Typically, the extraterritorial applicability of economic, social and cultural rights emerges in situations where state involvement is less direct.[74]

The Committee on Economic, Social and Cultural Rights (hereinafter CESCR) has been particularly vocal, through its General Comments and Concluding Observations, in affirming the extraterritoriality of the obligations contained in the Covenant. In what regards state participation in international organisations, the CESCR has asserted that it should be exercised in conformity with human rights norms,[75] with particular emphasis being placed on the states' obligation

72 Regarding the Human Rights Committee, see *López Burgos v. Uruguay*, Communication No. 52/79, 29 July 1981 and also General Comment No. 31, UN Doc CCPR/C/21/Rev.1/Add.13, 26 May 2004. At the regional level, relevant cases decided by the Inter-American Commission on Human Rights include: *Coard et al. v. United States*, Case No. 10.951, 29 September 1999 and *Armando Alejandre Jr. et al. v. Cuba*, Case No. 11.589, 29 September 1999. As for the European Court of Human Rights, mention should be made to *Loizidou v. Turkey (Merits)*, Application No. 15318/89, 18 December 1996; *Bankovic and Others v. Belgium and 16 other Contracting States*, Application No. 52207/99, 12 December 2001; *Issa and others v. Turkey*, Application No. 31821/96, 16 November 2004; *Ilascu and others v. Moldova and Russia*, Application No. 48787/99, 8 July 2004 and *Al-Skeini and others v. United Kingdom*, Application No. 55721/07, 7 July 2011.

73 S. Nerula, 'International Financial Institutions, Transnational Corporations and Duties of States', in M. Langford, W. Vandenhole, M. Scheinin and W.V. Genugten (eds), *Global Justice, State Duties: The Extraterritorial Scope of Economic, Social, and Cultural Rights in International Law*, Cambridge University Press, Cambridge 2012, pp. 124, 125.

74 M. Heijer and R. Lawson, 'Extraterritorial Human Rights and the Concept of 'Jurisdiction'' in M. Langford et al. (note 73), p. 186.

75 See, for example: General Comment No. 19 on the Right to Social Security, UN Doc. E/C.12/GC/19 (2008), para. 58; General Comment No. 18 on the Right to Work, UN Doc. E/C.12/GC/18 (2005), para. 30; General Comment No. 15 on the Right to Water, UN Doc. E/C.12/2002/11 (2002), para. 36; and General Comment No. 14 on the Right to the Highest Attainable Standard of Health, UN Doc. E/C.12/2000/4 (2000), para. 39.

of international assistance and cooperation,[76] embodied in Article 2 (1) of the Covenant. Essentially, state parties to the Covenant are generally required to 'take due account' of the rights prescribed therein, and to 'ensure' that the operations of international financial institutions 'promote and do not interfere with' those rights.[77]

Short in specific normative guidance, the CESCR's interpretations are in any case worth retaining inasmuch as they assume the extraterritorial reach of the rights contained in the Covenant, and conflate them with the notion of diligent state conduct. Notably, the CESCR highlights the role of states as guarantors of the human rights conformity of the policies and practices of international financial institutions. Indeed, all policy reforms and investment decisions within the WB are approved by member states (through the representation of Government officials), and thus, steering WB performance in a human rights-oriented manner is mainly dependent upon what is prioritised and politically acceptable within and among member states. The question therefore relates to how (member) states use their *power* and *capacity to influence* the institutional behaviour of the WB.[78]

4.2. ESTABLISHING RESPONSIBILITY

Some of the circumstances whereby the WB may be found responsible for internationally wrongful conduct have been discussed above. Establishing WB responsibility does not mean, however, that a finding of member state responsibility for the same, or other, sets of circumstances is thereby excluded.[79]

---

76 The CESCR has advised several state parties that as a member of international financial institutions 'to do all it can to ensure that the policies and decisions of those organizations are in conformity with the obligations of states parties under the Covenant, in particular the obligations […] concerning international assistance and cooperation' (emphasis added). See, for example Concluding observations of the Committee on Economic, Social, and Cultural Rights on the Fourth Report of the U.K. (UN Doc. E/C.12/1/Add.79, para. 26), 5 June 2002.

77 General Comment No. 19 on the Right to Social Security (note 75).

78 As put forward by Heijer and Lawson (note 74), p. 190, an appraisal of available case law on human rights obligations in an extraterritorial context suggests that 'it is not the fact of the affected person having earlier been subjected to the authority of a State, but rather the relationship of the State with a particular set of circumstances being of such a special nature, which is decisive in considering the State to be under a duty to use its influence, knowledge or other resources at its disposal to prevent the manifestation of human rights violations, provided that the State is indeed legally and factually capable to do so'.

79 ILC, Report of the International Law Commission on the Work of its Fifty-fifth Session, UNGAOR, 58th Session, Supplement No. 10 (A/58/10), p. 47, para. 8. Importantly, according to the ILC, only in the case of an intervening act by the member states that influences the commission of a wrongful act by the international organisation (see Arts. 58–62 (1) (a) of the ARIO) can the member state be held responsible. Hence, membership does not entail, as such, the responsibility of states – be it secondary or concurrent – for internationally wrongful acts of the international organisation.

When assessing the position of member states vis-à-vis the WB for responsibility purposes, it is important to recall what has almost become a truism: after having transferred competences to the organisation, member states do not leave their human rights obligations at home.[80] Such an understanding has been particularly emphasised by the ECtHR, according to which: the Convention 'does not exclude the transfer of competences to international organisations provided that Convention rights continue to be 'secured'. Member states 'responsibility therefore continues even after such a transfer'.[81] A fairly adequate criteria has been developed by the Court whereby member states should guarantee that, within the international organisation, human rights receive at least an 'equivalent protection' to that provided by the Convention.[82]

The jurisprudence of the ECtHR suggests that member states are bound by a duty of due diligence, according to which they must ensure that while entrusting an international organisation with certain competences, they will still have at their disposal sufficient tools to oversee the impacts of the organisation's activities on human rights.[83] In practice, such a duty would generally entail that the formulation of strategies, the definition of project-specific standards and the design of inspection mechanisms correspond to the 'equivalent protection' criteria and ensure, at a minimum, that human rights are respected and protected throughout the activities of the WB.[84]

Especially important for the purposes of the present chapter is the way by which member states participate in the Bank's decision-making processes. Among the secondary rules contained in Part Five of the ARIO, both the provisions on 'aid and assistance' (Article 58) and 'direction and control' (Article 59) could be relevant in this context. With regard to the former, in order for the vote to amount to aiding or assisting, it would have to actually facilitate the commission of the wrongful act by the Bank, which implies that the act in question could not have been adopted without the state's vote.[85] As for direction and control, the ILC's

80 It should be mentioned at the outset that any clauses limiting member state liability for the activities of an international organisation, such as the liability clause contained in the IBRD's Articles of Agreement (Art. IV, Section 9), do not apply in the context of human rights violations as they are not opposable to third parties.

81 ECtHR, *Mathews v. the United Kingdom*, Application No. 24833/94, ECHR Reports 1999-I, 12–13, para. 32.

82 See, inter alia, ECtHR *Bosphorus Hava Yollari Turzim Ve Ticaret Anonim Sirketi v. Ireland*, Application No. 45036/98, ECHR Reports 2005-VI, paras. 154–155.

83 Cf. P. Klein, 'The Attribution of Acts to International Organizations' in J. Crawford, A. Pellet and S. Olleson (eds), *The Law of International Responsibility*, Oxford University Press, Oxford 2010, pp. 312–314.

84 M. Salomon, 'International Economic Governance and Human Rights Accountability' in M. Salomon, A. Tostensen and W. Vandenhole (eds), *Casting the Net Wider: Human Rights, Development and New Duty-Bearers*, Intersentia, Antwerp 2007, p.181.

85 Klein (note 83), p. 308.

interpretations of both concepts are rather stringent, and would hardly apply to the relationship between international organisations and their members: on the one hand, 'direction' cannot be understood as mere incitement or suggestion; on the other hand, to establish 'control', it is necessary to prove domination and not simply the exercise of oversight.[86]

The ILC has in any case rejected both hypotheses when it comes to establishing member state responsibility for institutional conduct in the decision-making context, determining that '[an] act by a state member of an international organization done in accordance with the rules of the organization does not as such engage the international responsibility of that state'.[87] The ILC acknowledged, however, that member states are not free to ignore their international obligations, and that any breach committed by them in such capacity could entail their responsibility on the basis of the general international rules on state responsibility.[88] Accordingly, rather than *piercing* the veil of the organisation's decisions, one may have to look *underneath* the institutional veil, and assess member states' voting behaviour as a parallel sphere of conduct meriting legal analysis in its own right. Importantly, such construction allows for the establishment of state responsibility independently from the commission of an internationally wrongful act by the international organisation,[89] whose human rights obligations are far from being equivalent to those of states.

As advanced in section 1, decision-making processes within the Bank are instances whereby the pursuit of member states' preferences can be materialized. In this light, the exercise of voting rights by state representatives – or the assumption of a certain position in consensus decision-making – can be understood as a mechanism through which governmental powers are exercised in the external domain. For instance, with regard to the UK, its policy lines taken at the WB are formally decided in London by the Department for International Development. Based on analytical support from country offices and policy division teams, the Department instructs the UK Delegation when participating in decision-making processes at the Bank.[90] On the basis of such type of examples, it can be stated that the decision of an Executive Director acting under the instructions of his constituency(ies) 'will be held to be an act of his home state'.[91]

86 See para. 7 of the commentaries to Art. 17 of the ASR (note 54). As clarified in para. 2 of the commentaries to Art. 59 of the ARIO, Art. 17 of the ASR served as the basis for Art. 59.

87 Art. 58 (2) and 59 (2) of the ARIO.

88 Para. 5 of the commentary to Art. 58 of the ARIO, which also applies to Art. 59.

89 Except for Art. 61 dealing with circumvention.

90 Bretton Woods Project, 'The UK's role in the World Bank and IMF Department for International Development and HM Treasury', 13 March 2013, http://www.brettonwoodsproject.org/art-537382.

91 I. Seidl-Hohenveldern, 'Responsibility of Member States of an International Organization for the Acts of that Organization' in *Collected Essays on International Investments and on*

It is important to note that while the vote, as such, is to be considered as state conduct, it should be differentiated from the final decision adopted – which emerges as an expression of the international organisation's distinct will. Accordingly, whilst the final decision is attributable to the organisation, the vote is still linked to the member state's own action and is therefore attributable to it.[92]

Surely, member state voting behaviour can only be deemed to breach international law obligations where these prescribe specific courses of State action in an institutional setting. Such a violation was precisely at issue in the 2011 ICJ Case *Application of the Interim Accord of 13 September 1995 (The Former Yugoslav Republic of Macedonia v. Greece).*[93] The contention was based on the non-acceptance of FYROM's candidacy for membership in NATO, due to the opposition of Greece. Among other issues, the ICJ had to determine whether such decision was to be considered as a collective decision taken by NATO (where the unanimity rule applies), or if it should rather be assessed independently of NATO's decision, as an autonomous conduct of the member state – and thus attributable to the latter and not to NATO as a whole. Understanding that the question before it did 'not concern … the conduct of NATO or the member states of NATO, but rather solely the conduct of the Respondent',[94] the ICJ concentrated on Greece's voting behaviour and reviewed it on the basis of the (member) State's own international law obligations, ultimately concluding for a violation of the latter.

Concentrating on the human rights regime, and complementary due diligence prescriptions, it can be claimed that voting (or expressing consent) in favour of a loan where the WB member State has not taken any preventive measures to avoid possible harm, for example, by omitting any consideration of the environmental or human rights impacts of the project at hand, may give rise to state responsibility, for a violation of its positive obligation to exercise due diligence in protecting human rights abroad. In the particular case at stake, a standard of

---

International Organizations, Kluwer, The Hague 1998, p. 66. Albeit rarely upheld in the doctrine, this view has recently been advanced by P. Palchetti, Sulla Responsabilità Di Uno Stato Per Il Voto Espresso In Seno Ad Un Organizzazione Internazionale (2012) XCV *Rivista di Diritto Internazionale*, 354 and 355 and F. Naert, *Binding International Organisations to Member State Treaties or Responsibility of Member States for Their Own Actions in the Framework of International Organisations*, Accountability for Human Rights Violations by International Organisations, Intersentia, Antwerp 2010, pp. 162–166. For a discussion of the interplay between international organisations and their member states in institutional decision-making processes, see A.S. Barros and C. Ryngaert 'The Position of Member States in (Autonomous) Institutional Decision-Making: Implications for the Establishment of Responsibility', (2014) 11 *International Organizations Law Review* 1 (forthcoming).

92 Barros and Ryngaert (note 91).

93 ICJ, *Application of the Interim Accord of 13 September 1995 (The Former Yugoslav Republic of Macedonia v. Greece)* (Judgement), ICJ Reports 2011, p. 644.

94 Ibid., paras. 42 and 43.

care will have to be determined, by questioning whether the state (acting singly or in concert) either *knew* or *should have known* that the adopted decision could result in harmful conduct, and whether it could have reasonably averted it. Such constructive knowledge can be obtained by resorting to the reports prepared by the WB's staff on the basis of which Board members make their loan decisions: for instance, under the Bank's OP 4.01 on Environmental Assessment, referred to above, an evaluation of the environmental impacts of projects proposed for Bank financing is required 'to help ensure that they are environmentally sound and sustainable, and thus to improve decision making'.[95]

Such an understanding is in line with the jurisprudence of the ICJ, as reflected in the *Corfu Channel* Case and the *Genocide* Case aforementioned. In the former, Albania was held responsible for damage inflicted upon two British warships (and concomitant loss of life) which had collided with mines located in Albania's territorial waters. The decision was based on 'elementary considerations of humanity'; 'the principle of the freedom of maritime communication'; and, particularly relevantly, 'every State's obligation not to allow knowingly its territory to be used for acts contrary to the rights of other states'.[96] In light of the latter principle, Albania was found responsible for not having taken all the necessary steps to prevent harm, while it knew, or should have known (due to its close surveillance of the area), about the dangers posed in its territorial waters.[97] In the *Genocide* case, the ICJ described the duty to prevent (genocide) as a duty of conduct, calling for states to 'employ all means reasonably available to them' so as to prevent, as far as possible, a certain violation.[98] The Court interpreted the duty of due diligence as requiring an assessment of the state's 'capacity to influence effectively the action of persons likely to commit, or already committing' the violation and clarified that such capacity could only be determined *in concreto*.[99] Finally, for a state to incur responsibility on this basis, it is enough that the State 'was aware, or should normally have been aware',[100] of the serious danger inherent in the circumstances at stake.

In order to determine the responsibility of states for their voting behaviour, individuals may resort to a judicial review (by the courts of the donor country members) of executive decisions taken by the state entities responsible for directing the vote of the Executive Directors on the Boards of the WB, in light of the states' human rights obligations. Interestingly, member states of the WB

95 See para. 1 of OP 4.01 on Environmental Assessment, from January 1999 and revised on April 2013, http://web.worldbank.org.
96 *Corfu Channel* Case (note 64), p. 22.
97 Ibid., p. 23.
98 *Genocide* Case (note 55), para. 430.
99 Ibid.
100 Ibid., para. 432.

have already adopted national human rights legislation imposing certain duties on the Executive Directors representing them. For instance, the UK Human Rights Act imposes upon all UK government departments the duty to pursue respect for human rights in their work. As a public authority, the Department for International Development is thus bound by the Human Rights Act. According to a Guidance Note on the Human Rights Act issued in 2005,[101] when an act or a failure to act is incompatible with the ECHR, a human rights claim can be brought against the Secretary of State. With regard to the US, a Chapter of the US Code determines that: 'the United States government, in connection with its voice and vote in International Bank for Reconstruction and Development, the International Development Association, the International Finance Corporation [...] shall advance the cause of human rights [...]; 'The United States Executive Directors [...] are authorized and instructed to oppose any loan, any extension of financial assistance, or any technical assistance to any country [...], unless such assistance is directed specifically to programs which serve the basic human needs of the citizens of such country.'[102] In this light, by confronting national instructions with the information placed at the disposal of the Executive Director, it will be possible to conclude whether the required standard of care was respected in that particular occasion. In the end of the day, WB Executive Directors act on the basis of decisions that are taken in the territory of the member states they represent – and, in that sense, the conduct under scrutiny is not, as such, extraterritorial, but only its effects.

Having demonstrated in the previous sub-section that individuals impacted by WB operations fall under the jurisdiction of WB member states, owing to the power of the latter to influence WB performance, one cannot but conclude that WB member states have human rights responsibilities as development actors. The allocation of responsibility among multiple wrongdoing actors is of course not easy to determine: Executive Directors either act in single member constituencies or multiparty constituencies, and the *contribution* of each state to a certain damage may be difficult to assess.[103] Adding the WB to the equation as

---

101 The Human Rights Act: Building a Culture of Respect for Human Rights in DFID, Guidance Note, 2005.

102 US Code, 'Human Rights and United States Assistance policies with international financial institutions', 22 USC para. 262d.

103 As stated in Art. 47 (1) of the ASR (mentioned in note 54), '[w]here several states are responsible for the same internationally wrongful act, the responsibility of each State may be invoked in relation to that act'. This provision could possibly apply in the case of a wrongful vote cast by an Executive Director with a multiparty constituency, thereby engaging the responsibility of each member State independently. The ILC's provision does not however cater for situations where, through separate wrongful acts (i.e., separate votes) the member states contribute to same damage, i.e., damage that is indivisible. According to the terminology used by Nolkaemper and Jacobs, these are cases of shared responsibility stricto sensu. See A. Nolkaemper and D. Jacobs, 'Shared Responsibility in International Law: A Conceptual Framework' (2013) 34 *Michigan Journal of International Law*, 367, 368, 395–397.

a wrongdoer complicates things further. Be that as it may, the problem is not one that should be solved to the detriment of the victims, and thus, it is submitted that the principle of joint and several responsibility should be applied in these circumstances, thereby allowing individuals to invoke the responsibility of either of the joint wrongdoers for the whole or at least part of the damage.[104]

5. CONCLUSION

International law (and, in particular, international human rights law) imperatives dictate that the 'institutionalisation' of the common interest – through the creation of an international legal person such as the WB – be informed by a normative framework whereby: the exercise of powers by the international organisation and its member states is regulated; responsibility is linked to their operations; and access to remedies is provided for. Based on such an understanding, this chapter attempted to provide a clearer picture of how the WB and its member states contribute, each in their own capacity, to shaping the common interest in global sustainable development, for responsibility purposes.

Firstly, a deeper insight into the idiosyncrasies of the relationship between both actors was deemed necessary in order to enable a meaningful discussion regarding the contours of their human rights responsibility. Essentially, member states do not just vanish behind the veil of the legal personality of the international organisation they created. To the contrary, they maintain an active role in institutional undertakings. Accordingly, this chapter aimed to demonstrate that both the WB and its member states, as international legal persons, play important (and legally relevant) roles in the pursuit of global sustainable development. Owing to their power and authority, they are both in a position to impact upon the achievement of such common interest, and none can be fully responsible for it.

Sections 2 and 3 attempted to shed some light on how the human rights regime feeds into the operations of the WB and its member states. Based on the normative framework introduced by the due diligence principle, the human rights obligations of both actors were mainly discussed in their procedural dimension, which provides a practical and concrete framework against which their conduct may be judged. Next to this, attention was drawn to the circumstances under which the WB and its member states may be found responsible for internationally wrongful conduct. As the WB and its members are deeply implicated in the conduct of one another, each actor's responsibility can be established for/in connection with

104 On the meaning and implications of the principle, see Nolkaemper and Jacobs, ibid., pp. 422, 423, 428, 429.

the acts of the other, as the examples of shared responsibility, such as 'aid and assistance', demonstrate. This does not mean, however, that member State conduct cannot, in some instances, be evaluated in its own right. In fact, when it comes to member State participation in decision-making processes, the chapter purported to highlight that whenever State responsibility arises in these contexts, the act that is attributed to it is its own conduct (or abstention), and not the wrongful act of the WB – the only particularity being that the State's wrongful act was adopted in direct relation with the activities of the WB.

CHAPTER 9

THE COMMON INTEREST IN THE PROTECTION OF THE INTERNET: AN INTERNATIONAL LEGAL PERSPECTIVE

Matthias C. Kettemann

1. INTRODUCTION

During the general debate of the 68th session of the UN General Assembly in 2013, Dilma Rousseff, President of Brazil, chastised the United States of America for its surveillance programs that had targeted, inter alia, Brazilian citizens, Brazilian companies, the office of the President herself and communications of the Brazilian Permanent Mission to the UN in New York. "In the absence of the right to privacy, there can be no true freedom of expression and opinion", she said, "and therefore no effective democracy. In the absence of the respect for sovereignty, there is no basis for the relationship among Nations".[1] The situation represented both a "grave violation of human rights and of civil liberties [...] and especially of disrespect to national sovereignty".[2]

President Rousseff thus pointed out that both human rights, guaranteed by international law, and a traditional principle of international law, national sovereignty, were violated through the misuse of information and communication technologies (ICTs) by a state that had until then exercised its historical role as 'steward' of the Internet rather carefully: the USA.[3] Rightly presupposing that

[1] Statement by D. Rousseff, President of Brazil, UNGA, General Debate of the 68th Session, 24 September 2013, http://gadebate.un.org/68/brazil (report), http://gadebate.un.org/sites/default/files/gastatements/68/BR_en.pdf (document).

[2] Ibid.

[3] Whereas the EU Commission also sees the US as the Internet's steward (European Commission, Press Release, 12 February 2014, Commission to pursue role as honest broker in future global negotiations on Internet Governance, http://europa.eu/rapid/press-release_IP-14-142_en.htm), ICANN itself considers that the naming and addressing organizations, together with other actors, have "a shared or entangled responsibility for the stewardship of the common

international law applied to Internet governance,[4] Rousseff called for the United Nations to "play a leading role in the effort to regulate the conduct of states with regard to these technologies". She announced proposals "for the establishment of a civilian multilateral framework for the governance and use of the Internet and to ensure the effective protection of data that travels through the web". Such a "multilateral mechanism []" needed to ensure, inter alia, the protection of human rights, "open, multilateral and democratic governance", universality, cultural diversity and network neutrality.[5]

Her ideas were not new. There is a growing concern with realizing the promises of ICTs, and the Internet on which they run, for human rights, human security and human development. Especially as the first decade after the key World Summit on Information Society (WSIS) process of 2003–2005 comes to an end, the speed and normative intensity of policy developments related to the Internet, its regulation and governance, have notably intensified.[6]

Attempts to develop principles for Internet Governance abound.[7] Between 2010 and 2014 more than 25 declarations of Internet Governance principles have been published.[8] Key international organizations,[9] states[10] and civil

---

Internet infrastructure", cf. V.G. Cerf (Chair) et al., *ICANN's Role in the Internet Governance Ecosystem*, Report of the ICANN Strategy Panel, 20 February 2014, http://www.icann.org/en/about/ planning/strategic-engagement/governance-ecosystem/report-20feb14-en.pdf, 5.

4 Cf. Report of the Group of Governmental Experts on Developments in the Field of Information and Telecommunications in the Context of International Security, UN Doc. A/68/98 of 24 June 2013, para. 16.

5 Cf. Rousseff (note 1).

6 Internet Governance has been defined by the Working Group on Internet Governance as "the development and application by Governments, the private sector and civil society, in their respective roles, of shared principles, norms, rules, decision-making procedures, and programmes that shape the evolution and use of the Internet", Report of the Working Group on Internet Governance (2005), http://www.wgig.org/docs/WGIGREPORT.pdf.

7 Cf. M.C. Kettemann, *The Future of Individuals in International Law. Lessons from International Internet Law*, Eleven International Publishing, Utrecht 2013, pp. 126–128.

8 Cf. J. Baak and C. Rossini, *Issue Comparison of Major Declarations on Internet Freedom* (2013), http://bestbits.net/issue-comparison-of-major-declarations-on-internet-freedom.

9 For the UN, see UN General Assembly, Res. 67/195 of 21 December 2012, Information and communications technologies for development, UN Doc. A/RES/67/195 of 5 February 2013; for the EU, see European Commission, Communication from the Commission to the European Parliament, the European Economic and Social Committee and the Committee of the Regions, Internet Policy and Governance. Europe's role in shaping the future of Internet Governance, COM(2014) 72/4, http://ec.europa.eu/information_society/newsroom/cf/dae/document.cfm?doc_id=4453; for the Council of Europe, see Council of Europe, Internet Governance, Council of Europe Strategy 2012–2015, CM(2011)175 final of 15 March 2012, http://www.coe.int/t/dghl/cooperation/economiccrime/cybercrime/Documents/Internet%20Governance%20Strategy/Internet%20Governance%20Strategy%202012%20-%202015.pdf.

10 For the US, see US Department of State, 'Internet Governance 2020 – Geopolitics and the Future of the Internet', Remarks by Ambassador D.A. Sepulveda, U.S. Coordinator for International Communications and Information Policy, Bureau of Economic and Business Affairs, Department of State, Washington, DC, 23 January 2014, http://www.state.gov/e/eb/rls/rm/2014/220576.htm; for Germany, see Germany, Federal Foreign

society[11] and private sector[12] entities have submitted principles for Internet Governance. ICANN, the Internet's naming and addressing organization that manages key Internet resources, such as the Domain Name System and the root zone server under a contract with the US Department of Commerce, suggests its own globalisation in order to counter accountability deficits.[13] High-level committees[14] are engaged with the future of Internet governance and dynamic coalitions of international actors, including standard-setting bodies, individual states, the private sector and civil society representatives come together in multistakeholder conferences to discuss roadmaps for Internet governance.

The normative dynamization of the Internet's governance, however, suffers a key problem: The principles proposed by various actors are very diverse. They contain an eclectic mix of architectural principles, restatements of international law, references to human rights, and policy priorities. Consensus on a single set of principles is difficult to establish though the Multistakeholder Statement,[15] adopted by rough consensus at the conclusion of the Global Multistakeholder Meeting on the Future of Internet Governance, NetMundial, in late April 2014, is an important step towards common principles that transcend limited stakeholder interests. When presenting the Communication of the European Commission outlining the EU's policy approach to Internet Governance, Commission Vice-President Neelie Kroes underlined that "[t]he next two years will be critical in redrawing the global map of Internet governance".[16] This exercise – and the development and selection of principles – is premised upon a key assumption:

Office, Commissioner for International Cyber Policy, German Government Proposal on Global Internet Principles (February 2014), http://content.netmundial.br/contribution/german-government-proposal-on-global-internet-principles/32.

11 Cf. Internet Rights and Principles Coalition, Charter on Human Rights and Principles for the Internet (2011), http://internetrightsandprinciples.org/site/charter; and Necessary and Proportionate (2013), International Principles on the Application of Human Rights to Communications Surveillance, https://en.necessaryandproportionate.org/text.

12 Cf. IETF/IAB/W3C/ICANN et al., Montevideo Statement on the Future of Internet Cooperation, 7 October 2013, http://www.icann.org/en/news/announcements/announcement-07oct13-en.htm.

13 Cf. Special Meeting of the ICANN Board, 17 February 2014, Res. 2014.02.17.01 on President's Globalization Advisory Groups, http://www.icann.org/en/groups/board/documents/resolutions-17feb14-en.htm.

14 The two are the *Global Commission on Internet Governance*, https://www.ourinternet.org, and the *Panel on Global Internet Cooperation and Governance Mechanisms*. The latter has published its final report in May 2014, see 'Towards a Collaborative, Decentralized Internet Governance Ecosystem', Report by the Panel on Global Internet Cooperation and Governance Mechanisms, 2014, http://internetgovernancepanel.org/sites/default/files/ipdf/XPL_ICAN1403_Internet%20Governance%20iPDF_06.pdf.

15 NetMundial, NetMundial Multistakeholder Statement, 24 April 2014, http://netmundial.br/wp-content/uploads/2014/04/NETmundial-Multistakeholder-Document.pdf.

16 European Commission, Press Release, 12 February 2014, 'Commission to pursue role as honest broker in future global negotiations on Internet Governance', http://europa.eu/rapid/press-release_IP-14-142_en.htm.

that regulating and governing the Internet is somehow related to issues of global common interest.

The assumption is correct. Over the following section I will show why protecting the integrity of the Internet really lies in the global common interest.[17] I will do so in five steps: After defining what the Internet is (2), I will show that both the physical and the non-physical aspects of the Internet need to be protected as they are critical to its integrity (security, stability, resilience and functionality) (3). The protection of the Internet's integrity lies in the global common interest because it is essential for international peace and security, human rights, human security and human development (4). This has implications both for international law as it relates to the Internet and for Internet governance (5).

2. WHAT IS THE INTERNET?

"The Internet is that medium through which your e-mail is delivered and web pages get published", wrote Harvard law professor Lawrence Lessig in his definition of the Internet which resonates with most users, "[i]t's what you use to order books on Amazon [...]".[18] More technically, the Internet can be defined as

> [the] global data communication capability realized by the interconnection of public and private telecommunication networks using Internet Protocol (IP), Transmission Control Protocol (TCP), and the other protocols required to implement IP internetworking on a global scale, such as DNS and packet routing protocols.[19]

The Internet is a system, or network, of *inter*connected computer *net*works (hence the term *Internet*) that use a certain standard protocol (TCP/IP) to communicate. The connected networks are private and public, commercial and military. They are linked to each other through different technologies. When we say that we 'go on the Internet', we usually mean that we send emails, open our browser to access a page on the World Wide Web (WWW), use a hyperlink that connects

17 While I find Christina Voigt's arguments regarding the differences between common interest and common concern (See Ch. Voigt in this volume, chapter 1) very interesting, I do not subscribe to her conclusions regarding the differentiated legal consequences, to wit: common interests require international commitments, common concerns require coordinated action. I will argue that finding something to lie in the global common *interest* has international legal consequences and it is unnecessary to further show that there is also global 'concern' relating to it.

18 L. Lessig, *Code: Version 2.0*, Basic Books, New York 2007, p. 9.

19 M. Mueller, J. Mathiason and H. Klein, 'The Internet and Global Governance: Principles and Norms for a New Regime' (2007) 13 *Global Governance*, 237–254 (245). See also J. Mathiason, *Internet Governance: The New Frontier of Global Institutions*, Routledge, London 2008, p. 11.

one website to another or play an online game. Mail programmes, WWW, and online games are layered on top of the Internet as services of the Internet. The Internet enables them and its stability (actually, the stability of its naming and addressing system) ensures that we can use them.

We need to remember though that the Internet is essentially software that ensures *inter*connectivity, that is connectivity between largely privately owned and operated networks. Of course, the Internet needs physical infrastructure to run, but it does not 'consist' of it. However, without the physical infrastructure the Internet would not be able to function.[20] The Internet is not like the 'environment' or the 'sea' in that it was created by humans with a distinct purpose in mind. It is not an entity that, if left alone, would thrive on its own according to natural laws.

3. WHAT NEEDS TO BE PROTECTED?

Both the kinetic and the non-kinetic elements of the Internet are critical for our societies. The maintenance of vital state functions – such as ensuring energy security, defense, well-communicating emergency services – without a stable and secure communications infrastructure is impossible in today's highly technical world. The Internet is thus critical for itself and essential for the effective operation of other critical infrastructure.[21] Protecting the security, stability, robustness, resilience and functionality (thus: the integrity) of the Internet is an issue of critical information infrastructure protection. But what 'part' or 'dimension' of the Internet needs protection for it to function in light of its criticality for modern society?

What needs to be protected for the Internet to function effectively is made visible through the thought experiment of "destroying the Internet".[22] Such an attempt would be impossible because of the multiple redundancies built into the infrastructure.[23] Nevertheless, if one were to entertain the notion, an article suggests the following three steps: cutting the transcontinental Internet cables, disabling the root servers and destroying the data centers containing the physical data. The cables, the actual root servers, and the data centers are aspects of the Internet's physicality and need to be protected. They are thus critical Internet resources (CIR) – but not the only ones.

---

20 Cf. MUELLER et al. (note 19), p. 244.

21 Cf. European Commission, *Green Paper on a European Programme for Critical Infrastructure Protection*, COM(2005) 576 final, 17 November 2005, p. 19.

22 S. BIDDLE, 'How to Destroy the Internet', 23 May 2012, *Gizmodo*, http://gizmodo.com/5912383/how-to-destroy-the-internet.

23 Cf. ibid., *We just built it too well.*

For the Internet to function properly, non-kinetic Internet resources are to be protected as well. Non-kinetic CIRs include names and numbers (numerical addresses),[24] the addressing system that ensures they are properly resolved (i.e. decoded), the technical standards that ensure communication and the routing system. Protecting 'the Internet' thus also means protecting its kinetic and non-kinetic critical Internet resources. That these are largely controlled by private actors makes finding internationally acceptable principles to manage and govern them difficult,[25] but this lies outside the scope of this contribution.[26]

The Internet's integrity can be endangered by attacks against its kinetic resources, its key non-kinetic resources and by state efforts to exercise control over the Internet (censorship, blocking) or by governmentally ordered blackouts. The most effective "kill-switch" for the Internet thus lies less in its technical infrastructure alone than in a combination of control over physical infrastructure, such as servers, and institutional-legal authority.[27] As the example of Egypt in 2011 shows, Internet service providers could (technical vulnerability) and were ordered to (institutional vulernability) disable Internet connections to and from Egypt.[28] In a study on the 'dark side' of Internet governance, Laura DeNardis identifies eight levels of control of the Internet that can be attacked or interrupted unintentionally or through natural events.[29] These can be stratified according to four key aspects the Internet's integrity is meant to ensure: the Internet's basic functionality; access through a working addressing and routing system; communication and information through applications based on protocols ('use'); and transactions or transactionary functionality (see table 1).

---

24 L. DeNardis, Internet Points of Control as Global Governance (2013) 2 *CIGI Internet Governance Paper*, http://www.cigionline.org/publications/2013/8/internet-points-of-control-global-governance, p. 3.

25 Cf. M. Mueller, 'Ruling the Root: Internet Governance and the Taming of Cyberspace' (2002) *MIT Press*, Cambridge.

26 But see W. Drake, *Reforming Internet Governance: Perspectives from the Working Group on Internet Governance*, UN Publications, New York 2008; J. Mathiason, *Internet Governance: The New Frontier of Global Institutions*, Routledge, London 2008; R.H. Weber, *Shaping Internet Governance: Regulatory Challenges*, Springer, Vienna/New York 2009; E. Brousseau, M. Marzouki and C. Méadel, *Governance, Regulation, and Powers on the Internet*, Cambridge University Press, Cambridge 2012; L. DeNardis, *The Global War for Internet Governance*, Yale University Press, New Haven and London 2014.

27 Cf. DeNardis (note 26), p. 211.

28 Cf. M.C. Kettemann, 'Das Internet als internationales Schutzgut: Entwicklungsperspektiven des Internetvölkerrechts anlässlich des Arabischen Frühlings' (2012) 72 *Zeitschrift für ausländisches öffentliches Recht und Völkerrecht*, 469–548 (470).

29 Cf. DeNardis (note 26), p. 209.

Table 1. Internet Vulnerabilities[30]

Goal	Control question	Vulnerability	Attack vector
Functionality	Does the Internet work?	Physical infrastructure	undersea cables, power systems
		Institution-level outage	ISP service termination; cellular service disruption
Access	Can I access specific sites?	Domain Name System	DNS filtering, registries and registrars
		Switching-level infrastructure	routing infrastructure, IXPs
Use	Is my content transmitted?	Network management-disruptions	DDos attacks, DPI filtering
		Application-level blocking	email, social media sites, Skype
		Protocol-level blocking	VoIP, HTTP
Transactions	Can I pay for services?	Financial and transactional services outages	credit card transactions, payment systems

We thus see that apart from ensuring the security of the kinetic and non-kinetic resources of the Internet, we need to establish a *normative framework* regulating the behaviour of states and Internet content and access intermediaries (including Internet access providers and news portals, search engines and social networks) that ensures no actor negatively impacts the Internet's integrity. This, of course, raises the question of 'which' Internet should be protected and which interests should be prioritized: those of companies, of states, of individuals? Or only shared interests? Which Internet do we want: one that allows the efficient pursuance of economic interests of companies through swift broadband connectivity for all? One that provides a human rights-sensitive space for self-actualization of humans?[31] Or one that, as China and Russia argued in a 2011 letter to the UN Secretary-General, that allows states to "curb [...] dissemination of information which [...] undermines other countries' political, economic and social stability, as well as their spiritual and cultural environment"?[32]

This brings us to an essential finding: that the question 'which Internet' we want is wrong. The Internet has no sublime essence.[33] There is no intrinsic value to

30 Based on Figure 9.1., 'Inter Control Points Susceptible to Intentional or Unintentional Disruptions' (ibid.).

31 Special Rapporteur on the promotion and protection of the right to freedom of opinion and expression, F. La Rue, 'Promotion and protection of the right to freedom of opinion and expression', UN Doc. A/66/290 of 10 August 2011, http://www.ohchr.org/Documents/Issues/Opinion/A.66.290.pdf, para. 10.

32 Cf. Letter dated 12 September 2011 from the Permanent Representatives of China, the Russian Federation, Tajikistan and Uzbekistan to the United Nations addressed to the Secretary-General, UN Doc. A/66/359 of 14 September 2011, http://www.fmprc.gov.cn/eng/wjdt/wshd/t858978.htm, para. 3.

33 But see V. Mosco, *The Digital Sublime: Myth, Power, and Cyberspace*, MA: MIT Press, Cambridge 2005.

the Internet. The protection of the Internet's integrity is *functional*. We therefore have to ask, where the international community 'wants to go' with the Internet. In order to find an answer to this question we can rely on the one normative order that regulates issues lying in the global common interest: international law. The ultimate unit of international law is the person and it is in their interest that international law protects the integrity of the Internet. But what are the consequences of such a finding? Why exactly does protecting the Internet's integrity lie in the global common interest? This brings us to my next section.

4. PROTECTING THE INTEGRITY OF THE INTERNET LIES IN THE GLOBAL COMMON INTEREST

In 1998, experts working on behalf of the UNESCO posed the question whether the "United Nations General Assembly [could] affirm the principle of regarding cyberspace as 'the common heritage of humanity'"[34] and thus safeguard it. They failed to answer the question, which was well enough because it was the wrong one. It is not 'cyberspace' we should concern ourselves with, but rather the Internet itself; and rather than using the concept of common heritage of mankind, which presupposes a certain historical stability the Internet does not have, we rather need to firmly establish the reasons for why protecting the Internet actually lies in the global common interest.

During the World Summit on the Information Society (WSIS), which the UN convened in 2003 and 2005 to establish a normative trajectory for the Internet, states affirmed their common desire and commitment to build an information society that is "people-centred, inclusive and development-oriented" and in which individuals, communities and peoples can "achieve their full potential in promoting their sustainable development and improving their quality of life premised on the purposes and principles of the Charter of the United Nations and respecting fully and upholding the Universal Declaration of Human Rights".[35] We have here a first, clear answer to the question what 'vision' the international community pursues regarding the impact of the Internet.

Clearly, achieving world peace and international security (as enshrined in the UN Charter), ensuring human development (as codified in the Millennium Develop Goals and the Sustainable Development Goals) and respecting, protecting and implementing human rights (as normatively ordered in the UDHR) are in the

[34] UNESCO, Report of the Experts' Meeting on Cyberspace Law, Monte Carlo 29–30 September 1998, http://unesdoc.unesco.org/images/0011/001163/116300e.pdf, para. 9.

[35] WSIS, Geneva Declaration of Principles (2003), WSIS-03/GENEVA/DOC/4-E, 12 December 2003, para. 1.

global common interest. Different normative orders within international law contribute towards achieving these common interests. By establishing finalities for a normative order, such as WSIS has done for Internet governance, the normative development of that order is anchored in the finality of ensuring the common interest lying in peace, security and development. Creating a people-centred, development-oriented information society is thus part of the broader normative commitment in international law to protecting the common interest that is reflected in the concepts of international peace and security, the protection of human rights and the commitment to human development.[36]

We have thus established that there is a global common interest in ensuring a people-centred and development-oriented information society. But is protecting the Internet's integrity essential for reaching these goals? I will show that it is by detailing the impact of the protection of the Internet on human rights and development, economic growth, international security and cybercrime.

UN Special Rapporteur for freedom of expression, Frank La Rue, in a groundbreaking report on the impact of the Internet on freedom of expression, described the Internet as a "catalyst for individuals to exercise their right to freedom of opinion and expression". Freedom of expression on the Internet itself is a "facilitator of the realisation of a range of other human rights".[37] The multiple challenges that the Internet brings for human rights notwithstanding,[38] the absence of the Internet would seriously challenge the realization of human rights. There are important corollary rights that are premised upon exercising free speech on the Internet. These include the freedom of assembly and association online, the right to (digital) education and the right of access to digital knowledge.[39] From all these rights we can also derive a right to access to online information and communication which is crucial for human development.[40]

---

36 If one accepts Voigt's argument that only sustainable development is "*the* common interest of the 21st century" (and should, according to her, develop into "*the* common concern of the 21st century"), the same conclusion can be drawn. A people-centred, development-oriented information society contributes to sustainable development. Sustainable development is in the (or *the*) common interest. Thus governance approaches ensuring that information society is people-centred and development-oriented are also in the common interest.

37 F. La Rue, Report of the Special Rapporteur on the promotion and protection of the right to freedom of opinion and expression, UN Doc. A/HRC/17/27 of 16 May 2011, paras. 22 and 23.

38 See already R.F. Jørgensen (ed), *Human Rights in the Global Information Society*, MIT Press, Cambridge 2006; but also R. Deibert, J. Palfrey, R. Rohozinski and J. Zittrain (eds), *Access Controlled: The Shaping of Power, Rights, and Rule in Cyberspace*, MIT Press, Cambridge 2010; R. MacKinnon, *Consent of the Networked: The Worldwide Struggle for Internet Freedom*, Basic Books, New York 2012.

39 Cf. W. Benedek and M.C. Kettemann, *Freedom of Expression and the Internet*, Council of Europe, Strasbourg 2014.

40 Cf. St. Tully, 'A Human Right to Access the Internet? Problems and Prospects' (2014) *Human Rights Law Review*, 175–195.

Similar arguments have been voiced by courts and international organizations.[41] The Internet introduces new threat vectors to human rights, but greatly enhances the potential of people to realize their human rights. It is similarly a facilitator for human security.

The concept of human security deemphasizes the role of states as (the only) providers and referents of security. The United Nations have committed to the concept,[42] which the 2010 Secretary-General's report on human security describes as providing for "people-centred, comprehensive, context-specific and preventive responses" that "focus attention on current and emerging threats".[43] Human security approaches favour multistakeholder, bottom-up responses to threats and are targeted at protecting and empowering people and communities. The stability, security and functionality of the Internet is essential for certain aspects of human security. In light of the informationalization of critical infrastructure, and the character of the Internet as critical information infrastructure in its own right, serious threats to the security, stability and the functionality of the Internet can endanger human security.[44]

A similar case can be made with regard to human development. The General Assembly, in a 2012 resolution on ICTs and development,[45] acknowledged the "positive trends in the global connectivity and affordability of information and communications technologies, in particular the steady increase in Internet access to one third of the world's population" and reaffirmed the need to harness the potential of ICTs to promote achieving the MDGs "through sustained, inclusive and equitable economic growth and sustainable development". The General Assembly confirmed that ICTs have the

41 Cf. ECtHR, *Yildirim v. Turkey*, Application No. 3111/10, ECHR Reports 2012; Council of Europe, Parliamentary Assembly Res. 1877 (2012) on the protection of freedom of expression and information on the Internet and online media.

42 Cf. UN Press Release, General Assembly President Calls for New Culture of International Relations, with Principle of Human Security at its Core, During Day-long Debate, UN Doc. GA/10711 (2008), 22 May 2008, http://www.un.org/News/Press/docs/2008/ga 10711.doc.htm.

43 Cf. UN Secretary-General, Human Security. Report of the Secretary-General, UN Doc. A/64/701, 8 March 2001, para. 69.

44 The concept is also interesting in another light: human security approaches treat state failure and state fragility as serious threats to human security just as securitization by states (Cf. W. Benedek, 'Mainstreaming Human Security in United Nations and European Union Peace and Crisis Management Operations: Policies and Practice' in W. Benedek, M.C. Kettemann and M. Moestl (eds), *Mainstreaming Human Security in Peace Operations and Crisis Management. Policies, Problems, Potential*, Routledge, London 2010, pp. 13–31). Similarly a lack of regulation or regulatory failure can endanger the security of the Internet just as much as state overreach and nationalization of critical Internet resources.

45 UN General Assembly, Res. 67/195 of 21 December 2012, *Information and communications technologies for development*, UN Doc. A/RES/67/195 of 5 February 2013.

> [p]otential to provide new solutions to development challenges, particularly in the context of globalization, and can foster sustained, inclusive and equitable economic growth and sustainable development, competitiveness, access to information and knowledge, poverty eradication and social inclusion that will help to expedite the integration of all countries, especially developing countries, in particular the least developed countries, into the global economy.[46]

This reaffirms the commitment, already in the WSIS process, to the importance of development. It is difficult to empirically prove the positive impact of the Internet or of ICTs on human development because numerous other factors influence causality. Merely finding correlations between ICT use, as measured e.g. by Internet penetration, and development, measured e.g. by the Human Development Index, is unsatisfactory as well. It may well be impossible to scientifically establish a causal relationship between the increased use of ICTs and the elimination of absolute poverty, because of the complexity of the use of technology and its impact, because of the lack of useful data and because levels of absolute poverty are worryingly resistant.[47] A 2009 study by the Boston Consulting Group (BCG) on behalf of Telenor exemplifies these problems. The study concentrates on GDP growth arguing that a "10 percentage points increase in Internet penetration is *correlated* with a 1% increase in the annual rate of new business formation"[48] (my emphasis).

Development is more than GDP increases and new businesses. It is also more than the elimination of absolute poverty, namely the reduction of relative poverty and, more importantly, the increased freedom of people to realize their capabilities.[49] But even with a critical perception of the concrete impact of ICTs for development we can accept, with the United Nations and its Human Rights Council, that the potential of the Internet for development is great.[50] The importance of the Internet for development was affirmed by the latter in Human Rights Council Resolution 20/8 (2012)[51] and reaffirmed in Resolution 26/13 (2014), which recognized the globality and openness of the Internet as a "driving force in accelerating progress

46 Ibid., para. 1.

47 Cf. T. Unwin, *ICT4D: Information and Communication Technologies for Development*, Cambridge University Press, Cambridge 2009. Cf. also T. Unwin, 'The Internet and Development: A Critical Perspective' in W.H. Dutton (ed), *The Oxford Handbook of Internet Studies*, Oxford University Press, Oxford 2013, pp. 531–554, 533 (criticizing that most ICT-related studies are based on the "dominant hegemonic model of development").

48 Telenor/Boston Consulting Group, *Towards a Connected World. Socio-Economic Impact of Internet in Emerging and Developing Economies*, 2009, p. 7.

49 Cf. A. Sen, *Development as Freedom*, Oxford University Press, Oxford 1999.

50 Cf. Unwin (note 47), p. 549.

51 Human Rights Council, Res. 20/8, *The promotion, protection and enjoyment of human rights on the Internet*, UN Doc. A/HRC/RES/20/9 of 16 July 2012, para. 2.

towards development in its various forms".[52] The 2014 Resolution also called upon states to "address security concerns on the Internet in accordance with their international human rights obligations" so that the Internet remains free and secure and can continue to be a "vibrant force that generates economic, social and cultural development".[53] The HRC also confirmed the connection between development, human rights and the Internet by committing itself, in the 2012 Resolution, to further studying how the Internet can be an "important tool for development and for exercising human rights",[54] and, in the 2014 Resolution, by calling upon states to formulate their "Internet-related public policies" with the objective of ensuring "universal access and enjoyment of human rights".[55]

The BCG/Telenor study also points to the social benefits of increased Internet penetration, including improved education, better income and lifestyle opportunities and enhanced healthcare, especially in rural areas.[56] These benefits are usually presented anecdotally. The example of many African states shows how big (government) data and open data approaches are used by local start-ups in cooperation with local communities to monitor delivery of health services.[57] The Internet and Internet-based applications can be effective tools to visualize money flows and increase accountability of public officials, which in turn has positive effects on development.

This approach has emerged as a common theme in development policy. At the Rio+20 Summit in 2012, the United Nations Conference on Sustainable Development, states agreed to launch a process to develop sustainable development goals (SDGs).[58] These are discussed at the UN level in the Open Working Group on Sustainable Development Goals and should be integrated into the post-2015 development agenda.[59] As input to this process, the UN High Level Panel of Eminent Persons Report on the Post-2015 Development Agenda of 2013,[60] which tasked

52 Human Rights Council, Res. 26/13, *The promotion, protection and enjoyment of human rights on the Internet,* A/HRC/RES/26/13 of 26 June 2014, para. 2.

53 Ibid., para. 5.

54 Human Rights Council (note 51), para. 4.

55 Human Rights Council (note 52), para. 6.

56 Telenor/BCG (note 48), p. 8.

57 Cf. L. Treisman, 'Power to the people: how open data is improving health service delivery' (2013) *The Guardian,* 2 December 2013, http://www.theguardian.com/global-development-professionals-network/2013/dec/02/open-data-healthcare-accountability-africa.

58 General Assembly Res. 66/288, The Future We Want, UN Doc. A/RES/66/288, para. 248.

59 Cf. Open Working Group on Sustainable Development Goals, http://sustainabledevelopment.un.org/index.php?menu=1549, established under GA Decision 67/555 of 22 January 2013, UN Doc. A/67/L.48/rev.1.

60 UN High Level Panel of Eminent Persons Report (A New Global Partnership: Eradicate Poverty and Transform Economies through Sustainable Development, The Report of the High-Level Panel of Eminent Persons on the Post-2015 Development Agenda, 30 May 2013, http://www.post2015hlp.org/the-report.

itself with integrating the social, economic, and environmental dimensions of sustainability, underlined the importance of "harnessing innovation, technology, and the potential of private business to create more value and drive sustainable and inclusive growth.[61] This brings us back to the BCG report, which focuses on the positive impact of the Internet for private businesses. The High Level Panel, established by United Nations Secretary-General Ban Ki-moon, also called for a "data revolution for sustainable development, with a new international initiative to improve the quality of statistics and information available to citizens". ICTs were considered crucial for development as empowering tools: "new technology, crowd sourcing, and improved connectivity to empower people with information on the progress towards the [development] targets."[62] Disaggregated data to ensure that the "neediest [...] are receiving essential services" is necessary – and the "revolution in information technology over the last decade provides [us with] an opportunity to strengthen data and statistics for accountability and decision-making purposes".[63]

This is not to deny that digital inequalities are persistent and the different dimensions of the digital divide, even within developed societies, are difficult to bridge.[64] Rather, these issues have to be considered and dealt with, within the frame of international law, on a regional and national basis. The GA Resolution on ICTs and development expresses concerns about at the digital divide, the gender divide within the digital divide, and that the development promise of ICTs remains unfulfilled for the majority of the poor.[65] Targeted policies are required to ameliorate this situation but the finding does not detract from the validity of identifying the Internet's protection as lying in the common interest because of its potential for human development.

ICTs and their facility to organize data and draw societal benefits from data are thus accepted tools in pursuance of the UN's development goals. The Internet does not equal ICTs, but ICTs run on the Internet. Therefore, the use of ICTs is premised upon the protection of the Internet – which is in the common interest. Harnessing ICTs in order to realize human rights, human security and human development, as well as sustainable economic growth, is premised upon the integrity of the Internet. If the one is in the common interest – as it indubitably is – the other needs to be as well.

---

61 Ibid., 6.

62 Ibid., 7.

63 Ibid., 23.

64 Cf. E. Hargittai and Y.P. Hsieh, 'Digital Inequality' in W.H. Dutton (ed), *The Oxford Handbook of Internet Studies*, Oxford University Press, Oxford 2013, pp. 129–150.

65 UN General Assembly Res. 67/195, paras. 3–5.

Protecting the Internet is also essential for ensuring international security. The General Assembly, in Resolution 64/211 of 21 December 2009, promoted the creation of a global culture of cybersecurity,[66] and expressed concerns in light of growing threats to the reliable functioning of the Internet (technically: "of critical information infrastructures and to the integrity of the information carried over those"). These affect "domestic, national and international welfare". The resolution affirms that states are obliged to deal systematically with these threats and coordinate both with national stakeholders and internationally with the goal of facilitating the achievement of cybersecurity.

The 2013 report of the Group of Governmental Experts underlined that applying norms derived from "existing international law relevant to the use of ICTs by states is an essential measure to reduce risks to international peace, security and stability". The Charter of the United Nations is applicable to the whole gamut of socioeconomic activity on the Internet and in that "essential to maintaining peace and stability and promoting an open, secure, peaceful and accessible ICT environment".[67] Applying international law to the Internet lies in the common interest and safeguarding the Internet as such also lies in the common interest because a stable, secure and functional Internet is essential for international security.

Protecting the Internet's integrity by reducing the potential for criminal misuses of computers and networks is important in the international fight against cybercrime and cyber terrorism. It is well known that the Internet can be used for the coordination of terrorist attacks and the promotion of terrorist ideology.[68] At the same time the informationalization of many key infrastructure provision functions and of many industry control systems opens up new vulnerabilities within states that can threaten, if an attack is substantial, international peace and security. Similarly, the increased use of mobile devices, cloud computing and the use of social networks increases the vulnerability of citizens to acts of cybercrime.

These vulnerabilities are intensified through diverging levels of Internet security awareness and capabilities in different states. This is a concern to all states because of the interconnectedness of ICTs and the networked nature of the Internet. Only international cooperation in the protection of the Internet can help meet these

66 General Assembly Res. 64/211 of 21 December 2009, Creation of a global culture of cybersecurity and taking stock of national efforts to protect critical information infrastructures, UN Doc. A/RES/64/211 of 17 Mach 2010.

67 Report of the Group of Governmental Experts on Developments in the Field of Information and Telecommunications in the Context of International Security, UN Doc. A/68/98 of 24 June 2013, para. 19.

68 Ibid., para. 7.

challenges. This is a further reason for considering that the protection of the Internet's integrity lies in the common interest.

5. CONCLUSIONS FOR INTERNATIONAL INTERNET LAW AND INTERNET GOVERNANCE

As to international legal consequences of designating an issue as lying in the global common interest (or concern), I can point to the contribution of Christina Voigt,[69] respectively; for the international legal impact of pursuing human rights as a common interest in the framework of a humanized international law, I can recommend Wolfgang Benedek's.[70] What remains for me is to show briefly how international law, as it relates to the Internet – International Internet Law –, is influenced by the recognition of the global common interest in the Internet's integrity.

To the extent that a state controls Critical Internet Resources, it has to exercise this jurisdiction in a manner that ensures the common interest. To the extent that national politics (and policics) can impact the Internet negatively, a state has to refrain from their formulation and implementation. A state's sovereignty is reduced because of the limits the protection of the Internet as a common interest lays upon it. The US, as delegated manager of the Critical Internet Resources, therefore only has a 'custodial sovereignity'.[71] This implies that the US has to enter into consultations with other states with regard to the management of Critical Internet Resources and make sure that the management is transparent and accountable, ideally to the international community. All other states, insofar as they can endanger the Internet's stability, security and functionality, are preempted from doing so. In assessing whether politics may impact the Internet negatively, it makes sense to suggest the precautionary principle as a guide to decision-making.[72]

69 C. Voigt in this volume, chapter 1.

70 W. Benedek in this volume, chapter 10. 'What a human rights-based approach to the Internet means in practice is aptly illustrated by his work as a member of the Council of Europe's Committee of Experts on Rights of Internet Users (MSI-DUI) and the Committee's Draft Guide on Human Rights for Internet Users', 22 October, 2013, http://www.coe.int/t/informationsociety/Rights%20of%20Internet%20Users/Draft%20Council%20of%20Europe%20Guide%20on%20Human%20Rights%20for%20Internet%20Users.pdf.

71 Cf. W. Scholtz, 'Custodial Sovereignty: Reconciling Sovereignty and Global Environmental Challenges amongst the Vestiges of Colonialism' (2008) 3 *Netherlands International Law Review*, pp. 323–341. See also W. Scholtz's contribution, in this volume, chapter 7.

72 Cf. the work of the Council of Europe's Ad hoc Advisory Group on Cross-border Internet (MC-S-CI), http://www.coe.int/t/dghl/standardsetting/media/MC-S-CI/default_en.asp, especially its report: International and multi-stakeholder co-operation on cross-border Internet (2010).

A second consequence is that mankind – that is all actors making up the international community, and not only states – have a legitimate interest in making sure that all other actors, including the US as custodial sovereign, protect the Internet. Though sovereignty-oriented states have suggested exclusive sovereignty over national Internet segments, the character of the Internet as protected by international law as a common interest limits their sovereignty. The 2005 Tunis Agenda, though valuable in its description of the normative goals of the information society, still lays down that "policy authority for internet-related public policy issues" is a "sovereign right of states".[73] This needs to be qualified in light of a common interest approach to protecting the Internet in that the states' policy authority no longer is an exclusively sovereign right, but part and parcel of their sovereignty, to be exercised in the common interest. What sovereignty they have over Internet-related resources has to be understood in light of changing circumstances and the importance of the pursuance of common interests. As far as international law extends to non-state actors, these are also under obligation to confirm to, and support, the common pursuance of the global interest in safeguarding the Internet's integrity. This means, for example, that there is an international law-based duty, via the *Ruggie Principles*,[74] for companies to respect human rights and victims of business-related abuses a right to access to remedies.

In closing let us now turn to some conclusions related to Internet governance specifically. At some point in the normative ordering of a field, or regime, of international law, someone will call for its 'constitutionalization' or identify a certain moment as 'constitutional'.[75] Such a moment could be one in which agreement is reached on the regime's finality by, e.g., defining a global common interest. Though I have made the case for the recognition of the Internet's integrity as lying in the global common interest (functionally, not because of any essentialist characteristics), I do not suggest that there is a need for a 'constitutionalization' of Internet governance in the traditional, state-focused public law-inspired understanding of the word. In that, I agree with ICANN's own Strategy Panel report, which confirmed in 2014 that there is no need for such a constitutional moment[76] or a single constitutional document. Rather, what

---

[73] WSIS, *Tunis Agenda*, 2005, para. 35.

[74] Cf. Report of the Special Representative of the Secretary-General on the issue of human rights and transnational corporations and other business enterprises, J. RUGGIE, 'Guiding Principles on Business and Human Rights: Implementing the United Nations "Protect, Respect and Remedy" Framework', UN Doc. A/HRC/17/31 of 21 March 2011.

[75] For cyberspace, see D.G. Post, 'Cyberspace's Constitutional Moment, The American Lawyer', 1998, http://www.temple.edu/lawschool/dpost/DNSGovernance.htm. For the relevance of constitutionalist approaches to explaining and justifying the normative interaction of different regimes, see the approach based on systems theory by G. Teubner, *Verfassungsfragmente. Gesellschaftlicher Konstitutionalismus in der Globalisierung*, Suhrkamp, Frankfurt 2012, p. 255.

[76] Cf. Cerf et al. (note 3), p. 63 (the report adds that if there was a need, the moment had happened at WSIS in 2005).

Internet Governance needs, is the full application of international law in light of its protection of the Internet's integrity in the common interest. Furthermore, in the iterative commitment by all stakeholders to common principles and processes, based on international law, there lies something of normative and by argumentative extension, 'constitutional' dimension,[77] as these processes and principles aim at circumscribing in essence how international public (and semi-public) authority[78] is exercised and controlled. International law is the *ius necessarium* of the Internet, it is necessary to protect the integrity of the Internet as a matter of global common interest. It influences the processes of formulating both national Internet-related public policies and Internet Governance policy more broadly. As the Human Rights Council put it in its 2014 Resolution, states should consider "[f]ormulating through transparent and multi-stakeholder processes, and adopting national Internet-related public policies that affirm the global, open and interoperable nature of the Internet, and have the objective of universal access and enjoyment of human rights at its core[.]"[79]

International law helps us define what it means to 'affirm' the global, open and interoperable nature of the Internet and how to tailor policies so that they further universal access and the promotion, protection and enjoyment of human rights. This is important because normative approaches so far have largely relied on developing and affirming principles for Internet governance that have both evidenced a certain path dependency and a lack of international legal grounding. Admittedly, principles can stabilize normative expectations and, in their aggregate, evidence them. But ensuring the global common interest needs a firmer, more normative basis. Space does not allow for a comprehensive discussion of the various protective dimensions international law offers for the Internet and how they are intricately connected, including through the objective dimension of human rights protection and the interwoven network of extraterritorial human rights protection guarantees of states, independent of their human rights commiments internationally. Suffice it to say that we have to clarify what international legal rules apply to the governance and management of the Internet and how legitimacy of 'the rule' and 'the rules' of the Internet can be established

77 Though Teubner (note 76), p. 255, would argue that Internet Governance is a "transnational regime constitution" which "is exclusively tailored to one functionally differentiated sector of world society and thus constitutes a 'self-contained regime' […]". He defines 'regime constitutions' as 'partial constitutions' which do not have a backing in "gesamtgesellschaftlichen Prozessen", that is those oriented towards the "Gemeinwohl", the public good. I feel that the 'regime constitution' of the Internet has a broader impact on the pursuance of the global common interest than, say, the regime of the exploitation of fisheries in the North Sea.

78 Cf. G. Handl, 'Extra-territoriality and Transnational Legal Authority', in G. Handl, J. Zekoll and P. Zumbansen (eds), *Beyond* Territoriality. Transnational Legal Authority in an Age of Globalization, Martinus Nijhoff, Leiden/Boston 2012, pp. 3–12 (8).

79 Human Rights Council (note 52), para. 6.

in light of the normative parameters of the Internet, notably the multistakeholder justification narrative.[80]

International law has arrived at a point in its development where pursuing the common interest, as Bardo Fassbender put it, is the only reasonable answer to its *Sinnfrage*.[81] Ensuring a people-centric and development-oriented Internet is one of the key challenges for international law today. To that end, the protection of the integrity of the Internet as a common interest is essential.

It is especially essential at a time when the US is pursuing the transition of their stewardship function regarding key Internet naming and addressing functions to a multistakeholder-based institution. Prima facie, the US commitment is not to allow for the *internationalization*, but rather only the *globalization* of these obligations and its affirmation *not* to accept the replacement of its role with a "government-led or an inter-governmental organization solution"[82] might suggest that international law (as administered, for example, by an 'Internet United Nations') mattered less regarding the management of key Internet resources. But the opposite is true. We are currently in the process, within one international regime, with regard to one global common interest issue, of moving towards multistakeholder-based and globalized, and not state-centric and internationalized, administration. In this unparalleled process, there is an urgent need for international standards, provided by international law, to measure the normative outcome, to judge the legitimacy of the actors and institutions, and to safeguard the common interest.

80 I am pursuing these questions in the framework of a post-doctoral scholarship at the Cluster of Excellence 'Normative Orders' at the University of Frankfurt/Main (Germany).

81 Cf. B. Fassbender, 'Zwischen Staatsräson und Gemeinschaftsbindung. Zur Gemeinwohlorientierung des Völkerrechts der Gegenwart' in H. Münkler and K. Fischer (eds), *Gemeinwohl und Gemeinsinn im Recht: Konkretisierung und Realisierung öffentlicher Interessen*, Akademie Verlag, Berlin 2002, pp. 231–274, 231.

82 NTIA, NTIA Announces Intent to Transition Key Internet Domain Name Functions, 14 March 2014, http://www.ntia.doc.gov/press-release/2014/ntia-announces-intent-transition-key-internet-domain-name-functions.

CHAPTER 10

HUMANIZATION OF INTERNATIONAL LAW, HUMAN RIGHTS AND THE COMMON INTEREST

Wolfgang Benedek

1. INTRODUCTION

More than 65 years after the adoption of the Universal Declaration of Human Rights (UDHR), the protection of human rights can be considered as a widely recognized common interest of mankind. There are no international actors which oppose human rights as such, although there are differences with regard to the concept of human rights or the role of international institutions or foreign actors regarding their implementation. The compromise achieved some 20 years ago in the Vienna Declaration and Programme of Action (VDPA) still applies: all human rights are universal, indivisible, interdependent and interrelated and "while the significance of national and regional particularities and various historical, cultural and religious backgrounds must be born in mind, it is the duty of states, regardless of their political, economic and cultural systems, to promote and protect all human rights and fundamental freedoms".[1]

Since the adoption of the UDHR, the international system has experienced increasing cooperation, partly due to globalization, in particular since the fall of the Berlin Wall and the Iron Curtain in 1989. The common values of the UN Charter, like human dignity, justice, equality, rule of law, social progress, freedom and peace, have been largely enhanced by the human rights system created on the universal and regional level, which itself has contributed to a humanization of international law. Common values[2] are the basis for common concerns and common interests in international law. These values also serve as

[1] See *United Nations, World Conference on Human Rights, Vienna Declaration and Programme of Action*, June 1993, para. 5.

[2] See P.-M. Dupuy, B. Fassbender, M.N. Shaw and K.-P. Sommermann (eds), *Common Values in International Law*, Essays in honour of Christian Tomuschat, N. P. Engel Publishers, Kehl 2006.

a basis for the constitutional approach to international law, which, together with the communitarian approach, better accommodates humanitarian concerns than a sovereignty-based approach to international law.[3] This contribution aims at drawing the conclusions of these developments for the common interest in international law, with a particular focus on human rights. For this purpose, at first it looks at the progress made towards a humanization of international law and the impact of this process on the status of the individual in international law, then on the implications of the humanization of international law for the common interest, before finally engaging in a closer analysis of human rights as a common interest in international law, and ending with general conclusions.

2. HUMANIZATION OF INTERNATIONAL LAW FOR THE BENEFIT OF THE INDIVIDUAL

The increased status and role of the individual and its needs in international law as demonstrated in recent literature[4] are an expression of a basic change in international law through which the individual emerges as an actor in its own right, an object of common concern or as a holder of rights and bearer of duties. According to Antonio Augusto Cancado Trindade, "[s]tates exist for human beings (who compose them), and not vice versa".[5] Part VI of his teaching book on international law is entitled "Humanization of International Law", where he develops his ideas of basic considerations of humanity applied to various fields of international law. He also argues for humankind to be recognized as a subject of international law.[6]

A humanization of international law can be observed in the area of human development, where the "Human Development Report" of the United Nations Development Programme (UNDP) contributed to a humanization of the development discourse[7] and the Human Development Index has shifted the

---

3 See J. Rauber, 'On Communitarianism and Constitutional Approaches to International Law' (2013) 26 *Leiden Journal of International Law* 1, 201–217. See also St. Stec, 'Humanitarian Limits to Sovereignty: Common Concern and Common Heritage Approaches to Natural Resources and Environment' (2010) 12 *International Community Law Review* 3, 361–389.

4 See M.C. Kettemann, *The Future of Individuals in International Law*, Eleven, Utrecht 2013, A. Peters, *Jenseits der Menschenrechte, Die Rechtsstellung des Individuums im Völkerrecht* (Beyond Human Rights, The Legal Position of Individuals in International Law), Mohr Siebeck, Tübingen 2014, A.A.C. Trindade, *The Access of Individuals to International Justice* (2011) and A. Clapham, 'The Role of the Individual in International Law' (2010) 21 *European Journal of International Law* 1, 30.

5 A.A.C. Trindade, *International Law for Humankind, Towards a New Jus Gentium*, 2nd ed, Martinus Nijhoff Publishers, Leiden 2013, pp. 179, quoting from his Separate Opinion in the ICJ Advisory Opinion on the Declaration of Independence of Kosovo and pp. 275 et seq.

6 Ibid., pp. 391–528.

7 See for example UNDP, *Human Development Report 1999*, which sets out with „Globalization with a human face", UNDP, New York 1999, at p. 1.

focus to a human rights-oriented approach.[8] In the area of human security, the protection of civilians, in particular of women and children in armed conflict, can be regarded as a common concern, expressed in several resolutions of the Security Council and the General Assembly.[9] Furthermore, the focus on the individual as the main subject of security has resulted in a stronger attention to human rights in armed conflict. Also the parallel development in international humanitarian law, part of which always had a focus on the protection of vulnerable persons and which increasingly opened up to human rights concerns, should be mentioned in this context.[10]

In the area of international criminal law the individual has gained importance as a duty-bearer, as can be seen from the creation of specialized criminal tribunals in several countries and of the International Criminal Court, which can be regarded as representing a common interest of the international community to hold individuals responsible for major violations of the laws of war and of human rights.[11]

With regard to Transnational Corporations (TNCs), there is also a development to hold them responsible if not liable for human rights violations, either in the context of the UN Framework on Business and Human Rights or of other mechanisms like the Global Compact or various Corporate Social Responsibility (CSR) standards.[12]

Obviously, for the humanization of international law the mainstreaming of human rights has played a major role. After the period of standard-setting, which so far resulted in nine major United Nations conventions, the focus shifted to strengthening the implementation of these standards. In 1997, Secretary-General

---

8 See UNDP, Human Development Report, UNDP New York, annually, and W. Benedek and L. Heschl, 'Mainstreaming Human Rights: A Human Rights-Based Approach to the post-2015 Development Agenda' in J. Kozma, A. Müller-Funk and M. Nowak (eds), *Vienna +20, Advancing the Protection of Human Rights. Achievements, Challenges and Perspectives – 20 Years after the World Conference*, NWV/Intersentia, Vienna/Graz 2014, pp. 239–251.

9 See SC Res. 1894 of 11 November 2009, adopted on the initiative of Austria, while being a member of the Security Council. See also W. Benedek, 'Mainstreaming Human Security in UN and EU Peace and Crises Management Operations, Policies and Practice' in W. Benedek, M.C. Kettemann and M. Möstl (eds), *Mainstreaming Human Security in Peace Operations and Crises Management, Policies, Problems, Potential*, London and New York 2011, pp. 13–31 and generally, G. Oberleitner, Human Security: Idea, Policy and Law in M. Martin and T. Owen (eds), *Routledge Handbook of Human Security*, Routledge, London/New York 2013, pp. 319–330.

10 See Th. Meron, *Humanization of International Law*, Martinus Nijhoff Publishers, Leiden 2006.

11 See W.A. Schabas, *An Introduction to the International Criminal Court*, Cambridge University Press, Cambridge 2011.

12 See, for example, O. De Schutter, *Towards Corporate Accountability for Human and Environmental Rights Abuses*, Discussion Paper, 2007.

Kofi Annan announced the mainstreaming of human rights in all spheres of UN action as a major objective of UN reform. Since then, human rights have been integrated in the action of the UN, in the fields of development and peace-keeping in particular. A human rights-based approach to development or human rights training and child rights advisors in peace-keeping missions have resulted from these efforts of mainstreaming. In other areas like Business and Human Rights, mainstreaming of human rights has become important and is operationalized in the form of Human Rights Impact Assessments for larger investments. All these developments have contributed to the humanization of international law. The UN Human Rights Council, in its resolution on "enhancement of international cooperation in the field of human rights" recently called on all states to "further advance initiatives aimed at enhancing international cooperation in the field of human rights on issues of common interest and concern".[13] This can be taken as a reconfirmation of the duty to cooperation in the field of human rights, although it is not clearly identified what issues of common interest and concern the resolution, which was sponsored by the Non-Aligned Movement (NAM), had in mind. The position proposed here, however, is that not only certain issues of human rights are of common interest, but the concept of human rights protecting human dignity as such. In this context, particular emphasis should be put on those human rights which are identified as peremptory norms.

As a next step, the concept of common interest will be clarified before pursuing the question of the implications of the humanization of international law for the common interest. Starting from Simma, "community interest" is understood as a "consensus ... recognized and sanctioned by international law as a matter of concern to all states".[14] That standard may be difficult to achieve in practice, while it may be easier to talk of a "common interest", which a group or the large majority of states is sharing. For example, in the context of the WTO, the concept of common interest has been used to describe the WTO as a club based on reciprocity and common interest.[15] Also in the field of foreign investment, "common concerns" have been identified.[16] As the use of the concepts of common concern and common interest appear not to be consistent in practice, no particular distinction is made for the purposes of this contribution and both concepts are used interchangeably.[17]

---

13 See UN HRC, Doc. A/HRC/RES/23/3 (21 June 2013).

14 See B. Simma, 'Reciprocity' (2008) *Max Planck Encyclopedia of Public International Law.*

15 P.-T. Stoll, 'The World Trade Organization as a Club: Rethinking Reciprocity and Common Interest' in U. Fastenrath et al. (eds), *From Bilateralism to Community Interest,* Essays in Honour of Judge Bruno Simma, Oxford University Press, Oxford 2011, pp. 172–183.

16 See T. Treves, F. Seatzu and S. Trevisanut (eds), *Foreign Investment, International Law and Common Concerns*, Routledge, London 2014.

17 See, however, the contribution of Ch. Voigt, in this volume, who develops some distinctions with regard to sustainable development.

3. IMPLICATIONS FOR THE COMMON INTEREST

The humanization of international law contributes to a trend towards the humanization of international relations.[18] The discipline of international relations is rather concerned with interests than with rights. However, such interests increasingly go beyond state interests and include also the interests of individuals, like the protection of their human dignity and rights as a common interest. A humanization of international relations would also benefit the individual. Accordingly, the humanization of international law also contributes to the common interest, i.e. strengthening the human dignity of the individual.

One related area is the Rule of Law, which is identified already in the Preamble of the UN Charter as a major objective of the United Nations, although the Charter only talks about the establishment of "conditions under which justice and respect for the obligations arising from treaties and other sources of international law can be maintained". Also, the principles of pacta sunt servanda and bona fides in Article 2 of the Charter, regarding the obligations in the Charter, constitute a basis for the Rule of Law. Therefore, a common interest in the Rule of Law in international law can be identified. It contributes to much needed legal security for political as well as economic relations. This has inspired the work of the International Law Commission as well as of the United Nations at large, which has established a Rule of Law Coordination and Resource Group, assisted by a Rule of Law Unit, and discusses Rule of Law matters regularly in the General Assembly based on reports of the Secretary General.[19] Among other fields, the Rule of Law applies also to human rights.

However, there is also the objective and central concept of human dignity in the Charter, which complements the Rule of Law with a value basis, which is largely provided by human rights. As there is a common interest of states in respect for their sovereignty, there is a common interest of all individuals for the respect of their human dignity. This common interest has found international recognition by the UN Charter, the UDHR and the human rights system, which emanated from it. The UDHR accordingly describes its content as "a common standard of achievement for all peoples and all nations".[20] Although international relations are often more concerned with the national interest, this national interest can merge into a community interest, reflecting various common interests, among them the

18 See W. Benedek, 'Challenges of a Humanization of International Relations by International Law' in M. Pogacnik (ed), *Challenges of Contemporary International Law and International Relations,* Liber Amicorum in Honour of Ernest Petric, Europska Pravna Fakulteta u Novi Gorici, Nova Gorica 012, pp. 81–92.

19 See, for example, the report of the UN Secretary General, Annual Report on Strengthening and Coordinating United Nations Rule of Law Activities, UN Doc. A/64/298.

20 See the Preamble of the UDHR, proclamation of the UDHR, last indent.

interest in the respect of human rights. Indeed, a general trend has been observed towards community interests in international law, as academic literature, "but also law-developing agencies like the International Law Commission today [...] almost exclusively focus on 'operationalizing' community interests".[21] Human rights can be seen as both a common as well as a community interest; community interests emphasizing the multi-stakeholder nature of the international community. Multi-track diplomacy often uses multi-stakeholder approaches, which are more likely to give public or community interest higher attention.[22]

4. HUMAN RIGHTS AS A COMMON INTEREST

Human dignity and human rights have emerged as cornerstones of the international order today. The UN Charter in its preamble speaks of human dignity, which is reconfirmed by the UN Millennium Declaration which in para. 2 talks about a "collective responsibility to uphold the principles of human dignity, equality and equity at the global level". No country denies recognition to the UDHR as reconfirmed by the VDPA. This is proven in particular by the general acceptance of the review of national human rights performances by way of the Universal Periodic Review (UPR). This regular peer review, in which with the assistance of the UN Secretariat and the involvement of civil society all UN member states are scrutinized on their human rights record ending with numerous recommendations to be implemented before the next review,[23] can be seen as the best proof of human rights being recognized as a common interest, based on a common concern.

Certain countries and organizations like the US and the EU have developed their own human rights policies and reviews, which can go more-in-depth and be more demanding.[24] For example, the EU human rights policy as exemplified

---

21 See Ch. Tams, 'Individual States as Guardians of Community Interests' in Ulrich Fastenrath et al. (eds), *From Bilateralism to Community Interest*, Essays in Honour of Judge Bruno Simma, Oxford University Press, Oxford 2011, pp. 379–405, p. 405.

22 Cf. W. Benedek, 'The Relevance of Multi-stakeholder Approaches and Multi-Track Diplomacy for Human Rjghts Diplomacy' in M. O'Flaherty, Z. Kedzia, A. Mueller and G. Ulrich (eds), *Human Rights Diplomacy: Contemporary Perspectives*, Martinus Nijhoff, Leiden 2011, pp. 252–261.

23 See E. McMahon and M. Ascherio, 'A Step Ahead in Promoting Human Rights?' (2012) 18 *The Universal Periodic Review of the UN Human Rights Council, Global Governance*, 231–248 and UN GA Res. 60/251 of 15 March 2006, which also established the Human Rights Council. See also R. Freedman, *The United Nations Human Rights Council, A Critique and Early Assessment*, Routledge, Abingdon & Oxon 2013, pp. 253–282, p. 253 et seq.

24 See, for the US, U.S. Department of State, *Country Reports on Human Rights Practices for 2013*, http://www.state.gov/j/drl/rls/hrrpt/humanrightsreport/#wrapper and for the EU, *Annual Report on Human Rights and Democracy in the World*, http://eeas.europa.eu/top_stories/2013/250613_eu_hr_report_2012_en.htm.

by its Strategic Framework and Plan of Action of 2012[25] with about 100 concrete commitments and about 40 ongoing human rights dialogues can also be taken as an indicator that human rights are a common concern for an important part of the international community.

However, it is also important to point out existing limits. The UPR is still quite general and lacks a proper enforcement mechanism and the national or regional human rights mechanisms are sometimes incoherent and disputed. But this can be said for practically any area of common interest. What remains is that human rights, together with several other important concerns, have become a common concern as well as a common interest of the international community. Major human rights violations may trigger a "responsibility to protect", a concept adopted by the United Nations in 2005.[26] Certain human rights represent erga omnes obligations and in some cases have reached the level of ius cogens, like in the case of the prohibition of genocide, of racism or of slavery. Accordingly, the strongest concepts of international law are available for their protection, while the respective instruments and procedures still lack effectiveness. In this context, the creation of an International Court of Human Rights has been proposed in order to fill the gap of efficient remedies.[27] However, the community of states so far does not seem ready for such a court. For example, even the UN High Commissioner for Human Rights has not as yet endorsed the idea.

Let us now turn to international jurisprudence confirming certain human rights as common interests.

In its Advisory Opinion on Reservations to the Genocide Convention of 1951, the International Court of Justice (ICJ) held that it is important to consider the object of the convention, which was to safeguard the existence of certain human groups and to confirm the most elementary principles of morality with a universal scope:

> In such a convention the contracting states do not have any interests of their own; they merely have, one and all, a common interest, namely, the accomplishment of those high purposes, which are the raison d'etre of the convention.[28]

---

25 See Council of the European Union, *EU Strategic Framework and Action Plan on Human Rights and Democracy*, Luxembourg 2012, https://www.consilium.europa.eu/uedocs/cms_data/docs/pressdata/EN/foraff/131181.pdf.

26 See *World Summit Outcome*, UN GA Res. A/60/1 of 24 October 2005.

27 See M. Novak, J. Kozma and M. Scheinin, *A World Court on Human Rights-Consolidated Statute and Commentary*, Neuer Wissenschaftlicher Veralg, Vienna 2010.

28 ICJ, *Reservations to the Convention on the Prevention and Punishment of the Crime of Genocide* (Advisory Opinion), ICJ Reports 1951, p. 15.

Such a *"common interest"* can be seen in all major human rights conventions which are to benefit the higher "humanitarian and civilizing"[29] purpose of protecting human rights. In the recent case of *Belgium v. Senegal* concerning the obligation of trial or extradition of the former head of state of Chad, Hissen Habré, suspected also of responsibility for torture, the ICJ found that

> [the] States parties to the convention [against torture] have a common interest to ensure, in view of their shared values, that acts of torture are prevented and that, if they occur, their authors do not enjoy impunity.[30]

In that case, the ICJ had to consider objections by Senegal to the admissibility of the case with the argument that, as none of the alleged victims were Belgian nationals at the time when the acts were committed, Belgium should not be permitted to invoke the international responsibility of Senegal. According to the Belgian position, which was upheld by the Court, the nationality of the victims was irrelevant, because every state party to the Convention Against Torture (CAT) can request that other states parties meet their obligations under the CAT.[31] The Court followed this position by finding that

> [the] common interest implies that the obligations in question are owed by any State party to all the other states parties to the Convention. All the states parties "have a legal interest" in the protection of the rights involved (ILC, *Barcelona Traction, Light and Power Company, Limited (Belgium v. Spain)* (Judgement), ICJ Reports 1970, 32, para. 33). These obligations may be defined as "obligations erga omnes partes" [...].[32]

A community interest or common interest can also explain why some universal and all regional human rights conventions in Europe, the Americas and Africa give their parties the possibility of state complaints against alleged violations of the convention. On the level of the United Nations, based on procedures going back to the 70s, situations of serious human rights violations can be discussed in the Human Rights Council.

29 Ibid., p. 7.

30 ICJ, *Questions Relating the Obligation to Prosecute or Extradite (Belgium v. Senegal)* (Judgment), ICJ Reports 2012, p. 422, para. 68.

31 Ibid., para. 64.

32 Ibid., para. 68. In the ICJ, *Barcelona Traction* Case (*Barcelona Traction, Light and Power Company Limited* (New Application, 1962), *Belgium v. Spain* (Merits) (2nd phase) (Judgment), ICJ Reports 1970, p. 3) the Court refered to the existence of "obligations of a State towards the International Community as a whole", i.e. erga omnes obligations.

Indeed, according to Article 48 para. 1 (a) of the Articles on State Responsibility[33] any such obligation can be invoked by any state belonging to a group of states to which the obligation breached is owed, i.e. the CAT parties, if the obligation "is established for the protection of a collective interest of the group", while Article 48 para. 1 (b) covers obligations owed to the international community as a whole, i.e. erga omnes obligations,[34] based on ius cogens, i.e. peremptory norms of general international law according to Article 53 of the Vienna Convention on the Law of Treaties and Article 26 of the Articles on State Responsibility. Among these obligations are also the prohibitions of certain major human rights violations such as slavery or genocide.[35]

Outside the membership of UN Human Rights Conventions, some of which like the Convention on the Rights of the Child have reached universal membership,[36] the major human rights as contained in the UDHR can be considered as having reached the status of customary law.[37] This is also strongly indicated by the UPR review, which uses the UDHR as one basis of assessment.

The UDHR follows a universal approach as the Preamble speaks of the Universal Declaration of Human Rights as a

> [c]ommon standard of achievement for all peoples and nations, to the end that every individual and every organ of society, keeping this Declaration constantly in mind, shall strive by teaching and education to promote respect for those rights and freedoms and by progressive measures, national and international, to secure their universal and effective recognition and observance [...].

Accordingly, the actors called upon to promote and secure human rights are not only states, but also "*every individual and every organ of society*". Particular attention is put on teaching and education of human rights, which, more than 60 years later, has been responded to by the UN Declaration on Human Rights Education and Training of 2011, which recognizes human rights education as "*a*

---

33 See UN GA Res. 56/83 of 12 December 2001, adopting the draft articles of the International Law Commission on responsibility of states for internationally wrongful acts.

34 See S. Villalpando, 'The Legal Dimension of the International Community: How Community Interests are Protected in International Law' (2010) 21 *European Journal of International Law* 2, 387–419 at 407 et seq.

35 See J.A. Frowein, 'Jus cogens' *Max Planck Encyclopedia of Public International Law*, Oxford University Press, Oxford 2010.

36 The only major ratification missing is the one of the United States.

37 Compare H. Charlesworth, 'Universal Declaration of Human Rights (1948)' (2008) *Max Planck Encyclopedia of Public International Law*, Oxford Public International Law, para. 16.

collective commitment to all stakeholders" and sets out in Article 1 by stating that everyone should have access to human rights education and training.[38]

5. CONCLUSIONS

In conclusion, human rights can be seen as a common interest at least of all states and as a community interest of a larger group of international stakeholders, including individuals and civil society, based on a contemporary understanding of international law. As the example of the UPR shows, all those states have accepted the regular review of their human rights performance, which allows to conclude that human rights have been recognized as a common interest of all UN member states. As per its Charter and the UDHR, human rights have been a common interest of the United Nations from its beginning. This is also reflected in the fact that according to UN practice, human rights concerns regarding situations in member states are not considered to fall under the principle of non-interference in Article 2, para. 7 of the UN Charter. This means that the principle of state sovereignty is being transcended or qualified when human rights are at stake. This finding is in line with the concept of sovereignty as interpreted by Anne Peters, who concludes that "*a humanized state sovereignty implies responsibility for the protection of basic human rights ...*".[39] In a similar way, Benvenisti, referring to Huber and Vattel, develops the concept of "sovereigns as trustees of humanity" – a concept which inherently is based on the existence of a common interest.[40] The humanized sovereignty is a responsible, sometimes custodial sovereignty,[41] which also takes common interests like human rights globally into account. This also means that human rights necessarily transcend territorial sovereignties and become a general, global concern of the international community, consisting of state and non-state actors.

A reconfirmation of a common interest in the protection of core human rights can be seen in the recent judgment of the ICJ in the case of *Belgium v. Senegal* regarding the obligations to prosecute or extradite under the UN Convention against Torture.

---

38 United Nations Declaration on Human Rights Education and Training, GA Res. 66/137 of 19 December 2011. See also the World Programme of Human Rights Education, GA Res. 60/1 of 2005.

39 See A. Peters, 'Humanity as the A & Ω of Sovereignty' (2009) 20 *European Journal of International Law* 3, 513–545, 513 and 543 et seq.

40 See E. Benvenisti, 'Sovereigns as Trustees of Humanity: The Concept and its Normative Implications' (2013) 107 *American Journal of International Law*, 295–333, 307 et seq.

41 Cf. the contribution by W. Scholtz, in this volume, at p. 127 et seq.

This development is also visible from the increasing understanding of human rights as transnational obligations.[42] They can be considered as extraterritorial obligations (ETO), which are not limited to the territory of the signatory of the obligation, but, under certain conditions, also contain obligations towards human beings beyond territorial sovereignty.[43]

Such an approach is better suited to integrate new duty bearers of human rights, like TNCs or international organizations, into the legal regime of human rights.[44] For example, the Tilburg Guiding Principles on the World Bank, the IMF and Human Rights, which are being revised, start from the assumption that there is a universal responsibility for implementing human rights, "which concern all-state and non-state-actors" whose activities may affect peoples' lives. The Maastricht Principles on Extraterritorial Obligations of states in the area of Economic, Social and Cultural Rights of 2012[45] develop this approach for states, while significant legal research has also elaborated on the human rights responsibility of transnational corporations acting abroad.[46] This shows that human rights are a common interest of the international community and all states individually, going beyond state borders.

This is also reflected in the fact that human rights are not only a concern of member states of the UN. As can be seen from the work of Amnesty International and the large number of other NGOs, civil society has a major role in promoting and monitoring human rights. The development of human rights today is the result of a multi-stakeholder approach involving actors like international organizations and private actors as well, who can be duty bearers or beneficiaries.[47]

Consequently, human rights have become more than just a common interest of states, they have developed into a common interest of the international community. As community interests, human rights benefit from the respective

---

42 See 'Tilburg Guiding Principles on World Bank, IMF and Human Rights' in W. Van Genugten, P. Hunt and S. Mathews (eds), *World Bank, IMF and Human Rights*, Wolf Legal Publishers, Nijmegen 2003, p. 247 at seq.

43 See M. Langford, W. Vanderhole, M. Scheinin and W. Van Genugten (eds), *Global Justice, State Duties, The Extraterritorial Scope of Economic, Social and Cultural Rights in International Law*, Cambridge University Press, Cambrigde 2012.

44 See W. Vandenhole, *Emerging Normative Frameworks on Transnational Human Rights Obligations*, European University Institute Working Paper, Global Governance Programme, Florence 2012.

45 See *ETOs Consortium for human rights beyond borders*, www.eto_consortium.org/en/library/maastricht-principles.

46 See, for example, K. Buhmann and C. Ryngaert, 'Human Rights Challenges for Multinational Companies Working and Investing in Conflict Zones' (2012) 6 *Human Rights and International Discourse* 1, 3–13.

47 See W. Benedek, 'Multi-stakeholderism in the Development of International Law' in U. Fastenrath et al. (eds), *From Bilateralism to Community Interest*, Essays in Honour of Judge Bruno Simma, Oxford University Press, Oxford 2011, pp. 172–183.

legal concepts of protection as for example state responsibility for violations of erga omnes obligations or of ius cogens. The existence of human rights as a common concern, as well as a common interest accordingly legitimizes this development in international legal doctrine. Within the international community, states as well as non-state actors, in particular NGOs, may act as custodians of the common interest, as did Belgium in order to defend the freedom from torture and to fight against impunity in the case of Hissène Habré before the ICJ. And successfully so, as Senegal in February 2013 finally inaugurated the Extraordinary Chambers in Dakar, which in July 2013 charged Hissène Habré with crimes against humanity, torture and war crimes.[48]

[48] See *Human Rights Watch, Senegal: Case Against Habré Set to Continue*, www.hrw.org/habre-case.

CHAPTER 11

POLITICAL ACTIVITY, EXTRADITION AND THE COMMON INTEREST

Henning Bang Fuglsang Madsen Sørensen

1. INTRODUCTION

Extradition is an important part of international criminal law. Most countries do not want to be a safe haven for criminals, while most countries, on the contrary, want to shelter political dissidents. Many extradition treaties therefore contain a political offence clause, which blocks extradition when the criminal charges are related to political activities.

It has however remained a state prerogative to decide whether a specific act should be considered as a criminal offence, for which extradition should be granted, or as a political offence, for which extradition should be denied. State practices therefore vary, leading to a fragmented and complicated situation for states as well as citizens when determining whether an act should be considered as a criminal offence or a political offence.

The protection of the political offender has now become so complex that former NSA-employee Edward Snowden applied for asylum in no less than 21 different countries after fleeing from the US as he had leaked sensitive information about US surveillance programs.[1] The American government considers Mr. Snowden a criminal offender and has thus charged him for espionage[2] while others consider him as a political offender and hold the case of Mr. Snowden as a prominent example of the need to develop the political offence exception in extradition law

[1] The Guardian, 4 July 2013: Edward Snowden asylum: countries approached and their responses, http://www.theguardian.com/world/2013/jul/02/edward-snowden-nsa-asylum-application-list-countries.

[2] *United States of America v. Edward J. Snowden*, United States District Court for the Eastern District of Virginia, Case No. 1:13 CR 265 (CMH).

to a concept suitable for practical use in an open and global world order.[3] The support for another renowned whistle-blower, Australian Julian Assange, is more complicated as he is not requested for extradition because of his whistleblowing activities but on charges for having raped two women.[4]

These two cases also show how the protection of a political offender has moved to the global scale as Mr. Snowden is now granted asylum in Russia after having requested protection in 21 different countries while Mr. Assange is staying at the Ecuadorian embassy in London,thus involving at least five different states. But the protection of the political offender is more than a political problem or a challenge for asylum law. The protection of the political offender is also a matter of protecting political dissidents, thus shielding the prerequisite of democracy itself while also making sure that those criminal offenders will face justice in order to protect the security of that very same democracy.

But the state-centric construction of international law is not capable of handling the global dimension of whether an act should be considered as a political or a criminal act, thus granting the offender protection from being extradited. If the development and protection of democracy is considered a global common interest, the protection of the political offender must also be a matter of global common interest – as well as the need to prosecute criminals and prevent states from being safe havens.

This text analyses the scope of the political offence clause as well as the possibilities for protecting the political dissident through asylum law and the right to a fair trial. The paper calls for a redefinition of the political offence, a right to not only a fair but also a just trial and the impartial control of the protection of political dissidents by ensuring the claimed political dissident the possibility to ask international courts such as the European Court of Human Rights (ECtHR) to examine whether the criminal case against him or her may be considered as fair as well as just.

2. THE PURPOSE OF THE POLITICAL OFFENCE CLAUSE

The right to be politically active must be considered as one of the most important rights in a modern society. The Universal Declaration of Human Rights contains

3 M.D. Kielsgard, 'The Political Offence Exception: Punishing Whistleblowers Abroad' (2013) *EJIL: Talk!*, 14 November 2013.

4 K. Ambos, 'Diplomatic Asylum for Julian Assange' (2012) *EJIL: Talk!*, 11 September 2012.

the right to freedom of thought, conscience and religion,[5] the right to freedom of opinion and expression[6] and the right to peaceful assembly and association, followed by the right to take part in the Government by Article 21.[7] These rights are repeated in the Covenant on Civil and Political Rights as Article 18 ensures the right to freedom of thought, conscience and religion and Article 19 ensures the right to opiniion and expression, while the right to take part in the conduct of public affairs is protected by Article 25.[8]

The Convention for the Protection of Human Rights and Fundamental Freedoms contains similar provisions in Articles 9–11, while Article 16 protects the political activities of aliens. The African Charter on Human and Peoples Rights, Article 8, ensures the right to freedom of conscience and religion, while Article 9 (2) ensures the right to express and disseminate one's opinions within the law and Articles 10 and 11 ensure the right to free association and assembly, followed by the right to participate in Government by Article 13. Article 24 of the Arab Charter on Human Rights ensures every citizen the right to freely pursue a political activity, to freely form and join associations with others and the freedom to association and peaceful assembly while Article 30 ensures everyone the right to freedom of thought, conscience and religion. Similar provisions are found in the American Declaration of the Rights and Duties of Man, the American Convention on Human Rights and the ASEAN Human Rights Declaration.

When a state endorses the protection of human rights, the state must also accept the responsibility to protect the right to be politically active. But a state also has an obvious need for being able to prosecute and punish citizens who violate the laws of the state. However, some suspects may try to escape justice by fleeing to other states. The states have responded to this by concluding conventions on extradition, where they oblige each other to extradite persons requested for prosecution in their home state. But as most states acknowledge the right to be politically active as a basic human right, the states also have included an option to deny extradition in cases where the authorities of the state to which the citizen has fled are convinced that the criminal charges are related to the political activities of the citizen. This is the political offence clause. The political offence clause is therefore also a matter of protecting basic human rights.

Yet the political offence clause also serves another important goal in the relationship between the two states involved in the extradition process. If the state

---

5 The Universal Declaration of Human Rights, http://www.un.org/en/documents/udhr/index.shtml, Art. 18.
6 Ibid., Art. 19.
7 Ibid., Art. 20.
8 International Covenant on Civil and Political Rights, adopted by UN General Assembly Res. 2200A (XXI) of 16 December 1966.

of origin is tempted to request the extradition of the political dissident with the intent to use criminal law against a political opponent, then the state of origin will perhaps also be tempted to disregard normal requirements to a fair trial. It would however be considered as a violation of the sovereignty of the requesting state and thus a breach of international law if the state to which the person has fled evaluated whether the legal system of the requesting state would respect the normal requirements to a fair trial. The clause therefore also protects the requested state from having to assess whether the requested person will have a fair trial in the requesting country, thereby violating the sovereignty of the requesting state.[9]

The purpose of the political offence clause is thus three-fold: protection of fundamental rights, protecting the dissident and respect for the sovereignty of the requesting state. Cases like Assange and Snowden show how difficult it is to decide whether a person who claims to be pursuing a higher political goal should be considered as a political activist, who should be protected in respect of fundamental rights, or should be considered as a simple criminal, who should be extradited and prosecuted in respect for the sovereignty of the requesting state.

3. SCOPE OF PROTECTION

The clause dates back to 1833, when Belgium as the first country in the world passed an Extradition Act. The clause did however not survive in the original form for long, as Belgium in 1856 was forced to limit the clause to not cover attacks on heads of states and their families. This change came following the refusal of a French request for extradition of two men who were believed to have attacked Napoleon Bonaparte and his family in 1854.

The general clause has thereafter been accepted worldwide[10] with the European Convention on Extradition[11] as one of the most general examples. The UN Extradition Model Treaty[12] also contains the political offence clause but without the "attentat clause". There has however never been consent on what a political offence is, and states have therefore developed different approaches to this question. A consensus has only developed on the division between pure political

9 G.S. Gilbert, 'Terrorism and the Political Offence Exemption Reappraised' (1985) 34 *International and Comparative Law Quarterly*, 695.

10 Ch. van den Wyngaert, *The Political Offence Exception to Extradition: The Delicate Problem of Balancing the Rights of the Individual and the International Public Order*, Deventer, Kluwer, The Hague/Boston 1980, p. 163.

11 European Treaty Series, No. 24, European Convention on Extradition (1957), Art. 3.

12 UN General Assembly Res. A/RES/45/116 of 14 December 1990, para. 3(a).

offences and relative political offences.[13] Treason, sedition and espionage are considered as purely political offences, for which the political offence clause in general is applicable.[14]

But the relative political offence, where the claimed political offence includes a common crime, has been more difficult to handle. Three different methods have emerged. Anglo-American law has applied an incidence test, where the common crime must be related to an ongoing riot or uprising. French law has applied an objective test, where the common crime must target a political right or the state itself.[15] And Swiss law has applied a motivation test, where the motive of the offender must be political[16] even though the Swiss test is also labelled the proportionality test that implies a demand for certain proportionality between the political objective and the common crime.[17] A closer look at the American jurisprudence shows however that the American courts are using the incidence test in different ways, causing a call for a Supreme Court ruling on the matter[18] as the incidence test is called "an interpretive nightmare".[19] The same goes for the French courts, which in certain cases have replaced the objective test with the motivation test.[20] Some researchers even claim that French courts in general use the motivation test while Swiss courts in general use the objective test and then call for a fourth test called "the mixed approach".[21]

The political offence clause came under new pressure as the uprising in Northern Ireland in the late 1970s and early 1980s forced a number of IRA members to flee to the USA, where they joined the Irish minority. These IRA members were protected from extradition to the UK by the political offence exception in the extradition treaty between the US, the UK and Ireland.[22] The UK however protested against

13 V. DeFabo, 'Terrorist or Revolutionary: The Development of the Political Offender Exception and Its Effects on Defining Terrorism in International Law' (2012) 2 *American University National Security Law Brief*, 68–104, 76.

14 Ch. Cantrell, 'The Political Offence Exemption in International Extradition: A Comparison of the United States, Great Britain and the Republic of Ireland' (1977) 60 *Marquette Law Review*, 777, 780.

15 Cf. DeFabo (note 15), p. 79.

16 M.R. Garcia-Mora, 'Nature of Political Offences: A Knotty Problem of Extradition Law' (1962) 48 *Virginia Law Review*, 1226, 1239–1256.

17 Cf. DeFabo (note 15), p. 78.

18 G. Gilbert, *Transnational Fugitive Offenders in International Law: Extradition and Other Mechanisms*, Martinus Nijhoff Publishers, Leiden 1998, p. 230.

19 D.M. Lieberman, 'Sorting the Revolutionary from the Terrorist: The Delicate Application of the Political Offence Exception in U.S. Extradition Cases' (2006) 59 *Stanford Law Review*, 181–212, 189.

20 J.J. Kinneally III, 'Political Offence Exception: Is the United States-United Kingdom Supplementary Extradition Treaty the Beginning of the End' (1987) 2 *American University Journal of International Law and Policy*, 203, 210.

21 Cf. van den Wyngaert (note 12), pp. 120–124.

22 A.C. Petersen, 'Extradition and the Political Offence Exception in the Suppression of Terrorism' (1991) 67 *Indiana Law Journal*, 767, 778.

this, drawing attention to the fact that PLO members were regularly extradited from the USA to Israel on the same charges as the IRA members were wanted for in the UK. This was obviously a problem for the USA and the UK as close ally and friend of the US.

A supplementary treaty was therefore concluded between the USA, the UK and Ireland that a list of common crimes could not be considered as political crimes per se. Among these were murder, kidnapping and the use of bombs or firearms,[23] excluding most former IRA members from being protected by the political exception clause. The concept of listing certain crimes on a negative list had already been used in multilateral conventions on international crimes, excluding genocide,[24] war crimes and crimes against humanity,[25] financing of terror[26] and terrorist bombings[27] from being political offences. The supplementary treaty marked however a change in bilateral agreements on extradition, as the supplementary treaty limited the general protection of the political offence clause by omitting any offence from being seen as a political offence if the offence contained one of the offences from the negative list regardless which obvious political goal the perpetrator may have pursued.

The next deterioration appeared in the Convention relating to extradition between the member states of the European Union,[28] which with a strong inspiration from the Nordic countries[29] prohibited the use of the political offence clause between the EU member states. This convention was replaced by the European Arrest Warrant in 2002,[30] which contains no basis for refusing surrender of the wanted person because of the political elements in his deeds. The European Arrest Warrant was amended in 2009,[31] without bringing any changes in regard to the political offence clause.

---

23 Petersen (note 22), p. 779.

24 United Nations, Treaty Series, Vol. 78, p. 278, Art. VII.

25 United Nations, Treaty Series, Vol. 754, p. 73, Art. III.

26 United Nations, Treaty Series, Vol. 2178, p. 197, International Convention for the Suppression of the Financing of Terrorism, Art. 6.

27 United Nations, Treaty Series, Vol. 2149, p. 257, International Convention for the Suppression of Terrorist Bombings, Art. 5.

28 Official Journal C 313, 23/10/1996, p. 11, Council Act of 27 September 1996 Drawing up the Convention Relating to Extradition between the Member States of the European Union, Art. 5.

29 G. Mathisen, 'Nordic Cooperation and the European Arrest Warrant: Intra-Nordic Extradition, the Nordic Arrest Warrant and Beyond' (2010) 79 *Nordic Journal of International Law*, 1–33.

30 Council Framework Decision of 13 June 2002 on the European Arrest Warrant and the Surrender Procedures between Member States, 2002/584/JHA.

31 Council Framework Decision of 26 February 2009 Amending Framework Decisions 2002/584/JHA, 2005/214/JHA, 2006/783/JHA, 2008/909/JHA and 2008/947/JHA, Thereby Enhancing Rights of Persons and Fostering the Application of the Principle of Mutual Recognition to Decisions Rendered in the Absence of the Person Concerned at the Trial.

The member states of the EU and 19 other European countries are also members of the ECHR. The ECHR contains a number of provisions which protect the person charged with political offences. Article 3, which prohibits the use of torture, Article 5, which ensures the right to liberty and security, and especially Article 6, the right to fair trial, are of immense importance for the person who is facing criminal charges because of his or her political activities. The European Court of Human Rights has also made it clear that the requested country is responsible for violations of the right to a fair trial according to Article 6[32] and the prohibition against torture according to Article 3.[33] The risk of torture will on the other hand be of no relevance if the extradition case was heard in American courts,[34] meaning that the US will allow extradition even though the requested person faces a real and well-founded risk of being tortured.

The political offence clause was created 180 years ago. An examination of the scope of the protection offered today shows a rather complex result. The actual protection depends upon whether the charges can be considered as pure or relative political offences, which test the requested country most often uses and whether the surrender is taking place to or from an EU member state, a state that has acceded to the ECHR or any other state. It is therefore very difficult, if not impossible, to assess whether or not the protection from the political offence clause can be expected in a specific case. It is easier to tell what a political offence is not, rather than what it is.[35] Instead, it has been left open for each national legislator to decide what may or may not be considered as a political offence in each country.[36]

This ambiguity relates to severe as well as minor common crimes. A call for an international consensus on a definition of "terrorism" has been issued as the lack of a widely accepted definition makes it almost impossible to decide whether a person is a revolutionary or a terrorist.[37] The same goes for minor offences as one can wonder if the common crime in question is of such limited importance that

---

32 ECtHR, *Soering v. The United Kingdom*, Application No. 14038/88, ECHR Reports 1989, para. 113; ECtHR, *Drozd and Janousek v. France and Spain*, Application No. 12747/87, ECHR Reports 1992, para. 110; ECHR, *Mamatkulov and Askarov v. Turkey*, Application Nos. 46827/99 and 46951/99, ECHR Reports 2005, para. 90.

33 ECtHR, *Soering v. The United Kingdom*, ECtHR Application No. 14038/88, ECHR Reports 1989, para. 91; ECHR; *Cruz Varas and Others v. Sweden*, ECtHR Application No. 15579/89, para. 69; ECHR, *Mamatkulov and Askarov v. Turkey*, Application Nos. 46827/99 and 46951/99, ECHR Reports 2005, para. 67; ECHR, *Saadi v. Italy*, Application No. 37201/06, ECHR Reports 2008, para. 126.

34 J.T. Parry, 'International Extradition, the Rule of Non-Inquiry, and the Problem of Sovereignty' (2010) 90 *Boston University Law Review*, 1973, 1975.

35 J. Hopkins, 'Case and Comment' (1996) 55 *Cambridge Law Journal*, 417, 419.

36 I. Foighel, 'Politiske Forbrydelser Og Udlevering' in J.P. Buhl and others (eds), *Festskrift til Stephan Hurwitz*, Juristforbundets Forlag, Copenhagen 1971, pp. 243–255, p. 247.

37 Cf. DeFabo (note 15), p. 104.

the actual penalty makes it irrelevant to consider whether he or she should be protected by the political offence clause.

This must be considered as unacceptable as the purpose of the clause was to protect the individual from being prosecuted because of his or her political deeds, thereby suppressing the opposition and democracy itself. However, the purpose of the political offence clause can never have been to grant a general impunity for any common crime. Even though a person may be even deeply involved in political activities, the same person must still face justice if he or she commits a common crime without any connection what so ever to the political activities. The basic problem is therefore how to separate the political offender from the common criminal offender as it is a matter of common interest to protect the first and to prosecute the latter.

The situation of today is, however, very different from the situation in 1833, when the political offence clause was introduced. Media, the internet and the speedy way news travel around the globe within seconds have changed the possibilities for a despot to oppress his people and use unfair criminal trials as a mean to destroy the opposition. Ever since the "attentat clause" politics and extradition law have unfortunately also tended to get mixed up[38] with the *Assange* case[39] as a recent example. The *Snowden* case has also given reason to question whether the political offence exception is capable at all of protecting whistleblowers as Snowden was charged with theft of government property when he fled from the US and laid open the American Intelligence Services wiretapping on friends and foes around the world.[40]

The legal ambiguity, the use of negative lists in extradition conventions and the increased awareness of the protection of fundamental rights have also changed the relevance and the need for the political offence clause. Perhaps the time has come to abandon the clause altogether and consider other options to protect the political activist.

---

38 J. Hartmann, 'II. The Lugovoy Extradition Case' (2008) 57 *International and Comparative Law Quarterly*, 194.

39 US Trade Benefits for Ecuador Seen at Risk in *Assange* Case, Reuters, 14 August 2012, http://www.reuters.com/article/2012/08/14/ecuador-assange-usa-trade-idUSL2E8JEDOO20120814 [accessed 27 August 2012].

40 M.D. Kielsgard, 'The Political Offence Exception: Punishing Whistleblowers Abroad' (2013) *EJIL: Talk! – Blog of the European Journal on International Law*, http://www.ejiltalk.org/the-political-offence-exception-punishing-whistleblowers-abroad/ (accessed 13 December 2013).

4. TWO ALTERNATIVES TO THE POLITICAL OFFENCE CLAUSE

Two options are worth considering if the protection of the political dissident should be ensured by other means than the political offence clause. The first option is to deny extradition if the requested person is given status as a refugee because of his or her political opinion. This will couple the legal status of the requested person with the protection against extradition. This seems like an easy and effective way to handle the issue of extradition since the individual right to protection follows immediately from the legal status of the person. The other option is to deny extradition if the requesting state cannot guarantee a fair trial. Being a political activist does not grant a "free ride" regarding any offence, political or not, and the political offender must therefore stand trial as any other citizen if he commits a criminal offence without any relation to his political activities what so ever.

The following analysis will examine whether these two options may be useful in the protection of the political activist.

5. ASYLUM AND EXTRADITION

This section will describe how asylum and extradition were developed following the ending of World War II and how these two elements of international law have developed along different paths in the following years to an extent where the differences between asylum and extradition seems to complicate both national as well as international procedures.

5.1. NEW LEGISLATION FOLLOWING WWII

World War II made the need to prosecute war criminals obvious, and the UK, the US and Russia made, as early as in October 1943, a declaration saying that those responsible for atrocities in the German occupied territories had to face justice.[41] The United Nations General Assembly, which in February 1946 decided on a resolution regarding the extradition and punishment of war criminals[42] as well as a resolution regarding the question of refugees,[43] repeated this call for bringing war criminals, traitors and quislings to justice while any other refugee should return safely to his or her country of origin.

41 The Moscow Conference, 1943, Statement on actrocities.
42 Res. A/RES/3(I) of 13 February 1946.
43 Res. A/RES/8(I) of 12 February 1946.

The General Assembly then established the International Refugee Organization in December 1946,[44] which should facilitate the return of displaced persons and the protection of persons who were unable to return to their country of origin at present. It was clear from the establishment of the organization that ordinary criminals who were extraditable by treaty would be of no concern of the organization. The definition of "ordinary criminals" was apparently not discussed in detail, as the parties seemed to be in general consensus that this text was enough to distinguish asylum from extradition.[45] The organization also provided an *eligibility manual*, which elaborated on the definition by stating that the following crimes were to be considered as extradition crimes: murder, poisoning, rape, arson, forgery, issuing counterfeit money, perjury, theft, bankruptcy, receiving stolen goods, embezzlement, bigamy, assault, grave injury and malicious destruction.[46] The use of a negative list was however not in line with the extradition treaties referred to in the constitution of the organization as these treaties in general used the different kinds of tests described above. This discrepancy did unfortunately not seem to attract any attention at the time.

A further important step forward was the adoption, by the General Assembly, of the Universal Declaration on Human Rights on 10 December 1948. Article 14 ensures and limits the right to asylum by stating that:

(1) Everyone has the right to seek and to enjoy in other countries asylum from persecution.
(2) This right may not be invoked in the case of prosecutions genuinely arising from non-political crimes or from acts contrary to the purposes and principles of the United Nations.

The International Refugee Organization was then replaced by UNHCR.[47] Para. 6 of the UNHCR statute defines the competence of the UNHCR to include persons who were considered as refugees under the Constitution of the International Refugee Organization, while para. 7 excludes a person if there are serious reasons for considering him or herresponsible for a crime covered by Article 14, para. 2 of the Universal Declaration of Human Rights.

Another important development took place during the same period, as the United Nations concluded the adoption of the United Nations Convention Relating to

---

44 Res. A/RES/62(I)-(III) of 15 December 1946.

45 S. Kapferer, 'Article 14 (2) of the Universal Declaration of Human Rights and Exclusion from International Refugee Protection' (2008) 27 *Refugee Survey Quarterly*, 53–75, 61, doi:10.1093/rsq/hdn045.

46 G.S. Goodwin-Gill, *The Refugee in International Law*, 3rd ed, Oxford University Press, Oxford/New York 2007, note 188, p. 172.

47 Res. A/RES/319(IV) of 3 December 1949.

the Status of Refugees.[48] Article 1. A (2) of this convention defines a refugee as a person, who

> [as] a result of events occurring before 1 January 1951 and owing to well-founded fear of being persecuted for reasons of race, religion, nationality, membership of a particular social group or political opinion, is outside the country of his nationality and is unable or, owing to such fear, is unwilling to avail himself of the protection of that country; or who, not having a nationality and being outside the country of his former habitual residence as a result of such events, is unable or, owing to such fear, is unwilling to return to it.

The date limit set to 1 January 1951 has now been abolished by a protocol, so the status of a refugee is determined by the convention regardless of whether the person has left his or her home country as a result of events before or after this date.[49]

According to the convention, a person is thus to be considered as a refugee if there is a well-founded fear that the person will be persecuted for reasons of his or her membership of a particular social group or for having a certain political opinion. A person who is to be extradited, being suspected of having committed certain crimes falling within the political offence clause, will therefore have a possibility for requesting asylum as a refugee within the scope of the refugee convention.

Article 1. F (b) excludes however any person, for whom there are serious reasons for considering that "he has committed a serious non-political crime outside the country of refuge prior to his admission to that country as a refugee".

A person may thus still be protected by the country to which he has fled if the person is suspected of having committed a political crime. The convention gives no guidance on how to decide whether or not a specific criminal offence may be considered as a political crime and the basic problem therefore remains unsolved.

The wording of the article was debated during several meetings, where different models were considered.[50] One possibility was to just have a plain reference to Article 14 (2) of the Universal Declaration of Human Rights, which however was considered undesirable in the text of a legally binding convention. Another possibility was to just refer to the extradition conventions, but the parties did not want the refugee convention to interfere with bilateral extradition obligations. It was not until at a rather late stage of the negotiations the parties became aware

48 United Nations Treaty Series, Vol. 189, p. 137.
49 United Nations Treaty Series, Vol. 606, p. 267.
50 Cf. Kapferer (note 45), p. 70.

of the possibility that a state could use extradition to request a political refugee for prosecution. The Danish delegate then argued for the need to balance the seriousness of the offence against the dangers to the individual, but the issue was not discussed any further and Article 1. F (b) was given the wording mentioned above.

5.2. ASYLUM LAW AND THE POLITICAL OFFENCE CLAUSE

UNHCR has also published a Handbook on procedures and criteria for determining refugee status under the convention.[51] This handbook has no legally binding character, but is nevertheless important in order to understand the convention. The handbook elaborates on the situation where a person is charged with a political offence. If an act has been committed with a political motive and the punishment for this act is in general conformity with the law, the sole fear of being prosecuted for this act is not enough to consider the person in question as a refugee. According to para. 86 this will depend on a number of factors, including the personality of the person, his or her political opinion, the motive behind the act, the nature of the act, the nature of the prosecution and the motives of the prosecution and the nature of the law on which the prosecution is based.

The question of how to determine whether an offence is a political or non-political offence is further developed in para. 152. The nature and purpose of the offence, the motive of the offence and the personal gain from the offence are mentioned as important factors, but also a close and direct casual link between the crime committed and the political purpose and object is important. The proportionality of the political element compared to the common crime element of the offence should also be taken into account.

The understanding of a political offence as a matter of granting a person the status of a refugee is thus far more developed in asylum law than the understanding of a political offence in extradition law. The latter applies the incidence test, the objective test or the motivation test unless the offence is listed on a relevant negative list, while the former takes a more holistic approach to the matter. The variety of factors that may be included in the assessment of whether the offence may be considered as political makes it however also very difficult to assess whether a person will be granted protection as a refugee before a formal application has been processed by the authorities in the refuge country. This is

[51] UNHCR, Handbook on Procedures and Criteria for Determining Refugee Status under the 1951 Convention and the 1967 Protocol Relating to the Status of Refugees, HCR/IP/4/Eng/REV.1 Reedited, Geneva 1992, UNHCR 1979.

especially a problem as the person in question runs the risk of being arrested and extradited to the requesting country for further prosecution if the offence should be considered as a non-political crime under asylum law.

The option of using the legal status of the person as being a refugee because of his or her political deeds in his or her home country will thus only replace one of the three narrow tests with a holistic test and thus not provide the needed clarity for the person in question. This result is further complicated by the development of extradition law starting from the amendment of the USA-UK-Ireland treaty from 1987, as extradition law now often uses one of the three described tests along with a negative list. It seems thus that the international law of asylum and the international law of extradition in general are "out of sync", thereby leaving the individual in a vacuum as to whether or not he or she can expect to be protected by the state to which he or she has fled or extradited to his or her home state for prosecution. Following this approach, one has to object to a claim that Article 1. F (b) *"is simply a means of bringing refugee law into line with the basic principles of extradition law"*.[52] Even though this seems true at first glance, a more thorough analysis reveals that the practical result is far from bringing refugee law and extradition law in line with each other. Replacing the political offence clause by international asylum law will only be possible if extradition treaties refer directly to the refugee convention and state that a person who may be granted asylum because of his or her political background cannot be extradited. But even this manoeuvre will not ensure the needed clarity as to whether or not a person may rest assured that he or she will be granted protection as the holistic test of asylum law also leaves a wide discretion as to whether or not grant asylum.

Should the requested person be found to be a refugee because of his or her political opinion or alleged political crimes, then he or she will be protected from extradition not only by the political offence clause in the extradition conventions, but also by Article 33 of the refugee convention, which states that a person should not be expelled if his or her life or freedom were threatened because of his or her political opinion. The protection ensured by the refugee convention is thus comparable with the protection ensured by the extradition conventions.

5.3. EXTRADITION AND ASYLUM IN A EUROPEAN CONTEXT

UNHCR has done a preliminary study on the relationship between extradition and asylum. This study shows once again how national legislation uses different criteria to determine whether a person should be granted asylum or should be

52 J.C. Hathaway, *The Law of Refugee Status*, Butterworths, Toronto 1991, p. 221.

extradited, but the main focus on the study are the procedural issues and the study seems therefore not to have been followed by suggestions on new legislation or on the consequences of using these different criteria.[53]

The relationship between extradition and expulsion has afterwards been given attention by the Council of Europe, as the PC-OC: The Committee of Experts on the Operation of European Conventions on Co-Operation in Criminal Matters (PC-OC) considered whether a state may be tempted to proceed with an expulsion procedure if the extradition procedure failed. The PC-OC noted that extradition ensures the individual a number of safeguards, such as the rule of speciality and the demand for double criminality, while expulsion is a right for the Sovereign that may be used with a relatively wide discretion. The experts of PC-OC also noted that it was in compliance with the ECHR as well as in compliance with at least some member states' national laws to run a procedure for extradition and a procedure for expulsion as parallel processes so that expulsion could be initiated if the extradition procedure failed.[54] A small survey covering national procedures in seven countries also showed that individuals facing extradition often applied for asylum as a way to delay or perhaps even avoid extradition as the administration of extradition and the administration of asylum are handled by different national authorities. Therefore decisions may be taken by one authority which may cause unnecessary problems and delays for the other authority while the involved authorities also may have problems when they need to share information about the individual in question.[55]

The PC-OC will continue to develop the relationship between extradition and expulsion by providing examples of good practice and obstacles in this area. It is however at present not clear whether the PC-OC will make formal proposals for international legislation on this issue.[56]

5.4. CONCLUDING REMARKS REGARDING ASYLUM LAW AND EXTRADITION

Asylum law and extradition were considered to supplement each other in the years following World War II so that a person would be considered as a political

[53] S. Kapferer, *The Interface Between Extradition and Asylum*, UN High Commissioner for Refugees (UNHCR), Geneva 2003.

[54] PC-OC (2012) 08 Rev. 2, Note on the Relationship between Extradition and Deportation/expulsion (disguised Extradition), 2012.

[55] PC-OC Mod (2013) 06 Rev. 2, Information Received from States on Practical Problems Encountered as Regards the Interaction between Extradition and Asylum Procedures, 2013.

[56] PC-OC (2013) 14: List of Decisions Taken at the 65th Meeting of the PC-OC, 2013, p. 3.

refugee and therefore protected by the state of refuge or as a criminal and therefore extradited.

These two areas of law have however developed along different paths in the following decades. Today, the two areas of law seem to almost have lost any connection to each other what so ever. Nowadays, there are at least three different ways to decide whether a person should be protected by the political offence clause found in extradition law, whereas asylum law has developed a completely different approach to this question.

A person wanted for extradition may therefore apply for asylum as a way to fight the extradition decision and thereby have his or her case assessed on completely different criteria even though the two assessments rest upon the same facts. Furthermore, as extradition is handled by law enforcement authorities and asylum is handled by the refugee authorities, these two authorities often do not share case files due to national legislation, traditions or confidentiality in each area. The two assessments are therefore not coordinated, causing a lengthy and costly procedure.

European experts therefore once again reopened the debate in 2013 of whether there is a need to align these two areas again.[57] The PC-OC has now initiated further analysis of good practice and obstacles in preparation of a special session on the interaction between extradition and asylum to be held in 2014. It is too early to predict how this debate will develop, but it certainly seems to be justified to ask whether the lack of coordination between asylum law and extradition causes unnecessary costs and delays for the authorities as well as for the individuals in question, who will risk not only costs and delays but also a violation of human rights.

6. THE RIGHT TO A FAIR TRIAL

The political offence clause relieved the requested state from the burden of deciding whether or not the criminal case in the home state would be fair as this would be considered as a violation of the sovereignty of the requesting state. However, as the protection of the right to be politically active is a fundamental human right and as such a matter of common interest, it should be considered whether states can uphold this position or whether states must accept the scrutiny of other states in regard to whether criminal law is being abused against the opposition.

57 PC-OC Mod (2013) 06 Rev. 2, Information Received from States on Practical Problems Encountered as Regards the Interaction between Extradition and Asylum Procedures, 2013.

The problems of defining what a political offence actually is and the findings that a political offence in the context of criminal law may be something completely different than what grants the very same person the status of being a political refugee could give reason to considering whether the political offence clause in the extradition treaties should be completely replaced by a general demand for fair trial.

A closer look at what constitutes a fair trial is however necessary before it is possible to decide whether or not this is an option as a right to a fair trial may not be the same as a right to a just trial. A state may criminalise certain political activities and then prosecute individuals from the opposition, who engage in these activities. Being ensured a fair trial will not be of much help if this right cannot protect citizens from being met with criminal charges based solely on political activities.

An example of the right to a fair trial is found in ECHR Article 6, which guarantees a person charged with a criminal offence a right to a fair and public hearing within reasonable time in front of an independent and impartial tribunal established by law. Article 6 (3) is more specific, as the charged person here is guaranteed a number of minimum rights. These include the right to be informed promptly and in detail of the nature and cause of the accusation against him or her, the right to have adequate time and facilities for the preparation of his or her defence, to defend him- or herself with legal assistance, to examine witnesses against him or her and to have free assistance of an interpreter. These rights are repeated in the Charter of Fundamental Rights of the European Union, Article 47, and the American Convention on Human Rights, Article 8. The African Charter on Human and Peoples' Rights, Article 7, ensures the right to a fair trial although with a different wording and a slightly different approach, while the Universal Declaration of Human Rights, Article 11 (1) ensures the right to a public trial at which the charged person has all the guarantees necessary for his or her defence.

The right to a fair trial thus *only* relates to procedural issues like the right to examine witnesses,to have sufficient legal aid during the trial and so forth. The right to a fair trial is not a right to only be charged in a just trial understood as a trial, where criminal law is not used as a means to attack a person for his political beliefs by charging him or her with more or less obscure criminal offences.

If the requesting state includes the use of certain symbols belonging to the opposition, participation in certain organizations with close relations to the opposition and so forth in national criminal law, then the requesting state can press charges against members of the opposition for what seem to be criminal offences, but what in real terms must be considered as political offences. If the charged person has fled his home country and now is requested to stand trial for this kind of charges, then the requested state may be asked to refuse the extradition as the person claims that the trial as a whole is unjust due to the political nature of the offences he is charged with. It will be of little help for the political dissident when the requested state limits this analysis to the procedural rights of the trial, as the requesting state may be able to ensure these rights on an international level even though the criminal case as such rests upon the criminalisation of opposition as such. The case may then be procedurally fair even though the case as such must be considered as unjust.

An examination of whether a criminal case is based on the desire to use criminal law to persecute members of the opposition will be seen as a violation of the sovereignty of the prosecuting state. It is up to the individual state to decide whether a certain behaviour shall be included in the criminal code, and obligating other states to examine whether criminalisation of certain acts are done in respect for the right to engage in political activities may therefore at first glance appear to be a full scale attack on the sovereignty of the state in question.

This may however be questioned by including two observations.

The first observation relates to the obligation to criminalise the most severe crimes like genocide, crimes against humanity, war crimes and torture. A majority of states[58] have now included universal jurisdiction on these crimes in their national criminal codes, accepting the responsibility to prosecute and punish offenders who are under suspicion of having participated in these severe crimes. Including these crimes under the universal jurisdiction will give the national criminal courts jurisdiction in these cases, and a person being prosecuted can therefore not escape criminal liability by referring to the fact that the sovereign state, where the acts apparently were committed, has refrained from criminalising these acts. State sovereignty is thus secondary to the call of international criminal law on states to make sure perpetrators will face justice in these cases, and the state sovereignty is therefore not absolute in international criminal law. Certain acts must be criminalised regardless of state sovereignty.

The second observation relates to the obligation to protect citizens from other violations of fundamental rights. One of the most profound examples is the prohibition against torture, which is found in the torture convention.[59] According to Article 3 (1), no state shall extradite a person to another state, where there are substantial grounds for believing that the person would be in danger of being

58 Amnesty International: Universal Jurisdiction – A preliminary Survey of Legislation around the World, Amnesty International Publications, 2011, p. 13.

59 Convention against Torture and Other Cruel, Inhuman or Degrading Treatment or Punishment, adopted and opened for signature, ratification and accession by General Assembly Res. 39/46 (10 December 1984).

tortured. A person, being requested to be extradited to face criminal charges in a country may thus enact this protection and avoid extradition if he or she can substantiate reasons for fearing that he or she will be subjected to torture in case he or she is extradited. The domestic court in the state requested to extradite the person will have to make a decision on this matter, which will only be possible after the court has decided on whether the legal as well as the practical safeguards against torture in the requesting state can be found adequate to protect the citizen against torture. Such procedural safeguards belong to the sphere of the sovereign state, but it is nevertheless a well integrated part of international criminal law that states must accept the fact that foreign courts have the competence to examine whether the requesting state has made a satisfactory guarantee for the requested person not to be subjected to torture. Certain fundamental rights must thus be protected regardless of state sovereignty.

For example, the question of whether a person will be subjected to an unjust trial, based on a criminalisation of his or her political activities can be included among the questions a domestic court may consider before a decision is made concerning extradition of the person. This could still be considered as a violation of the sovereignty of the requesting state as international criminal law stands today. But, as the last two observations have demonstrated, this sovereignty is not absolute as the national legislation and procedural safeguards of the requesting state in some situations are subjected to scrutiny in domestic courts in the requested state despite the fact that these questions in general are considered as belonging to the exclusive sphere of the sovereign state.

7. CONCLUSION

The analysis has shown that asylum law and extradition law have developed from the same starting point in the late 1940s and early 1950s, when the two law regimes were supposed to be supporting each other.

Extradition law has developed during the last 60 years so that we now have three different ways of deciding whether or not a requested person may be successful in claiming protection by the political offence clause. The political offence clause is furthermore limited by the use of negative lists in the various conventions, while the EU member states all together have decided to abolish the use of the political offence clause. A person who wants to flee to a country where he or she may hope for protection against extradition must therefore engage in a highly complicated legal assessment of the law and jurisprudence of the state to which he may consider fleeing before he may be able to predict whether or not he will be offered protection in that specific state.

Asylum law has also developed during the last 60 years, so the question of whether or not a person will be successful in a claim for asylum because of his or her political opinion is now decided by the use of a number of different factors, including the nature and the purpose of the deed, the motive, the personal gain, the link between the crime and the political motive and the proportionality of the crime committed. However, asylum law also operates with a negative list of offences which cannot be considered as political offences. A person claiming asylum because of his or her political opinion and involvement in politically motivated offences will therefore again be facing a highly complicated assessment of jurisprudence by the country of refuge before he or she may be able to predict whether or not he or she can expect to be given asylum.

The person in question will thus face a complicated legal assessment of law and jurisprudence of extradition law as well as asylum law. The assessment is further complicated by the fact that the assessment must be made regarding the national law and jurisprudence of the country to which he may be fleeing, which for the person most likely will be a foreign country with a foreign language and foreign legal traditions. It may be difficult, if not impossible, for the average citizen to make this assessment on his or her own, and he or she will instead have to flee and just hope that the authorities of the country of refuge will be evaluating his or her case with a positive result.

His last or her hope, the right to a fair trial, will then only help him or her if he or she can establish a reasonable argument claiming that he or she will not be given a fair trial if he or she is extradited and then prosecuted. If the prosecuting country grants him or her all the procedural rights necessary to ensure a fair trial, then he or she will not be able to fight the extradition by claiming that the case as a whole is unjust.

The basic idea of the political offence clause in extradition law and the possibility of granting asylum because of political opinion was the protection of the right to be politically active as this must be considered a basic fundamental right in a democratic society. The analysis of extradition law and asylum law reveals however that a person who asks for protection on this account has chosen a very risky strategy where he or she is in urgent need of advanced legal support as the actual protection will depend on a complex assessment of laws and jurisprudence in the country of refuge. And on top of all this is the fact that the right to a fair trial is limited to the procedural issues and not the question whether or not the case as a whole can be considered as fair or whether his or her government abuses criminal law in order to pursue its own political goals.

The present state of the protection of the political offender seems unacceptable, and an improvement in this protection must be seen as a matter of common interest for all democratic states.

8. HOW CAN THE PROTECTION OF THE POLITICAL OFFENDER BE STRENGTHENED?

A reasonable protection for the political dissident will only be possible if at least three different but related measures are taken into consideration.

First of all, it seems necessary to realign asylum law with extradition law. Asylum law is supposed to be the way to protect the political dissident and he or she must then also be protected against extradition, just as well as he or she must be secured asylum if his or her extradition is denied because of the political character of his or her offence. This is not the present state of law, and a realignment of these two areas is therefore needed. Extradition law is considered as part of international law, and states must therefore reach an agreement which of the three tests should beapplied or whether the more advanced test of asylum law should also be used in extradition law. The states must also decide on the use of negative lists in extradition law as well as in asylum law. It is of eminent importance that the citizens can foresee whether or not a certain action will be accepted as political or non-political and also whether the common crime element in a certain action will make the action as such non-political.

Second, the contracting states have to consider if a case where criminal law is abused to suppress the opposition can be seen as fair or just. The traditional concept of *fair trial*, as this is developed as a fundamental right, only relates tothe procedural issues of the case. But as the protection of fundamental rights must now be considered as going beyond the national state, time may have come where the concept of *fair trial* has to be developed so that it will include not only the question of whether the trial will be fair, but also whether the case as a whole is just on an international level. Abusing criminal law as a means to suppress the opposition can never lead to a just trial, regardless whether or not the charged person is granted the procedural rights as demanded in the traditional concept of fair trial.

Third, the national states must acknowledge that the question of whether a certain common crime is political is not only a legal problem, but also a political problem. The political pressure from the requesting state, when a state is considering whether an individual should be granted asylum or should be extradited, may be very intense and work on political, diplomatic and economic levels at the same time. This pressure may give reason to concern that the final decision of whether to grant asylum or to extradite may be influenced by other factors than the facts of the case. It must of course be a matter for the national authorities and courts to decide first, but it will be important to have an external safeguard that can ensure that only the relevant legal arguments are used to make this decision. ECtHR, the Inter-American Court, the African Court, the ASEAN Intergovernmental Commission on Human Rights and the Human Rights Committee under the ICCPR are all examples of bodies which may function as external safeguards. A citizen who faces extradition on criminal charges with a political element could be given the possibility to ask these institutions to decide upon whether the case as such may be considered as politically motivated, followed by a decision whether or not to allow extradition. In such cases, the requesting state would then have to argue its case concerning the criminal charges in the context of the respect for the citizen's right to be politically active. The protection of the political dissident will thus be submitted to international control, external to the single state.

The first proposal that asylum law and extradition law are in urgent need of being realigned is the least controversial of the three proposals. Asylum law and extradition law had the same purpose and the same scope at the end of World War II, but have since then developed in different ways. The proposal is thus just a matter of "updating" the two bodies of law so that they can give each other the mutual support that they each were based upon 60 years ago. That is not to say that this project will be easy, it will most likely be a very challenging task. But it is necessary to consider asylum and extradition within the same framework and also to elaborate on the question of how a person in a certain situation can foresee his or her extradition or can rely on the access to asylum.

The second proposal is more controversial as this will take the question of *fair trial* to a level beyond what today is considered to be included in *fair trial.* But the concept is shaped by the history of the last 60 years and reflects the fact that the ECHR and many of the other human rights conventions and charters were a response to the horrors of World War II. The main focus was how to secure the rule of law of a nation state. But the current development in the protection of human rights takes the responsibility of this protection beyond the single nation state, which also gives reason to consider whether the concept of *fair trial* should now be developed to include the notion of whether a trial is not only fair but also just. A trial where criminal law is abused to suppress political opponents cannot by any means be considered as just, and the right to a fair and just trial must now be developed so that the protection against such abuse is taken beyond the individual national state.

The third proposal, to let an international court or tribunal have the powers to consider whether the political offence clause is applicable in a case after the national courts have considered the case, is the most controversial of the three proposals as this will be only possible if the national states delegate such competence to the relevant tribunal. The national courts of the requested state must of course be given an opportunity to decide whether the requested person should be extradited or granted asylum. If the decision of the national court does not satisfy the requested person or the requesting state, these two parties should be able to ask the international tribunal to rule on the matter. States that have submitted themselves to external supervision by regional human rights institutions like the ECtHR could refer the case to this regional institution, while other states must be referred to the Human Rights Committee.

These recommendations may be seen as far-reaching and will only be possible if the national states accept an international responsibility for protecting the political dissident from being prosecuted through an abuse of criminal law. States must also acknowledge that the question of prosecuting political opponents may be highly controversial in a political context so that the national states must subject themselves to impartial international supervision. This may of course be considered highly controversial in certain national states, but the development over the last 60 years has led to a situation where the political dissident may very well end up being left in legal vacuum. Democracy is only possible if there is a real and active opposition present in a national state, and the matter is therefore not only a matter of respecting the sovereignty of a national state but also a matter of protecting the basis of democracy itself. Setting a clear legal basis of the political offence clause is therefore not only a matter of international criminal law or asylum law, but a matter of common interest in the protection of democracy itself and therefore a responsibility that goes far beyond the single nation state.

CONCLUSIONS: THE COMMON INTEREST IN INTERNATIONAL LAW – PERSPECTIVES FOR AN UNDERVALUED CONCEPT

Wolfgang Benedek, Koen De Feyter,
Matthias C. Kettemann and Christina Voigt

1. DEFINITION OF COMMON INTEREST

This book has shown that in international law the common interest has many faces. Nevertheless, a definition can be attempted: either in abstract terms, through a description of essential features of the concept, or by identifying the substantive content of the common interest, or of several common interests that are currently protected in international law, or may be deemed worthy of such protection in the future. This task is essential because nothing says so much about a social order than the definition of what interests the order pursues and its members have in common. Yet we do not postulate, as a precondition to our analyses of common interest in international law, that the international legal order undergirds a distinct international community with a clearly defined finality. Our approach is more modest and thereby more realistic. Defining common interests in international law does indeed help us draw conclusions as to certain aspects of the finality of the international order, such as the protection of human survival. We do not, however, in defining and discussing certain common interests, exclude all other possible interests the present and future international society may have 'in common'.

When defining the common interest in abstract terms, a first option is to ground the common interest in common values. In this approach, international law is perceived as a legal system underpinned by strong moral values. Such common values are the basis for the identification of the common interest that is protected in international law through cooperation and collective commitment, and the frustration of which is considered to be an issue that affects the community as a whole.

A second option is to take the measure of support that an interest enjoys within the international community as a criterion: common interests are those that are backed by a communal legal spirit – the opinio iuris communis. Interests are common interests because states, international organizations and private actors generally agree that some form of legal protection of these interests is required, and that these interests should be taken into account in their own behavior, for reasons that may vary. Widely ratified international treaties identifying interests as common interests are an indicator of support, but in this somewhat sociological approach soft law instruments and positions taken at international fora by actors that are not necessarily regarded as international legal persons are also relevant.

A third option is to designate interests as common when they can only be safeguarded through common action. Common interests are those interests that can only be managed effectively through cooperation by all actors that constitute the international community. As it is also in the interest of humanity as a whole that common interests are protected, a reasonable expectation arises that an international agreement on burden-sharing can be reached. As states vary in their capacities and responsibilities, the means they command to protect a common interest may vary accordingly. International agreements that address access to common resources or sharing of burden and benefits in accordance with states' responsibilities and capabilities are a necessary tool to create an equitable legal framework. The need for joint action makes the interest a common interest, and this finding acts as an engine for law and policy-making even if current awareness still lags behind.

The three different approaches to identifying common interests may lead to similar, but not identical results: although the protection of a world cultural heritage site does not always require global action, its preservation is nevertheless considered to be in the global interest; although free migration can only be safeguarded through common action, it has not so far been recognized as a global common interest.

In any case, a note of caution on the process of identification of common interests is in order, as the history of international law demonstrates. When common interests are grounded in values particular to some, or are supported only by specific (typically dominant) actors, they may be used for suppressive ends. Those on the receiving end of suppression in the past may have reason to greet the current invocation of the common interest with some skepticism. There is a risk that the process of identification of common interests falls prey to power relationships. Power relationships may offer a less defensible but nevertheless potent explanation of why some interests are deemed common and others not.

Is there an overarching common interest from a substantive point of view? An argument can be made that the long-term survival of humankind qualifies as the common interest that public international law needs to protect. The emphasis on long-term survival allows taking into account the interests of future generations as well; whether the formula also sufficiently captures the increasing recognition of the non-anthropomorphic value of nature is less clear.

The notion of sustainable development may be used to bring some order to the fragmented recognition of common interests in international law so far. However, in the absence of an international legislature and of a system of courts with compulsory jurisdiction, the current piecemeal approach is bound to continue with different common interests being recognized at different points in time in various international instruments and by various international courts. In any case, the recognition of common interests does not appear to be particular to any specific area of international law. Referral to the common interest acts as corrective to the overly state-centric nature of public international law, and may thus potentially be of relevance to any area of the law. In this edited volume alone, authors have relied creatively on a common interest, i.e. to argue, for protection of groups and individuals against states and abuses of their sovereign powers; or for the protection of the kinetic and non-kinetic elements of the Internet; or to suggest an adequate response to trans-border forced migration of vulnerable people; to ensure the rule of law and legal security, and to protect democracy by requiring that trials are not only fair, but also just.

2. THE SEARCH FOR THE COMMON INTEREST IN THE SOURCES OF PUBLIC INTERNATIONAL LAW

The current system of sources of international law, as epitomized by Article 38 of the Statute of the International Court of Justice and understood in international jurisprudence and by the majority of the 'invisible college' of international lawyers, creates difficulties for the protection of common interests, given the importance it attaches to state consent. Treaties cannot impose obligations on states that do not consent to a treaty even if that treaty deals with a common interest; the consent and practice of the general community of states is required to establish customary law. Non-state actors are largely ignored: they can usually not directly contribute or become a party to a treaty, nor is the practice of non-state actors deemed relevant for the establishment of customary law.

Publicists interested in protecting common interests through international law have therefore paid particular attention to two other sources of international law listed in Article 38: general principles of law, and judicial decisions. They have also looked beyond Article 38 to concepts that are not explicitly included there, such as ius cogens/erga omnes obligations (derived from custom), soft law and multistakeholder approaches with variable normative geometries.

General principles of law hold promise because they allow involving non-state actors, regardless of whether the principles are understood as principles deriving from municipal law across the globe (as municipal law is well-equipped to deal with non-state actors) or as principles underlying international legal relations (in which non-state actors participate). In addition, differently from custom, general principles of law are not dependent on state practice. When general principles are construed as a reflection of the evolving opinio iuris of the international community as a whole, and are thus constituted not only on the basis of state opinions, but also duly consider the opinio of IGOs, NGOs, business associations etc., they are a useful instrument for designing the common interest in such a way that it reflects more than the lowest common denominator that can be arrived at through bargaining by states protecting their national interest.

Only a minority of legal disputes is settled by judicial bodies, and judicial decisions are only a secondary source in the Article 38 framework. On the other hand, international judicial bodies are independent from states, offer some opportunities for participation by non-state actors, and are in a position to use the sources of international law creatively. The rules on treaty interpretation, for instance, offer a degree of flexibility to the international judge: evolutionary object and purpose interpretations may enable the judge to go beyond balancing the interests of the parties, and to take into account the common interest. This does not mean, however, that judges necessarily make use of the space available to them. With the possible exception of human rights bodies, judicial practice appears to be rather timid. Some examples of judicial activism for the protection of the common interest were identified, both with regard to procedural decisions (the adoption of provisional measures going beyond those requested by the parties in order to prevent injury to a common interest, generous granting of standing) and with regard to decision-making on the merits (growing importance awarded to the state duty to cooperate).

It is doubtful whether the catalogue of sources identified in Article 38 suffices if international law is to properly protect the common interest of the international community as a whole. This is not surprising. Article 38 was essentially drafted in 1920, when the Statute of the Permanent Court of International Justice was adopted; the erstwhile Article 38 is very similar to the current one. In 1920 the world was a different place, and public international law was a different law: there were fewer states in colonial times, and few non-European legal traditions that were taken seriously; international law regulated the co-existence rather than the cooperation between this limited number of states; non-state actors remained largely outside of the realm of the legal regime.

Still, in international law there are rules that are meant to express an idea of international public policy (ordre public in municipal law) by setting limits to the freedom to contract, and requiring not just co-existence, but the cooperation of all actors in the international community. For example, the concept of ius cogens was codified in 1969 in Article 53 of the Vienna Convention on the law of treaties. Ius cogens norms were defined as norms 'accepted and recognized by the international community of states as a whole [...] from which no derogation is permitted'. Another example is the concept of erga omnes obligations. In 1970, the ICJ, in the Barcelona Traction case, spoke of 'obligations of a State towards the international community as a whole' (at para. 33), and this statement echoes in the Articles on state responsibility (adopted in 2001) that speak of the invocability of obligations 'owed to the international community as a whole' (in Article 48 (1) (b)). However, while – arguably – all ius cogens norms are applicable erga omnes, not all norms with an erga omnes character amount to ius cogens. For all the above, however, a common interest lies behind their normative force. As a consequence, in theory, such obligations should be enforceable by all actors, but enforcement in practice still runs for a large part through state-centric procedures within a state-centric international structure. Nevertheless, even the much more limited concept of obligations erga omnes partes (i.e. the notion that a violation of a [common interest] treaty provision by one state party injures every other state party to the treaty) may prove useful, particularly when the relevant treaty is widely ratified. De lege ferenda, a common interest approach suggests the expansion of the recognition of the international legal personality of participants of international law, thus opening up avenues for a broader variety of actors taking up the legal defense of the common interest in the future.

It is a paradox of public international law that the more inclusive the rule making process is, the less binding the outcome might be. This flies in the face of discursive theories of justice. Further, from a common interest perspective, inclusive rule-making crucially establishes the legitimacy of a normative approach to 'managing' a concern shared by the international community as a whole. Declarations on issues of common concern that are adopted at the United Nations General Assembly or at world conferences by consensus or by large majorities provide convincing evidence of the existence of a global common concern. Even if such soft law norms may be of modest use in judicial dispute settlement, they may well have a significant impact on the behavior of states and of non-state actors. Similarly, credible multi-stakeholder initiatives that adopt hybrid instruments are significant in the establishment of global common concerns, and in organizing international cooperation for their protection. They also contribute to stabilizing normative expectations, contribute to the body of international law broadly understood and can be used as effective advocacy tools by both state and non-state actors.

3. LEGAL AND OPERATIONAL IMPLICATIONS OF A COMMON INTEREST APPROACH: RESPONSIBILITIES AND REMEDIES

If the responsibility for protecting the common interest is shared by all, how is it divided over the various actors? Does a particular state that factually has the capacity to safeguard a common concern more effectively than others (say, a big emitter of certain greenhouse gases) have a differentiated responsibility? And if certain actors fail in their obligations, are remedies available? Treaty regimes organizing responsibility for the common interest differ, but some essential features of a 'common interest approach' may be identified.

One option is to entrust the governance of the common interest to a global body: rights in the resources of the deep seabed are vested in mankind as a whole, and an international organization, the International Seabed Authority, administers these resources on behalf of mankind; no state is allowed to exercise sovereignty over the Area or its resources. The more usual option is, however, to work through sovereignty. The state that has established national jurisdiction is required to act as the custodian of the common interest, while the international community has the right to monitor the relevant state's exercise of responsible sovereignty and has the duty to assist.

As agents of the international community, sovereigns are entrusted with the responsibility to take the common interest into account. The state is restricted in its actions by the common interest, both internally, with regard to its own population and territory, and externally, in its relations with other actors. The sovereign's obligation to protect the common interest is, however, a contextual one. As capacities of states and conditions within states differ, states are granted a degree of policy space in the implementation of their obligation as a custodian. The duty of the international community to assist is triggered, when the custodial state is unable to fully protect the common interest on its own.

In a common interest approach, the international community includes other states, intergovernmental organizations and private actors. Private parties have an ancient pedigree in public international law, even if their historical participation in the legal regime has become somewhat obscured by the Westphalian discourse and its focus on the application of international law among European states only.

Other states hold a legal interest in the responsible exercise of sovereignty by the state holding national jurisdiction. The protection of the common interest is not a matter falling exclusively within domestic jurisdiction. Other states are, as a minimum, entitled to monitor and criticize the exercise of sovereignty by the custodial state. They have, in certain circumstances, the right to initiate legal proceedings in the common interest, or may even have the right to enforce the protection of the common interest. Co-operation is, however, preferred over unilateral action: in essence the protection of the common interest requires joint action, rather than separate action, suggesting that negotiations with a view to producing agreement will be more fruitful than unilateralism.

In any case, other states also have a duty to assist the custodial state in protecting the common interest. As a minimum, this duty implies a requirement to exercise due diligence, i.e. to assess the impact of their own actions on the capacity of the custodial state to protect the common interest, in order to avoid harm. In a number of treaty regimes, states with stronger capacities have clear duties of assistance to states with lesser capacities. These duties of assistance may be of a financial nature, require transfer of technology or knowledge, or require a contribution to capacity-building in the custodial state. In a number of regimes, and progressively in customary law, duties of consultation and cooperation regarding the management of common interests also emerge. They are related to due diligence duties and, when connected to untested technologies or phenomena beyond comprehensive human understanding, normatively influenced by a variation of the precautionary principle.

When states cannot, by themselves, manage the common interest resources in a way that respects their international legal obligations, they may be required to enter into institutionalised cooperative relationships. An underlying factor in the exponential growth of intergovernmental organizations after the Second World War may be that their founding fathers believed that an institutional framework was necessary for the protection of a common interest. The UN Security Council and the World Bank group, but also many of the UN specialized agencies not discussed here, may fit the category. But also other bodies, including the International Court of Justice, the Human Rights Council, the Special advisers on the prevention of genocide and on the responsibility to protect come to mind. It could be argued that the operational impact of the common concern approach is more important than its normative impact.

The institutionalization of the common interest brings its own risks. The mandates of the organizations may reflect a particular, rather than a shared understanding of the common interest. Decision-making processes within the organization may be unequal or exclusive. The participation by non-state actors may be poor. The practice of implementation of the protection of the common interest by these organizations may be selective. In any case, intergovernmental organizations – particularly those entrusted with operational capabilities in the field – tend to develop a degree of independence, and therefore questions of responsibility arise, even when they purportedly serve the common interest. In order to address issues of adverse impact of intergovernmental institutions on the protection of the common interest, member states need to retain the tools to oversee the organization's impact. Ideally, the institutionalization of the common interest through the creation of an international organization includes mechanisms attributing responsibility and access to remedies.

More generally, the issue of remedies is the Achilles heel of current efforts to protect the common interest in public international law. Significant normative and operational developments are occurring, but the enforcement of compliance against those not acting in the common interest remains problematic. In many areas of international law, only limited means are available to ensure that the custodial state exercises sovereignty responsibly. That conclusion applies even more strongly to the enforcement of the responsibilities of the international community. On the other hand, as stated above, perhaps it is in the nature of the common interest approach that progress should be achieved primarily through dialogue, agreement and cooperation.

As shown in the different contributions to this volume, the identification and protection of the common interest is by itself an important task in the progressive development of international law. The increasing participation of non-state actors in this process corresponds to the development from a community of states to a proper international community, which increasingly pursues common aims as a matter of common interest. While there is a stronger consensus on some key areas like sustainable development or core human rights, other concerns are still in process of general recognition and still others might emerge in the future. They all contribute to strengthening the case of the common good in the international relations among states and non-state actors and thus the evolution of an international law, which is able to respond to common needs. In any case, this volume made a beginning in identifying the crucial issues and introducing the complexity of the legal regimes advancing the common interest in international law.

LIST OF CASES

EUROPEAN COURT OF HUMAN RIGHTS (ECHR)

Soering v. The United Kingdom, Application No. 14038/88, ECHR Reports 1989
Cruz Varas and Others v. Sweden, Application No. 15579/89, ECHR Reports 1991
Drozd and Janousek v. France and Spain, Application No. 12747/87, ECHR Reports 1992
Loizidou v. Turkey (Merits), Application No. 15318/89, ECHR Reports 1996
Waite and Kennedy v. Germany, Application No. 26083/94, ECHR Reports 1999-I
Mathews v. the United Kingdom, Application No. 24833/94, ECHR Reports 1999-I
Bankovic and Others v. Belgium and 16 other Contracting States, Application No. 52207/99, ECHR Reports 2001
Öcalan v. Turkey (Merits), Application No. 46221/99, ECHR Reports 2003
Issa v. Turkey, Application No. 31821/96, ECHR Reports 2004
Ilascu and others v. Moldova and Russia, Application No. 48787/99, ECHR Reports 2004
Mamatkulov and Askarov v. Turkey, Application No. 46827/99 and 46951/99, ECHR Reports 2005
Bosphorus Hava Yollari Turzim Ve Ticaret Anonim Sirketi v. Ireland, Application No. 45036/98, ECHR Reports 2005-VI
Saadi v. Italy, Application No. 37201/06, ECHR Reports 2008
Al-Skeini and others v. United Kingdom, Application No. 55721/07, ECHR Reports 2011
Yildirim v. Turkey, Application No. 3111/10, ECHR Reports 2012
Nada v. Switzerland, Application No. 10593/08, Judgment, ECHR Reports 2012

INTERNATIONAL COURT OF JUSTICE (ICJ)

Corfu Channel Case (United Kingdom of Great Britain and Northern Ireland v. Albania) (Merits), ICJ Reports 1949, p. 4
Reparation for Injuries Suffered in the Service of the United Nations (Advisory Opinion), ICJ Reports 1949, p. 174
Reservations to the Convention on the Prevention and Punishment of the Crime of Genocide (Advisory Opinion) ICJ Reports 1951, p. 15
Effects of Awards of Compensation made by the United Nations Administrative Tribunal (Advisory Opinion), ICJ Reports 1954, p. 47
South West Africa, Second Phase (Ethiopia v. South Africa; Liberia v. South Africa) (Judgment), ICJ Reports 1966, p. 6

Barcelona Traction, Light and Power Company Limited (Belgium v. Spain) (New Application: 1962) (2nd phase) (Judgment), ICJ Reports 1970, p. 3

Legal Consequences for States of the Continued Presence of South Africa in Namibia (South-West Africa) notwithstanding Security Council Resolution 276 (1970) (Advisory Opinion), ICJ Reports 1971, p. 16

Interpretation of the Agreement of 25 March 1951 between the WHO and Egypt (Advisory Opinion), ICJ Reports 1980, p. 73

Continental Shelf (Libyan Arab Jamahiriya v. Malta), Application to Intervene (Judgment), ICJ Reports 1984, p. 3

Case concerning the Frontier Dispute (Burkina Faso v. Mali) (Provisional Measures), ICJ Reports 1986, p. 554

Military and Paramilitary Activities in and against Nicaragua (Nicaragua v. United States of America) (Judgment), ICJ Reports 1986, p. 14

Application of the Convention on the Prevention and Punishment of the Crime of Genocide (Bosnia and Herzegovina v. Jugoslavia (Serbia and Montenegro)) (Provisional Measures) (Order of 13 September 1993), ICJ Reports 1993, p. 325

East Timor, Portugal v. Australia (Jurisdiction) (Judgment), ICJ Reports 1995, p. 90

Legality of the Threat or Use of Nuclear Weapons (Advisory Opinion), ICJ Reports 1996, p. 226

Land and Maritime Boundary between Cameroon and Nigeria (Cameroon v. Nigeria) (Provisional Measures) (Order), ICJ Reports 1996, p. 13

Gabcikovo-Nagymaros Project (Hungary v. Slovakia) (Judgment), ICJ Reports 1997, p. 7

Difference Relating to Immunity from Legal Process of a Special Rapporteur of the Commission on Human Rights (Advisory Opinion), ICJ Reports 1999, p. 62

Armed Activities on the Territory of the Congo (New Application: 2002) (Democratic Republic of the Congo v. Rwanda) (Provisional Measures) (Order), ICJ Reports 2002, p. 219

Legal Consequences of the Construction of a Wall in the Occupied Palestinian Territory (Advisory Opinion), ICJ Reports 2004, p. 136

Pulp Mills on the River Uruguay (Argentina v. Uruguay) (Provisional Measures (Order), ICJ Reports 2006, p. 113

Application of the Convention on the Prevention and Punishment of the Crime of Genocide, Bosnia and Herzegovina v. Serbia and Montenegro ('Bosnia Genocide Case') (Request for the Indication of Provisional Measures) (Judgment), ICJ Reports 2007, p. 43

Pulp Mills on the River Uruguay (Argentina v. Uruguay) (Judgment), ICJ Reports 2010, p. 14

Application of the Interim Accord of 13 September 1995 (The Former Yugoslav Republic of Macedonia v. Greece) (Judgement), ICJ Reports 2011, p. 644

Request for Interpretation of the Judgment of 15 June 1962 in the Case concerning the Temple of Preah Vihear (Cambodia v. Thailand) (Provisional Measures), ICJ Report 2011, p. 537

Questions Concerning the Obligation to Prosecute or Extradite (Belgium v. Senegal) (Judgment), ICJ Reports 2012, p. 422

Jurisdictional Immunities of the State (Germany v. Italy, Greece intervening) (Judgment), ICJ Reports 2012, p. 99

Questions Relating to the Obligation to Prosecute or Extradite (Belgium v. Senegal) (Judgment), ICJ Reports 2012, p. 422

INTERNATIONAL CRIMINAL TRIBUNAL FOR THE FORMER YUGOSLAVIA (ICTY)

Prosecutor v. Duško Tadić, Case No. IT-94-1, Decision on the Defence Motion for Interlocutory Appeal on Jurisdiction, 2 October 1995.

Prosecutor v. Anto Furundzija, Case No. IT-95-7/1, 10 December 1998

INTERNATIONAL TRIBUNAL FOR THE LAW OF THE SEA (ITLOS)

The M/V "Saiga" Case, Dissenting opinion of Judge Warioba, Case No. 2, 1 July 1999

Southern Bluefin Tuna Case *(New Zealand v. Japan; Australia v. Japan)*, Separate Opinion of Judge Wolfrum, Case Nos. 3 and 4, 27 August 1999

The MOX Plant Case (Ireland v. United Kingdom), Provisional Measures, Case No. 10, 3 December 2001

Seabed Disputes Chamber, Responsibilities and obligations of States sponsoring persons and entities with respect to activities in the Area, Advisory Opinion, Case No. 17, 1 February 2011

INTERNATIONAL COURTS AND BODIES

African Commission on Human and Peoples' Rights, *Centre for Minority Rights Development (Kenya) and Minority Rights Group International on behalf of Endorois Welfare Council v. Kenya*, Communication 276/2003.

Inter-American Commission on Human Rights, *Coard et al. v. United States*, Case No. 10.951, 29 September 1999

Inter-American Commission on Human Rights, *Armando Alejandre Jr. et al. v. Cuba*, Case No. 11.589, 29 September 1999

Human Rights Committee, *López Burgos v. Uruguay*, Communication No. 52/79, 29 July 1981

Court of Justice of the European Union, Joined Cases C-584/10 P, C-593/10 P and C-595/10 P, *Commission and Others v. Kadi*, Judgment of 18 July 2013

NATIONAL COURTS

United States of America v. Edward J. Snowden, United States District Court for the Eastern District of Virginia, Case No. 1:13 CR 265 (CMH)

R (on the application of Al-Jedda) (FC) (Appellant) v. Secretary of State for Defence (Respondent) [2007] UKHL 58 (2008); 1 AC 332; ILDC 832 (UK 2007)

BIOGRAPHIES

Wolfgang Benedek

Wolfgang Benedek is head of the Institute of International Law and International Relations of the University of Graz and director of the European Training and Research Centre for Human Rights and Democracy of the University of Graz (UNI-ETC). He is the managing co-editor of the European Yearbook on Human Rights and a regular lecturer at the Vienna Diplomatic Academy and the European Master Programmes on Human Rights and Democratisation in Venice and Sarajevo. His main research interests include human rights, human development and human security, on which he has published substantially.
Email: wolfgang.benedek@uni-graz.at

Claire Buggenhoudt

Claire Buggenhoudt received a Master's in Law, magna cum laude, from the University of Antwerp (Belgium) in 2009. She is currently employed as a PhD student and teaching assistant in public international law at the University of Antwerp. Her doctoral thesis examines the approach of international judicial bodies to public and common interest concerns in litigation on natural resource exploitation. Her research interests include international adjudication, human rights and environmental protection at the international level.
Email: claire.buggenhoudt@uantwerpen.be

Koen De Feyter

Koen De Feyter is the Chair of International Law at the University of Antwerp, and the founder of the Research Group on Law and Development at the same faculty.He coordinates an international research network on 'Localizing Human Rights' that includes socio-legal fieldwork in China, the DRC and India. In the area relevant to this book, he previously edited *Globalization and Common Responsibilities of States* (Ashgate 2013).
Email: koen.defeyter@uantwerpen.be

Ana Sofia Barros

Ana Sofia Barros is a PhD researcher at the Leuven Centre for Global Governance Studies, University of Leuven, since 2012. Her research focuses on the responsibility of member States of International Organisations and her academic interests include International Human Rights Law, the Law of International Organisations and International Environmental Law. Ana Sofia obtained her Law degree

from the Faculty of Law of the University of Lisbon and her Master's Degree in Human Rights and Democratisation from the European Inter-University Centre for Human Rights and Democratisation. Prior to joining the Centre, Ana Sofia worked in a Portuguese Law Firm and became a qualified lawyer in 2012. She has also done an internship at an international NGO (IRCT) and at the European Commission (Anti-Fraud Office).
Email: Sofia.Barros@ggs.kuleuven.be

Matthias C. Kettemann

Dr. Matthias C. Kettemann, LL.M. (Harvard) is post-doc fellow at the Cluster of Excellence "Normative Orders" at the University of Frankfurt/Main and lecturer at the Institute of International Law and International Relations, University of Graz. Matthias studied law in Graz and Geneva and was Fulbright and Boas Scholar at Harvard Law School. The scientific lead of international multistakeholder initiatives on the law and politics of the Internet, he publishes regularly on issues of Internet and the law. Recent publications include *European Yearbook on Human Rights 2014* (2014, co-editor), *Freedom of Expression on the Internet* (2014, co-author); *Netzpolitik in Österreich* [*Net Politics in Austria*] (2013, co-editor) and *The Future of Individuals in International Law* (2013).
Email: matthias.kettemann@gmail.com

Sten Schaumburg-Müller

Sten Schaumburg-Müller, professor, PhD and dr. jur. (habilitation). Worked as a private lawyer 1986–1997, as women's human rights advocacy advisor in Lusaka, Zambia, 1997–2000, at Aarhus University, Denmark, 2000–2014 and presently at Southern University of Denmark. Professor in media law, jurisprudence (Rechtslehre) and human rights. Previously board member of i.a. Danish Institute of Human Rights and Mellemfolkeligt Samvirke (Danish Association for Development Cooperation). Presently at the Danish Research Council.
Email: stsm@sarn.sdu.dk

Werner Scholtz

Werner Scholtz is a Professor of Law in the Department of Public Law and Jurisprudence of the University of the Western Cape (South Africa); a Research Associate at the South African Institute for Advanced Constitutional, Public, Human Rights and International Law (SAIFAC) and head of the Regional African Law and Human Security programme (RALHUS). His publications focus predominantly on international, regional (AU) as well sub-regional (SADC) environmental law. Scholtz serves on the editorial board of the SADC Law Journal and is inter alia a member of the International Law Association (ILA) Committee on the Legal Principles of Climate Change, the ILA Committee on Recognition/

Non-Recognition and the European Society of International Law (ESIL) Interest Group on International Environmental Law.
Email: werner.scholtz@yahoo.de

Henning Bang Fuglsang Madsen Sørensen

Henning Bang Fuglsang Madsen Sørensen is Ph.D. fellow at Aarhus University, department of Law. He is researching the right to compensation for violation of fundamental rights during international criminal law proceedings and has published a number of articles on this subject.
Email: henning@75862988.dk

Vito Todeschini

Vito Todeschini is a PhD fellow at Aarhus University, Denmark. He holds a law degree from the University of Ferrara, and the European Master's Degree in Human Rights and Democratisation (E.MA) from the European Inter-University Centre (EIUC), Venice. He has been legal intern with the International Commission of Jurists in Geneva, funded by the E.MA Scholarship. Vito's research project deals with the investigation and prosecution of international law violations in peace enforcement operations. His research interests cover international humanitarian law, human rights law, international criminal law, and the law on the use of force. His university thesis on the concept of terrorism in international law was awarded the 'Paolo Borsellino' National Prize and the Emilia-Romagna Region 'Renè Cassin' Prize.
Email: vito@law.au.dk

Jure Vidmar

Dr. Jure Vidmar holds a Leverhulme Early Career Fellowship in the Faculty of Law, University of Oxford, where he is a Research Fellow of St John's College. He is also an Extraordinary Lecturer at the Centre for Human Rights, Faculty of Law, University of Pretoria, and a Visiting Fellow at Harvard Law School. Previously, he was an Anglo-German Fellow at the Institute of European and Comparative Law, University of Oxford, and prior to that a post-doctoral researcher at the Amsterdam Center for International Law, University of Amsterdam. Jure's main research and teaching interests lie within international law, human rights, European law, and legal and political theory. Jure is the author of a monograph entitled 'Democratic Statehood in International Law: The Emergence of New States in Post-Cold War Practice' (Oxford, Hart, 2013) and co-editor (with Erika de Wet) of 'Hierarchy in International Law: The Place of Human Rights' (Oxford, OUP, 2012). He is also an editor of the Hague Yearbook of International Law.
Email: jure.vidmar@law.ox.ac.uk

Christina Voigt

Christina Voigt is Professor at the Department of Public and International law, University of Oslo, Norway. She is the author of "Sustainable Development as a Principle of International Law" (M. Nijhoff, 2009) and the edited volumes "Sustainable Development in International and National Law" (with H.C. Bugge, Europa Law Publishing, 2008) and "Rule of Law for Nature" (Cambridge University Press, 2013). Her teaching and research focus lies on international environmental law and public international law. She works in particular on legal issues of climate change, sustainability and the interface between environmental and trade law. Christina was awarded the International Union for the Conservation of Nature (IUCN) Academy of Environmental Law Junior Scholarship Prize in 2009. Currently, she is the program coordinator for environmental law at the Center of Excellence – Pluricourts – at the University of Oslo.
Email: christina.voigt@jus.uio.no

Law and Cosmopolitan Values

In this series, the editors envisage monographs and collections of essays that address fundamental topics in law and globalisation, which range over doctrinal as well as normative questions of International and European law, human rights, justice and democracy. A main purpose of the series is to encourage scholarship that explores and transcends the categories and assumptions on which contemporary debates on globalization are conducted, and to stimulate refl ection upon questions concerning the interplay between law, policy and principle. Recognizing that there is no occasion to distinguish sharply between theoretical and systematic work in the fi eld from an analysis of law in context, the editors welcome studies from a wide variety of methodological traditions. Contributions to the series, inevitably crossing disciplinary lines, will be of interest to students, researchers and professionals in public law, international law, human rights law, political science, legal and political philosophy. Although the series aims in the fi rst place to refl ect the diverse scholarly activity within the Centre for Law and Cosmopolitan Values, University of Antwerp, submissions of manuscripts by anyone who is working in the same fi eld are strongly encouraged.

Instructions to authors

Manuscripts can be forwarded to any member of the editorial board at any time.

If the entire manuscript or a minimum of 2 chapters are available then the author is required to submit a detailed table of contents and brief proposal (up to 3 pages) outlining methodology, likely public, and the contribution the book is or is likely to make. If no manuscript is available, then the proposal should, in addition to the above, contain summaries of all chapters (no longer than 10 pages).

Every contribution should be accompanied by a statement that it is the author's own original work, that it is not being considered for publication elsewhere, and that it does not constitute a substantial repetition of work published or to be published elsewhere.

Manuscripts that are deemed worthy of further consideration will be forwarded by the editors to a member of the advisory board or an external expert for a second review. Peer review reports are signed and should be detailed, describing and commenting on content, methodology, likely public, and the contribution the book makes or is likely to make. In case of disagreement between fi rst and second reviews, the editorial board will ask a third reviewer for a further opinion.

It is expected that the reviewing process will not exceed 2 months in each case.

Related links:
http://lcv.intersentia.com
Centre for Law and Cosmopolitan Values: www.lcv.ua.ac.be.